LONGITUDE AND EMPIRE

LONGITUDE AND EMPIRE

How Captain Cook's Voyages Changed the World

BRIAN W. RICHARDSON

UBCPress · Vancouver · Toronto

15 14 13 12 11 10 09 08 07 06 05   5 4 3 2 1

Printed in Canada on acid-free paper ∞

Library and Archives Canada Cataloguing in Publication

Richardson, Brian William, 1966-
   Longitude and empire : how Captain Cook's voyages changed the world / Brian W. Richardson.

Includes bibliographical references and index.
ISBN 0-7748-1189-7

   1. Cook, James 1728-1779 – Influence. 2. Voyages around the world – History – 18th century. 3. Discoveries in geography. I. Title.

G246.C7R47 2005   910'.92   C2005-901912-3

Canadä

UBC Press gratefully acknowledges the financial support for our publishing program of the Government of Canada through the Book Publishing Industry Development Program (BPIDP), and of the Canada Council for the Arts, and the British Columbia Arts Council.

This book has been published with the help of a grant from the Canadian Federation for the Humanities and Social Sciences, through the Aid to Scholarly Publications Programme, using funds provided by the Social Sciences and Humanities Research Council of Canada.

Printed and bound in Canada by Friesens
Set in New Baskerville by Artegraphica Design Co. Ltd
Text designer: Irma Rodriguez
Copyeditor: Andy Carroll
Proofreader: Rob Giannetto

UBC Press
The University of British Columbia
2029 West Mall
Vancouver, BC V6T 1Z2
604-822-5959 / Fax: 604-822-6083
www.ubcpress.ca

FOR GORDON

We should note the force, effect, and consequences of inventions
which are nowhere more conspicuous
than in those three which were unknown to the ancients,
namely, printing, gunpowder, and the compass.
For these three have changed the appearance and state of the whole world.

Francis Bacon, *Novum Organum*, Aphorism 129

Contents

Illustrations / ix

Acknowledgments / xv

Introductions / 2
  The Story / 8
  The Book / 12
  The Author / 16

1 **Points** / 20
  Rules of Exploration / 22
  Points along a Coast / 24
  The Coordinate System / 31
  Verification of Details / 36
  The Possibilities of Location / 41

2 **Shapes** / 46
  Grand Divisions / 48
  Extreme Places / 49
  The Oceanic Plane / 57
  Cook's Turn to Islands / 59
  Landscapes and Maps / 66
  The Move to Interiors / 75

3 **Nations** / 78
  The Orient, the Savage, and Europe / 79
  The Primacy of Place / 84
  Studying Nations / 90
  Classifying Nations / 101
  Explaining Nations / 104
  The Savage, the Noble Savage, and the Nation / 107

4   States / 110
   Hobbes / 112
   Locke / 114
   Rousseau / 116
   The Scottish Enlightenment / 117
   The Native State in Cook's Voyages / 118
   Kant / 124
   Finding and Creating the Territorial Nation-State / 130

5   Collections / 136
   The Cabinets of Curiosities / 139
   Collecting Nations / 140
   The Practices of the Collection / 142
   Boredom and the Collection / 147
   The Dangers of Relativism / 154
   The Persistence of Extreme Otherness / 159
   The Transcendence of the Collector / 163

6   Empires / 168
   Cook and Empire / 172
   Empire As Collection / 177
   Empire As Exchange / 180
   Empire As Cultivation / 189
   Empire As Panopticon / 192

Conclusions / 198

Notes / 201

Bibliography / 214

Index / 223

Illustrations

2   "Captain Cook," Engraving of Nathaniel Dance's portrait
of Captain Cook, from Walter Besant, *Captain Cook* (London:
Macmillan, 1925)

4   "A Chart of the Southern Hemisphere," from Admiralty, *A Voyage
towards the South Pole and round the World: Performed in His Majesty's
Ships* Resolution *and* Adventure, *in the Years 1772, 1773, 1774,
and 1775*, 2 vols., ed. John Douglas (London: W. Strahan and
T. Cadell, 1777)

20   "A Map of the East Indies," from William Dampier, *The Voyages
of Captain William Dampier*, 2 vols., ed. John Masefield (London:
E. Grant Richards, 1905)

42   Table of Coordinates from Pascoe Thomas, *A True and Impartial
Journal of a Voyage to the South-seas, and round the Globe, in His
Majesty's Ship the* Centurion, *under the Command of Commodore
George Anson* (London: S. Birt [etc.], 1745)

46   "Christmas Island," from Admiralty, *A Voyage to the Pacific Ocean.
Undertaken, by the Command of His Majesty, for Making Discoveries in
the Northern Hemisphere, to Determine the Position and Extent of the West
Side of North America; its Distance from Asia; and the Practicability of a
Northern Passage to Europe. Performed under the Direction of Captains
Cook, Clerke, and Gore, in His Majesty's Ships the* Resolution *and*
Discovery, *in the Years 1776, 1777, 1778, 1779, and 1780*, 3 vols., ed.
John Douglas (London: Printed by W. and A. Strahan for G. Nicol
and T. Cadell, 1784)

53   "The Ice Islands," from Admiralty, *A Voyage towards the South Pole
and round the World: Performed in His Majesty's Ships* Resolution *and*
Adventure, *in the Years 1772, 1773, 1774, and 1775*, 2 vols., ed.
John Douglas (London: W. Strahan and T. Cadell, 1777)

61   "Chart of the Island of Otaheite," from Admiralty, *An Account of the Voyages Undertaken by the Order of His Present Majesty for Making Discoveries in the Southern Hemisphere, and Successively Performed by Commodore Byron, Captain Wallis, Captain Carteret, and Captain Cook in the* Dolphin, *the* Swallow, *and the* Endeavour, 2 vols., ed. John Hawkesworth (London: W. Strahan and T. Cadell, 1773)

62   "Sketch of the Harbour of Samganooda on the Island of Oonalaska," from Admiralty, *A Voyage to the Pacific Ocean. Undertaken, by the Command of His Majesty, for Making Discoveries in the Northern Hemisphere, to Determine the Position and Extent of the West Side of North America; its Distance from Asia; and the Practicability of a Northern Passage to Europe. Performed under the Direction of Captains Cook, Clerke, and Gore, in His Majesty's Ships the* Resolution *and* Discovery, *in the Years 1776, 1777, 1778, 1779, and 1780,* 3 vols., ed. John Douglas (London: Printed by W. and A. Strahan for G. Nicol and T. Cadell, 1784)

65   "Chart of New Zealand," from Admiralty, *An Account of the Voyages Undertaken by the Order of His Present Majesty for Making Discoveries in the Southern Hemisphere, and Successively Performed by Commodore Byron, Captain Wallis, Captain Carteret, and Captain Cook in the.* Dolphin, *the* Swallow, *and the* Endeavour, 2 vols., ed. John Hawkesworth (London: W. Strahan and T. Cadell, 1773)

67   "A View of Streights Le Maire between Tierra Del Fuego and Staten Land," from George Anson and Richard Walter, *A Voyage round the World, in the Years M, DCC, XL, I, II, III, IV, by George Anson, Esq., now Lord Anson, Commander in Chief of a Squadron of His Majesty's Ships, Sent upon an Expedition to the South-Seas, Compiled from his Papers and Materials* (Ayr: Printed by J. Wilson, 1790)

68   "A Chart and Views of Pitcairn's Island," from Admiralty, *An Account of the Voyages Undertaken by the Order of His Present Majesty for Making Discoveries in the Southern Hemisphere, and Successively Performed by Commodore Byron, Captain Wallis, Captain Carteret, and Captain Cook in the* Dolphin, *the* Swallow, *and the* Endeavour, 2 vols., ed. John Hawkesworth (London: W. Strahan and T. Cadell, 1773)

69   "A View of the Indians of Tierra del Fuego," engraving by Giovanni Cipriani, from Admiralty, *An Account of the Voyages Undertaken by the Order of His Present Majesty for Making Discoveries in the Southern Hemisphere, and Successively Performed by Commodore Byron, Captain Wallis, Captain Carteret, and Captain Cook in the* Dolphin, *the* Swallow,

and the Endeavour, 2 vols., ed. John Hawkesworth (London: W. Strahan and T. Cadell, 1773)

70 "Easter Island," from Admiralty, *A Voyage towards the South Pole and round the World: Performed in His Majesty's Ships* Resolution *and* Adventure, *in the Years 1772, 1773, 1774, and 1775,* 2 vols., ed. John Douglas (London: W. Strahan and T. Cadell, 1777)

71 "Monuments in Easter Island," from Admiralty, *A Voyage towards the South Pole and round the World: Performed in His Majesty's Ships* Resolution *and* Adventure, *in the Years 1772, 1773, 1774, and 1775,* 2 vols., ed. John Douglas (London: W. Strahan and T. Cadell, 1777)

72 "Man of Easter Island," from Admiralty, *A Voyage towards the South Pole and round the World: Performed in His Majesty's Ships* Resolution *and* Adventure, *in the Years 1772, 1773, 1774, and 1775,* 2 vols., ed. John Douglas (London: W. Strahan and T. Cadell, 1777)

73 "Woman of Easter Island," from Admiralty, *A Voyage towards the South Pole and round the World: Performed in His Majesty's Ships* Resolution *and* Adventure, *in the Years 1772, 1773, 1774, and 1775,* 2 vols., ed. John Douglas (London: W. Strahan and T. Cadell, 1777)

78 "Man of the Island of Tanna," from Admiralty, *A Voyage towards the South Pole and round the World: Performed in His Majesty's Ships* Resolution *and* Adventure, *in the Years 1772, 1773, 1774, and 1775,* 2 vols., ed. John Douglas (London: W. Strahan and T. Cadell, 1777)

90 "Man in Christmas Sound, Tierra del Fuego," from Admiralty, *A Voyage towards the South Pole and round the World: Performed in His Majesty's Ships* Resolution *and* Adventure, *in the Years 1772, 1773, 1774, and 1775,* 2 vols., ed. John Douglas (London: W. Strahan and T. Cadell, 1777)

94 "The head of a New Zealander, with a comb in his hair, an ornament of green stone in his ear, and another of a fish's tooth round his neck," from Admiralty, *An Account of the Voyages Undertaken by the Order of His Present Majesty for Making Discoveries in the Southern Hemisphere, and Successively Performed by Commodore Byron, Captain Wallis, Captain Carteret, and Captain Cook in the* Dolphin, *the* Swallow, *and the* Endeavour, 2 vols., ed. John Hawkesworth (London: W. Strahan and T. Cadell, 1773)

105 "The Island of New Caledonia," from Admiralty, *A Voyage towards the South Pole and round the World: Performed in His Majesty's Ships* Resolution *and* Adventure, *in the Years 1772, 1773, 1774, and 1775,* 2 vols., ed. John Douglas (London: W. Strahan and T. Cadell, 1777)

106 "A View of Bolcheretzkoi in Kamtschatka," from Admiralty, *A Voyage to the Pacific Ocean. Undertaken, by the Command of His Majesty, for Making Discoveries in the Northern Hemisphere, to Determine the Position and Extent of the West Side of North America; its Distance from Asia; and the Practicability of a Northern Passage to Europe. Performed under the Direction of Captains Cook, Clerke, and Gore, in His Majesty's Ships the* Resolution *and* Discovery, *in the Years 1776, 1777, 1778, 1779, and 1780*, 3 vols., ed. John Douglas (London: Printed by W. and A. Strahan for G. Nicol and T. Cadell, 1784)

110 "The Landing at Mallicollo, one of the New Hebrides," from Admiralty, *A Voyage towards the South Pole and round the World: Performed in His Majesty's Ships* Resolution *and* Adventure, *in the Years 1772, 1773, 1774, and 1775*, 2 vols., ed. John Douglas (London: W. Strahan and T. Cadell, 1777)

136 "Various Articles of Nootka Sound," Admiralty, *A Voyage to the Pacific Ocean. Undertaken, by the Command of His Majesty, for Making Discoveries in the Northern Hemisphere, to Determine the Position and Extent of the West Side of North America; its Distance from Asia; and the Practicability of a Northern Passage to Europe. Performed under the Direction of Captains Cook, Clerke, and Gore, in His Majesty's Ships the* Resolution *and* Discovery, *in the Years 1776, 1777, 1778, 1779, and 1780*, 3 vols., ed. John Douglas (London: Printed by W. and A. Strahan for G. Nicol and T. Cadell, 1784)

148 "Taheitans, Sandwich Islanders, New Zealanders and Egyptian Merchant & Lady," from Jehoshaphat Aspin, *Cosmorama: A View of the Costumes and Peculiarities of All Nations* (London: J. Harris, 1827)

149 "Danes, Icelanders, Swedes and Finlanders," from Jehoshaphat Aspin, *Cosmorama: A View of the Costumes and Peculiarities of All Nations* (London: J. Harris, 1827)

161 "I Resolved to Make the Chief Alone Fall Victim to his own Treachery," from John Barrow, *Cook's Voyages of Discovery* (London: A. & C. Black, 1925)

162 "The Fatal Fight with Natives of Owhyhee," from C.G. Cash, *The Life and Voyages of Captain James Cook* (London: Blackie and Sons, 1905)

168 "We Hold a Vaster Empire Than Has Been," Canadian stamp from 1898

184 "The Landing at Tanna, one of the islands of New Hebrides," from Admiralty, *A Voyage towards the South Pole and round the World: Performed in His Majesty's Ships* Resolution *and* Adventure, *in the Years 1772, 1773, 1774, and 1775,* 2 vols., ed. John Douglas (London: W. Strahan and T. Cadell, 1777)

185 "The Landing at Erramanga, one of the islands of New Hebrides," from Admiralty, *A Voyage towards the South Pole and round the World: Performed in His Majesty's Ships* Resolution *and* Adventure, *in the Years 1772, 1773, 1774, and 1775,* 2 vols., ed. John Douglas (London: W. Strahan and T. Cadell, 1777)

Acknowledgments

In the time it took me to write this book, Captain Cook sailed around the world twice and was well on his way into a third attempt. He didn't survive, and without help, I probably wouldn't have either.

This book would never have been possible without a great dissertation committee: Mike Shapiro, Ben Finney, Phyllis Turnbull, Nevi Soguk, and Jon Goldberg-Hiller. Noenoe Silva should also be counted as a committee member, not only for her tireless engagement with every draft I produced, but also for her endless support throughout the whole project. And while they had little to do directly with this dissertation, Warren Magnusson, Rob Walker, Evelyn Cobley, and John Michelson had much to do with why I could think clearly enough to start it.

I'd like to thank my family, friends, and colleagues: Colleen Fox, who has made me miss more movies than I care to mention, my mother, Mary, my brother, Dave, my nephew, Trevor Richardson, Gordon and Dorothy Williscroft, Lois and Roy Ekstrom, my father, Bill, and stepmother, Nancy Richardson, Debbie Halbert, Dave Wright, Aquiles Garro-Jiminez, Decha Tangseefa, Neil Reimer, Andrew Crowe, Chris Flett, Frank Nutch, Tom Spreen, Harry Partika, Cora Iezza, Jim Tiles, Mary Tiles, Graham Parkes, Kathy Ferguson, Karen Peacock, Rebecca Knuth, Gina Pusateri, Clare Hanusz, Kennan Ferguson, Jorges Fernandez, Dean Schimpf, Joan and Harold Stubbs, Joan Sabanos, Tom Hawley, Kerry Burch, Sandy Schram, Angie Sorrell, Eileen Flett, Dave Flett, Donna Perrin, Carolyn Tabarrok, Tim Krutzmann, Sarah Harvey, Eric Sage and Bill Krauss, Rosarie Adams, Mel Bolen, Judith Stamps, Evan Leeson, Rod Neufeld, and Shane Gunster. I would also like to thank the faculty, staff, and students at Windward Community College, and in particular Nancy Heu, Tara Severns, Faye Watanabe, Gerry Mero, and Trudy Miyaji, for their support and patience. Lists, of course, are convenient, but they fail to capture the variety of debts that I owe to all of these people. The libraries at the University of Hawai'i and the University of Victoria must also be thanked for allowing me access to rare documents and permission to copy the images reprinted here.

Finally, I would like to thank the book's acquisitions editor, Jean Wilson, who made every step of the publishing process a pleasure, the two anonymous referees, whose criticisms and words of encouragement improved the final product immensely, and Camilla Blakeley and Andy Carroll for making the manuscript a much better book.

LONGITUDE AND EMPIRE

Introductions

An engraving of Nathaniel Dance's portrait of Captain Cook, showing the captain in full naval dress. Cook is pointing to the Friendly Islands on his chart of the southern hemisphere, produced during the second voyage.

We have all met Captain James Cook.

Portraits, statues, coins, and stamps have offered his likeness for over two hundred years. But we do not simply look at him. The impact of his three voyages into the Pacific, both as a series of events and as published documents, has been much more profound – it is through him, through the ideal that his voyages represent, that we understand how to look with him at the world.

One of the more famous and widely reproduced images of Cook was painted by Nathaniel Dance in 1776, during the time Cook was in England between his second and third voyages. The portrait represents Cook at the height of his glory, surrounded by icons of his success. He is sitting in an austere room with a view of the ocean to his side. The room, no more than a container bordered by the ocean, includes various scientific and naval symbols, such as his captain's jacket and three-pointed hat. While the hat rests on a bound book – one of the printed volumes of Cook's second voyage – Cook's hand points to a map of the Southern Ocean. The printed map, and the lines of Cook's voyages that are traced on this map, mark the central achievement of that voyage and Cook's primary, but far from only, justification for immortal fame.

The painting is a theoretical statement concerning the relationship between knowledge, authority, and the world. The austerity of the room suggests an epistemological ideal, a sense of how the world both ought to be arranged and ought to be known. The room is clean and clear, allowing the objects within to be viewed without the threat of confusion.

Cook is not looking directly at the viewer, but to one side. The connection between Cook and the viewer is not immediate, but is rather organized by a more complex arrangement between Cook and the objects around him. On the table is a captain's hat, which is resting on a book, which is itself resting on a chart. The hat, of course, evokes Cook's naval authority. The book evokes his authority over the texts of his voyages that

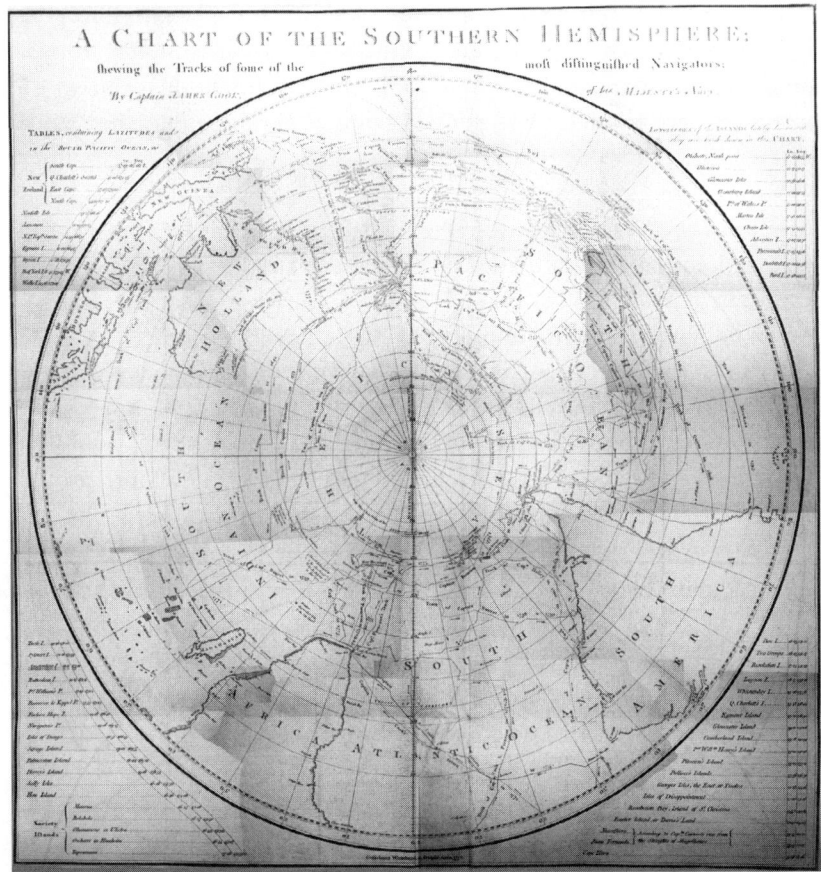

A Chart of the Southern Hemisphere, published in the official account of Cook's second voyage. The chart is centred on the South Pole and includes the tracks of Cook and earlier explorers. It was on the second voyage that Cook demonstrated the non-existence of a large southern continent.

were published at the time. The chart to which he points is of the southern hemisphere, an engraved version of which was included in the printed edition of the second voyage. By comparing this map to the chart in the portrait, the reader can determine that Cook's finger is resting somewhere on the South Pacific.

Cook is not simply pointing to his map; he is pointing to the Society Islands, a group of islands which includes modern-day Tahiti. These islands are a focal point for all three of Cook's voyages. Cook was not the first European to report back to Europe on the existence of Otaheite, as it was then called, but he added several islands in the group to European maps and, perhaps more significantly, his voyages extended European knowledge of what could be found in the islands. It is at this point in the portrait, where printed texts, printed maps, and the peoples and places of the world come together, that the broader conceptual and political importance of Cook's voyages, both as travels and as books, begins to make sense. Cook sits in his abstracted box, holding together global knowledge and power, and the nations of the Pacific are identified, described, and given a place in the world and in the book.

One important aspect of the picture that merits discussion is the direction of Cook's gaze. It is fixed and grave, but he is not looking at the viewer. While he appears to be looking out of his room, he is not looking towards anything in particular. But if we read the picture as part of a larger spatial arrangement, he may be looking back towards the Pacific, establishing a four-way relationship between the map, the navigator, the reader, and the place. We, as readers, are then to follow Cook's gaze, from his map through his vision towards the places he has provided an account of.

Alternatively, given that the ocean is behind him, if Cook is at the Naval Hospital in Greenwich, then his gaze could be directed away from the ocean and towards England, London, the Royal Society, and the palace of King George III. In this case, Cook is not showing the reader the places of the Pacific, he is exhibiting the places that were collected to the authorities that sent him out there in the first place. He is giving an official account of himself, his voyages, and the world, and we, again as readers, are allowed to follow along.

But the picture offers no clear evidence of who or what Cook is gazing at. As a result, we are encouraged to focus on the gaze itself, and whether he is looking at the natives of the South Pacific or the aristocracy of London, it is the gaze itself that fixes our attention. The gaze grounds the claims to truth, but only within a larger epistemological and political context, only within a world of books, of naval authority, of navigational tools, and of austere, purifying rooms that are bounded by the ocean.

THE THREE voyages into the Pacific that Cook commanded between 1768 and 1780 were carried out in the relatively peaceful period in European history between the Seven Years War, which ended in 1763, and the uprisings in the American colonies, which began while Cook was on his third voyage. Unlike those of his predecessors, Cook's voyages into the

Pacific were carried out with little concern for direct military challenges from other European powers. Rather, the challenges that were faced in the voyages arose from the dangers of open ocean navigation and from the interactions with native populations. While the voyages were not part of any recognized military campaign, they were nonetheless full of conflicts, successes, failures, and glory.

As a project to explore the world, Cook's voyages arose from a complex relationship between Cook's intentions, the contemporary interests of various people and institutions in Europe, the narrative forms that voyaging had taken in European literature, and the desire to create a reliable account of the world that could not only be shared with others, but that could also be useful to them for their own projects.

As both official and popularized accounts of the voyages would have it, Cook was sent into the Pacific ocean in response to three key scientific problems. In the first voyage, he was part of a global astronomical experiment to measure the time it took the planet Venus to cross the face of the sun, which would help astronomers determine the distance between the earth and the sun. In the second voyage, Cook was sent to determine with finality the existence or non-existence of a large southern continent. In the third voyage, Cook's goal was to finally determine the existence or non-existence of a Northwest Passage connecting the Pacific and Atlantic oceans.

Yet the three voyages were much more than responses to these specific problems. Building on the ability to determine longitude reliably, Cook's voyages mark a significant shift in how Europeans could know the world. Throughout his voyages, Cook demonstrates first to himself and his crew and then to his readers the existence or non-existence of places; he locates every place in a single, fixed grid of coordinates; he moves away from the continental coastlines into the fragmented plane of the Pacific Ocean; and he travels along watery tracks that prior European navigators could only dream of.

The engagement with the world and the world of knowledge is totalizing. Cook spends most of his time in places that had already been visited by other Europeans, but he incorporates and reworks these discoveries into a single updated description. He settles controversies of position. He describes the inhabitants of various places and notes where his descriptions agree or disagree with those already available. And Cook does this for places all around the Pacific and all along the routes that his ships take, from Batavia (now Djakarta) and the Cape of Good Hope, to Teneriffe and Brazil. Additionally, even if Cook does not specifically describe a place, he has left a blank space on the map for it that either he or someone else will fill in later.

In the end, Cook's voyages created a mathematical, scientific, and textual vision of the world's places that transcended the opinions and guesses offered by his predecessors. Cook's engagements with prior navigators also affirmed the status of his voyages and accounts of them as the culmination of all the information that was available, to which he added his own observations. As a result, the printed accounts of his voyages also became the ideal representation of scientific exploration literature. More than with any other voyage, Cook's travels and writings represented how an explorer *ought* to give an account of the world – while the voyages contain descriptions of distant places, they also discuss the practical and epistemological conditions under which certain kinds of descriptions are considered to be accurate and complete. Not only do the voyages summarize what has gone on before and offer answers to many of the problems that were posed in eighteenth-century Europe, they also create the conditions for exploration that will dominate the nineteenth century. Cook is concerned with the health of his crew, the relationship between Europeans and natives, the reliability of the newly developed chronometers, the maintenance of a ship and its crew on long voyages, and the nature of a wide range of meteorological, geological, and biological phenomena. In the words of Joseph Conrad, Cook's voyages offer responses to "the problems of our earth's shape, its size, its character, its products, its inhabitants."[1] The engagement is cosmological, encompassing the world and placing Cook at the centre, as both witness and judge.

The engagement is also moral and political. Cook's voyages, as they become parts of the textual terrain, mark significant reworkings of European discussions concerning humanity and power that support various images of political legitimacy, ethics of engagement, and accounts of global justice. The representations of the world in Cook's voyages have political implications. In Europe, the representations of the places in the South Pacific were used in debates over the limits and character of human nature, over the relationship between science and politics, and over the legitimate use of power, both at home and throughout the world.

One important aspect of Cook's voyages is the encounters with islands and ultimately the idealization of the island as such. Cook's descriptions of the islands of the South Pacific became a model for describing the world: descriptions grounded on reliable instruments, mathematically demonstrable methods, and verifiable observations. The South Pacific was the first section of the world to be included in the nineteenth-century imperial archive, and this helped to establish the conditions under which the rest of the world would be added. The Pacific also was held up as a mirror for European political ideals, in which fixed territorial and national identities came to play an increasingly important role. The idea of the pure nation was generally imagined as a natural spatial entity because islands had already been discovered, located, and described. What Cook found on the islands of the South Pacific, in other words, was used to idealize the natural political order that nationalists spent the next two centuries trying to create. The specific representations of the geographical and natural world offered to the readers of Cook's voyages were used to rework problems in political philosophy.

The printed accounts and artifacts from the voyages were many things to people in many disciplines. Associated with the scientific studies of humanity sponsored by the Royal Society, and with the laissez-faire economics of Adam Smith, the voyages were established as exemplars of an enlightened description of and relationship to the world. Rationalism and capitalism are intermingled throughout Cook's voyages. Also, the voyages contributed to the human sciences, not only in providing data but in exemplifying the form that such a science should take. But Cook's voyages are political treatises by other means, so a discussion of the political philosophy of the voyages will have to approach the question somewhat indirectly.

THE STORY

In keeping with Paul Carter's approach, the focus on the textuality of the voyage suggests that "travelling was not primarily a physical activity: it was an epistemological strategy, a mode of knowing."[2] Thus "the landscape that emerges from the explorer's pen is not a physical object: it is an object of desire, a figure of speech outlining the writer's exploratory impulse."[3] Carter does not distinguish manuscripts from printed books, and he mixes a discussion of texts that are handwritten diaries, recent printed transcriptions, and printed works from the eighteenth and nineteenth centuries. Members of the reading public, however, can only follow the voyages as they exist in print, so the distinction between the library and the archive is crucial. Our interest in Cook's voyages is not in the explorer's pen so much as the publisher's printing press, the draftsman's etching tools, and all of the material and institutional resources that took the manuscript accounts of the places of the world into the printed page, and persistently presented them to their readers.

One way in which the text of travel narratives can be studied is by analyzing the names that were given to places. Carter writes that "just as the geographical feature it [the name] brings into scientific circulation has its own unique place on the map, so the name occupies a unique place in the text."[4] Carter suggests that the names in Cook's voyages were neither random nor mathematical – the names were meaningful as markers for specific events in his voyages. In other words, the meaning of the name is not simply referential: "The significance of this overdetermination of meaning does not lie in the direction of Cook's psychology, but in the revelation of the fact that Cook moved in a world of language. He proceeded within a cultural network of names, allusions, puns and coincidences, which, far from constraining him, gave him, like his Pacific Ocean, conceptual space in which to move."[5] Not only does the printing press help establish precedence in discovery for particular places,[6] but, by bringing all the places of the three voyages into print, the books also help to create a system of names that covers the world. While landscapes may emerge from the pen, epistemological strategies and publicity also depend on creating printed books out of the written manuscripts. It is only when places from around the world are contained in printed texts that the dialogue with space and about space can be carried on by so many people in so many ways. It is often those who first publish a description of a place who can claim to have discovered it, or at least to have added it to "the map." Likewise, those who provide a superior description of a place can supersede the descriptions offered by those who came before – that is, those who published an account before. The practices of navigation and discovery involve much more than just moving. It is not enough to carry on a dialogue with space; the motion must be documented and those documents must be placed in the textual spaces created within a society of print and navigation.

In *The Songlines,* Bruce Chatwin described the way that aboriginal Australians articulate their relationship to the places between which they travel. Rather than relating to places in the world through a printed map and a published journal, the Aborigines relate to the land through songs, which are sung as they travel along lines that traverse the land. In theory, at least, the whole of Australia could be read as a musical score. There was hardly a rock or creek in the country that could not or had not been sung.[7] It is thus through song that the world comes into existence, and that each of the places in the world acquire their location. What the songs do, in other words, is trace the connections between places in the world, organizing the material world into a series of meaningful paths. Rather than being frontiers or borders, the songlines are sections of track over which specific people or groups have control. "Music," according to Chatwin, "is a memory bank for finding one's way about the world."[8]

And so it is with the printed book in Cook's world. The places and tracks on the page do not arise from songs, however. The regularized beats of the timepieces help determine coordinates, but the ways of knowing the world are very different. Space comes into meaningful existence through measuring, writing, drawing, and printing. The voyages of Captain Cook, in all the varieties of presentation, thus carry the reader along both physically and textually. And just as it is necessary to travel through the song to determine something's place, so too is it necessary to travel somehow through the text.

Nevertheless, the books produced from Cook's voyages are not simply continuous narratives. The books include tables of contents, which allow readers to skip from one chapter to another. The books also contain a wide assortment of lists and tables, which offer specific kinds of information all at once. Finally, the books contain landscapes, portraits, and maps, all of which may connect to the narrative, but which organize the information in a discontinuous way. A map provides a picture of a place all at once, and it may represent the progress of the narrative (as Cook's maps of New Zealand and the Southern Hemisphere do), but it does so in terms of space rather than time. Landscapes and portraits freeze the places and peoples, although they also provide additional information that the narrative can refer the reader to. This is the printed world that Cook's voyages built.

When Carter describes how Cook proceeded in a "cultural network of names, allusions, puns and coincidences, which ... gave him, like his Pacific Ocean, conceptual space in which to move,"[9] it must be recognized that a significant amount of this network was based on printed books. The *Endeavour*, the *Adventure*, and the *Discovery* were not simply ships, they were also libraries. Given the availability of books describing the paths of previous navigators, Cook is able to talk with previous authors, constructing a dialogue within his own narrative, where opinions are compared and debates are engaged. When these works are discussed, the genre of commentary (clarifications, confirmations, corrections, additions) is dominant. In William Dampier's account, for instance, both Joseph Banks, the ship's aristocratic naturalist, and Cook read the first printed European description of Australia. If nothing else, the other accounts make Cook's narrative more complicated than a simple accumulation of experiences over time, whether organized in terms of a travel narrative or not.

Subsequent navigators carried on Cook's process of revisiting places that had already been accounted for – correcting, articulating, and (with greater frequency) updating the information. The most immediate example is George Vancouver, who was the captain of a voyage into the Pacific roughly a decade after Cook. But Vancouver is not exceptional. The Russian navigators Ivan Kruzenshtern (or Krusenstern) and Otto von Kotzebue also refer to Cook, as do the French, English, and Americans. But in this system of citations, Cook's books are perhaps the most important of all, if only because Cook's voyages are the summation and correction of so many previous navigators, and thus form a core collection, a baseline, of texts on which all subsequent navigators can and must build. Cook builds on claims made in Dampier's voyages, but Matthew Flinders, who explored Australia's southern coast, does not. The printed account of Cook's voyages have subsumed Dampier's voyages in ways that Flinders' voyages could never hope to do to Cook's. Whereas Cook collects together a wide range of authors, whose accounts of the Pacific are partial, so that he can create a general image of the Pacific, Flinders takes this general image, finds a space that Cook has left empty, and fills it.

The success of Cook's voyages in the world of books resulted in their being taken as an exemplar whose status throughout the nineteenth and twentieth centuries was unrivalled. For many people, Cook is more than an explorer of the Pacific; he is also the last great navigator and the epitome of what exploration should be. In *Islands of History,* Marshall Sahlins writes of "the place Cook has assumed in Western folklore as a constituting being, responsible for the shape of the world as we know it."[10] Not only did people read Cook's voyages in one form or another, people who wrote travel narratives were often inspired, or at least influenced, by the voyages. Cook's voyages became a model of how to present both the narrative of the voyage and the information collected. Perhaps none of the forms of information are new, but they are done so well by him that it is these books that became the model, and it is this captain that became the voice of Enlightenment exploration.

THE BOOK

We must never forget that Cook and his voyages exist for the most part in print, that they came into being within a book culture and that they were, as a result, subject to the conditions and opportunities created by the printed word and the printing press. It is not simply that the remnants of Cook's voyages through the world have acquired, as if by accident, a textual form. The voyages and books were the intentional *products* of a book culture and their existence is unavoidably intertwined. Both the shape and the content of the world is inescapably textual – composed of printed words, tables, maps, illustrations, and numbers. It is through the printed book that readers are introduced to Cook and his account of the world.

The creation of the voyages as a series of printed texts depended on a wide range of other institutions and practices that gave books status, made them accessible, and conditioned how they were understood. Publishers are clearly central to the process. Printed books existed well before Cook was born. William Caxton had brought the first printing press to England in 1476, and by Cook's time an uncountable number of different titles had been produced. Some of the most successful of these books had been travel stories. More, Swift, and Defoe had already published and perished, and through the years an extensive print literature had accumulated. Thus, when Cook returned from the South Pacific, there was an already-waiting set of people, institutions, and technologies ready to take his texts, prepare them, and reproduce them as books for a public that had both the capacity and the desire to read them. The presence of Cook's voyages thus depended on the interaction between the reader, the text, and the social structures of reading that help produce both readers and texts.

Cook was an institutional explorer who was supported by key members of the English government, and it was to them that he reported back. His written words were taken over by people connected to the Admiralty, which used its power to organize the voyages, to turn them into public texts, and to use the information for further projects. It was the Admiralty, and Lord Sandwich in particular, who arranged to have John Hawkesworth produce the account of Cook's first voyage, and who decided that Cook would produce the account of the second with the help of John Douglas. It was also the Admiralty that ultimately decided which astronomers, painters, botanists, and other gentlemen were allowed to go on all three of the voyages. In this way, the Admiralty played an important role as a gatekeeper, determining who could help produce the information that the voyages made possible.

Not only did Cook's version of the second voyage carry the authority of the Admiralty and the King, it also included over sixty engravings that had been produced at the Admiralty's expense. High-quality engravings were not cheap, but they were both important to, and expected in, any serious published accounts of scientific voyages. The physical characteristics of the books, therefore, were significant not only because they made the books desirable, but also because they increased their cultural and intellectual status – these are important, weighty books that ought to be taken seriously. For the second voyage, in particular, the Admiralty helped create the most complete, well-designed printed account of a voyage that had been produced anywhere in the world up to that time. The account of the third voyage largely followed the pattern of the second.

While the Admiralty was focused on publishing the primary accounts of Cook's voyages, it also supported many other books connected to Cook's voyages and to the voyages undertaken after Cook. For instance, the Board of Longitude, which had nominated astronomers for the voyages, also published William Wales's 1777 account of some scientific observations from the second voyage entitled *The Original Astronomical Observations Made in the Course of a Voyage towards the South Pole, and round the World ...* Accounts of other voyages, such as those commanded by Bligh and Vancouver, were also published with Admiralty support.

Another important institution that conditioned the circulation and reception of Cook's voyages was the lending library. Not only was the high-quality production costly, even if subsidized, but print technology had not yet become mechanized, which would allow larger scale and less expensive print runs. In the eighteenth century, as the reading public expanded in size and as reading itself became a common entertainment, lending libraries became more numerous and accessible. One example is the Bristol Library, which was founded in the early seventeenth century and expanded considerably in the late eighteenth.[11] According to Paul Kaufman's calculations in his *Borrowings from the Bristol Library, 1773-1784*, the following were the ten most borrowed books during this period:

1 John Hawkesworth, *Voyages*, borrowed 201 times.
2 Patrick Brydone, *A Tour through Sicily and Malta*, borrowed 192 times.
3 Earl of Chesterfield, *Letters to His Son*, borrowed 185 times.
4 David Hume, *The History of England*, borrowed 180 times.
5 Oliver Goldsmith, *History of the Earth, and Animated Nature*, borrowed 150 times.
6 Guillaume Thomas François [abbé] Raynal, *A History of the Settlements and Trade of the Europeans in the East and West Indies*, borrowed 137 times.
7 William Robertson, *The History of the Reign of Charles V*, borrowed 131 times.
8 Laurence Sterne, *Tristram Shandy*, borrowed 127 times.
9 George Lyttelton, *The History of the Life of Henry the Second*, borrowed 121 times.
10 Henry Fielding, *Works*, borrowed 120 times.

While Hawkesworth's *Voyages*, which contained the official account of Cook's first voyage, was the most popular set of books in the collection, the library also had a considerable number of other books that were associated with Cook's voyages.[12] The Admiralty edition of Cook's second voyage was borrowed 113 times in this period. (The account of the third voyage had just been published in 1784, and it does not occur in the library's holdings list.) Georg Forster's account of the second voyage was borrowed 65 times. Sydney Parkinson's account of the first voyage was borrowed 17 times, as was John Reinhold Forster's *Observations Made during a Voyage round the World*. By comparison, George Anson's *A Voyage round the World* was borrowed 10 times, and Louis-Antoine de Bougainville's *Voyage round the World* (translated by John Reinhold Forster) was borrowed 48 times. Daniel Defoe's *Robinson Crusoe* was not part of the library's holdings, but this likely indicates the novel's widespread existence in personal libraries rather than its lack of popularity.

Popularity, of course, is not the same as significance or originality. However, when a text's popularity is connected to so many powerful institutions, as the accounts of Cook's voyages were, and when the text is related to profound changes in the way that many Europeans viewed the world, the popularity of the text then becomes a way to gauge the social and intellectual impact of the institutions that produced it.[13]

From the catalogue of the Bristol Library, it is also possible to construct a general image of what the reading public was engaged in during that period. The most popular genres, even excluding the accounts of Cook's voyages, were the "travel journals to" and the "accounts of" various places around the world, including Genoa, Iceland, Russia, Japan, Greece, and America.[14] For most of these travel books, the journey and the narrative are focused on a specific point that is the goal of the journey and the primary subject of the discussion. This organization was used as much for books about Sumatra as for books about Monmouthshire or Wales. In addition to the books about distant places, the library also housed books about different places in history. These books included the antiquarian collections of detail (of Scottish scenery, of the county of Dorset, and so on) and the multi-volume comprehensive history books (of Britain, of Rome, and of other places).

The Admiralty's accounts of Cook's voyages are somewhat exceptional: they were among the few travel books not focused on specific areas or places, some others being George Anson's *A Voyage round the World*, published in 1764, Louis de Bougainville's *Voyage round the World*, published in English in 1772, and two collections of voyages (one by Alexander Dalrymple, published in 1769, and another by Thomas Astley, published in 1745). In this way, Cook's voyages, much like Goldsmith's *History of the Earth, and Animated Nature*, published in 1774, offered an account of the world that brought many different places together.

The library itself created a similar collection of disparate places. It collected together books of travel and history and presented the world to the library's patrons, with the nations of Europe being described alongside distant places such as New Guinea, Bengal, the European colonies in the Americas, the Moluccas, Madeira, Jamaica, and Egypt. There were holdings lists of one form or another, and the books had to be put somewhere on the shelves. The organization of the books on the shelves was probably not geographical, as if the shelves could correspond to a map, yet the library would nonetheless have created a sense that the reader could access places throughout the world and move from one place to another at will.

One likely organization of the shelves would have been by author. Thus Edmund Burke's *Observations on the State of the Nation*, published in 1769, could have been on the shelf near James Boswell's *An Account of Corsica, the Journal of a Tour to That Island*, published in the same year, or on the shelf just above Hans Sloane's *A Voyage to the Islands of Madeira, Barbados ... and Jamaica,* published in 1707.[15] Even if these books were published years apart and described places that were even farther apart, the library brought them together and, by lending them to the people of Bristol, made them all accessible to a reading community. The library's collection is thus a statement, not only about the world, but also about the proper organization of knowledge about the world.

THE AUTHOR

Throughout this discussion, we must never forget that Cook was a character, the narrator in fact, in a story. Of course, there was once a time when Cook, as an officer of the Royal Navy, navigated ships from Britain to the South Seas and around the world. But the focus of the discussion here is on the printed texts and on Cook as an authorial voice in those texts. There will be no attempt to determine what really happened in the voyages or what Cook was really like. The issues that have animated recent Cook scholarship, which have been built on the journals, will thus not be engaged with in any sustained way. The focus here will be to determine how the voyages, as printed texts written in first person, with Cook as the main character, imagine the world.

One of the features typical of novels, according to Tzvetan Todorov, is the presence of many voices in the text. There are a wide range of characters who interact throughout a typical novel, giving a much greater sense of a dialogue than occurs, say, with a scientific treatise. In the printed account of Cook's voyages, there are also many voices. However, these voices are related and organized by the first-person voice of Cook, who becomes the sovereign centre around which the other voices are collected, quoted, organized, spoken to, and judged.

The drama of the voyages, it should be emphasized, is the drama of knowledge. As the voyages progress, the reader is offered a history of Cook's own engagements with both the world and previous texts. As the narrator of the voyage, Cook is thus fashioned into an ideal of the rational surveyor, someone who is able to enter into dialogue with alternative accounts (both in writing and conversation) but who retains the capacity to finally judge the truth. He appeals to grids in which he narrates his wanderings through time and space, discovering for himself not only discrete knowable objects, but also how it is possible to know anything.

But Cook does not simply present a true account of the world; he also narrates the process by which he arrives at that account, and the reader is encouraged to identify with this process. In *On Longing*, Susan Stewart has noted that with the rise of the novel in the eighteenth century, "a new process of reading evolves from this new form of realism, a reading which gives the reader the status of a character. The reader comes to 'identify with' the position of Tom Jones, Pamela, Joseph Andrews, with the 'proper name' and not with a lesson, a signified."[16] In the same way, readers are encouraged to identify with particular characters in the voyages, such as Banks, Anderson, and, most importantly, Cook himself. It is through these characters and the information that they provide that the reader is given not only a particular description of the world but also a sense of how proper descriptions of the world ought to be created. As both the author and subject of the voyages, therefore, Cook encourages his readers to see the world through his eyes. At the very least, we become his confidants.

When Cook refers either to himself or to others in the text, the references are couched in a narrative of trust, which is itself tied to the political and economic structures that locate people in different social classes. In the third voyage, for instance, Cook writes, "I am indebted to Mr. Anderson for a considerable share of what follows in this and in the following chapter. In other matters I have only expressed, nearly in his words, remarks that coincided with mine; but what relates to the religion and language of these people, is entirely his own."[17] Responsibility is, of course, an important aspect of this passage, as is the desire to give Anderson due credit for the information he supplied. But there is also an important strategy here, insofar as the creation of reliable authors is a crucial way to create reliability in an empiricist approach to the world.

While the European gentlemen are brought into the narrative with little or no skepticism, the natives and the sailors are presented as secondary characters (named or unnamed). One of the anonymous books describing the second voyage, attributed to John Rickman, includes the claims that, given the structures of authority, the sailors often were not even able to speak, at least to the officers and the gentlemen. He writes that "among the seamen on board a king's ship, there are always some expert navigators, whose judgment, ripened by experience, is much to be depended upon; but the misfortune is, that these men are never consulted, nor do they even dare so much as to whisper their opinion to their superior officer. Like gamesters standing by, they can see the errors of the game, but must not point them out till the game is over. This was the real case on board the *Discovery*."[18] No matter how many people were on the ship or were met with in the voyages, the number of characters included in the narrative is very small. At times we hear of sailors jumping ship and being brought back, but the accounts that they give of themselves are almost always from the captain's perspective; or, better yet, from the perspective of sovereign authority itself.

By focusing on the legal and sovereign organization of identities in the voyages, Cook is not simply a journalist or an important character. He is also the captain of the ship. Cook's relationship to the voyages, therefore, acquires a more proprietary and strictly representational character. His status depends on a combination of his (political) control over the ship and his (legal) representation of the voyage as such. Cook thus owns the actions of the people on board, and, in a sense, acquires both the responsibility and the credit for what happens. When he writes, "I sailed," we should understand the "I" in terms of sovereignty – the commonwealth that consolidates the identities of its members into a single person. On the ship, he is representing the Admiralty, the King, and the Country to other places. He is also representing the voyages back to the Admiralty, the King, and the Country. He not only commands but must give an account of his commands.

The continued presentation of Cook as the captain and the central author of the voyages is tied to various projects of celebration, in which Cook is portrayed as a great navigator, a humanitarian, a servant of the empire, and a key originator for distant colonies. But the celebration of Cook also ends up being self-congratulatory. Cook became a hero of the British empire. Not only was he directly connected to specific projects, such as the British colonization of Australia and New Zealand, he and his voyages, once again as both events and texts, were also used to cast a long shadow on the nature of British exploration as such. More than just the captain of a ship, Captain Cook, "the navigator without fear and without reproach,"[19] had become an icon. His status made it possible for others to write of the traveller's moral and spiritual relationship to movement in the world. He is deified, even on spots where he remained for only half an hour and did nothing remarkable. Cook has thus become a different kind of explorer, one who sets the stage for the global interactions of the nineteenth century, and one whose account of the world is not read simply because it is entertaining, but also because it is taken to be comprehensive, useful, and true. Cook is given credit, and the act of giving him credit also gives credit to the people and institutions that created and sustained him. The celebration of Cook's authority throughout the nineteenth century, in other words, is tied to the celebration of specific forms of knowledge and power that cover both the world and the printed page.

But before the celebration could commence, the voyages had to be undertaken, the journals organized, and the results published. Longitude had to be verified, artifacts had to be collected, and everything had to be returned to Europe and turned into a book, a travel journal, in which Cook's voice travels with the reader from place to place, from episode to episode, and from chapter to chapter. Cook is not a fictional character, and while his voyages imagine places, they do not describe imaginary places.

ONE

Points

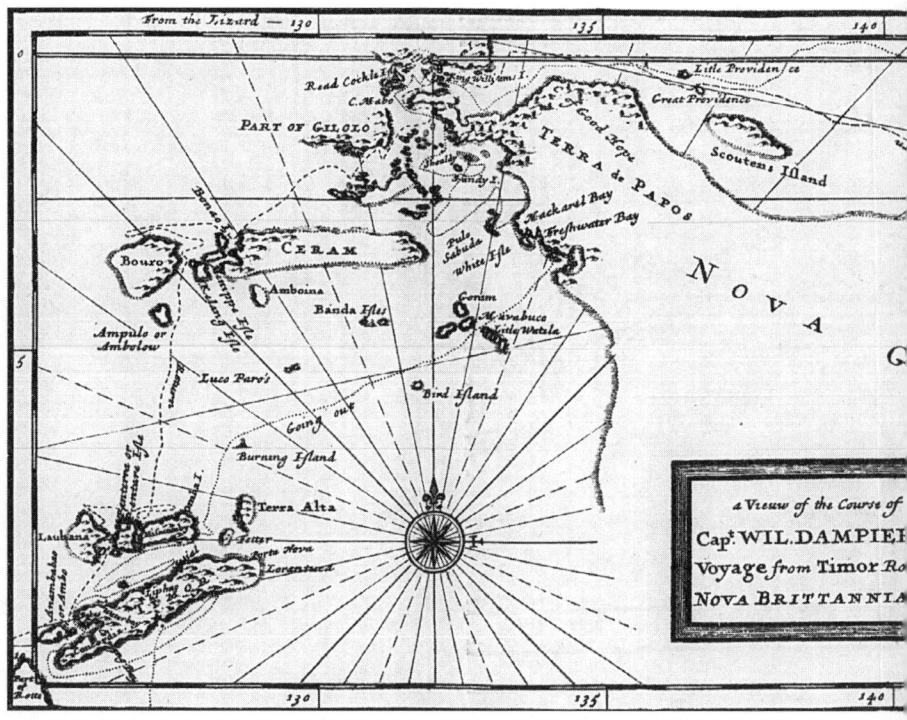

A view of the course of William Dampier. The coordinates are marked out to 5
degrees, and the coastline, while offering a rough estimate of location and shape,
lacks the detail that would become common in Cook's voyages.

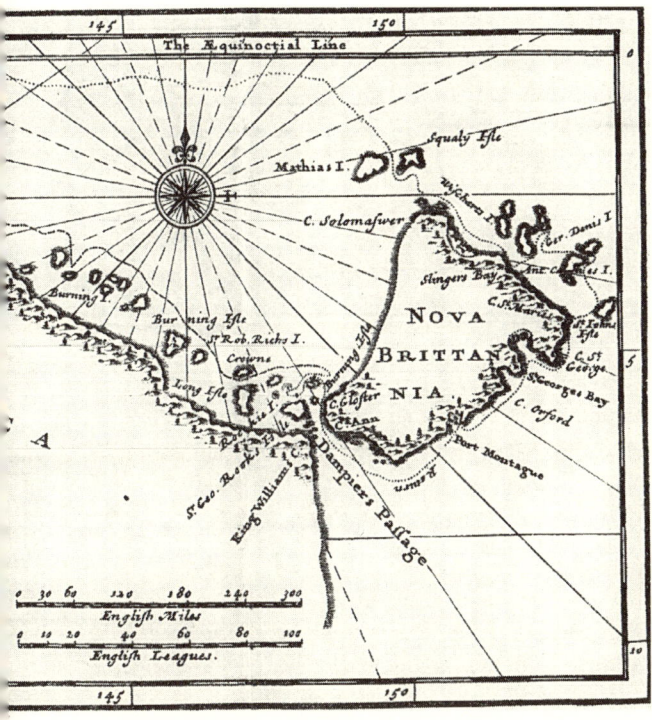

Coordinates are created by imagining the world divided into a grid of vertical and horizontal lines of longitude and latitude. Each point has a specific value, expressed in degrees, minutes, and seconds, that can be related to a point on the globe. However, it was not until Cook's time that techniques and instruments had been developed that allowed navigators to accurately measure longitude, making it possible to connect the mathematical arrangement to terrestrial space. The impact of the ability to calculate longitude reliably is typically discussed in its practical terms:

the safety and the knowledge created by the new accuracy. But longitude also changed the way that places were articulated and travel was narrated. The world changed.

To appreciate the impact of being able to reliably measure longitude, we must first consider the world of the navigator before Cook, such as can be found in the writings of John Locke, in which Europe's world is organized in terms of coastal trade routes and ports.

RULES OF EXPLORATION

In 1704, John Locke published *The Whole History of Navigation,* initially as an introduction to John Churchill's *Collection of Voyages.* Locke begins by quoting a list of directions written specifically for those engaged in oceanic navigation. These were close to being an official statement on how to proceed in such matters. As Locke explains, the directions were

> drawn up by Mr. Rook [Lawrence Rooke], a fellow of the Royal Society, and geometry professor of Gresham college, by order of the said society, and published in the *Philosophical Transactions* of the eighth of January 1665-6, being Number 8. They are as follow:
>
> 1. To observe the declination of the compass, or its variation from the meridian of the place, frequently: marking withal the latitude and longitude of the place where such observation is made, as exactly as may be, and setting down the method by which they made them.
>
> 2. To carry dipping needles with them, and observe the inclination of the needle in like manner.
>
> 3. To remark carefully the ebbings and flowings of the sea in as many places as they can, together with all the accidents ordinary and extraordinary of the tides; as, their precise time of ebbing and flowing in rivers, at promontories or capes, which way the current runs, what perpendicular distance there is between the highest tide and lowest ebb, during the spring tides and neap tides, what day of the moon's age, and what times of the year the highest and lowest tides fall out: and all other considerable accidents they can observe in the tides, chiefly near ports, and about islands, as in Saint Helena's island, and the three rivers there, at the Bermudas, &c.
>
> 4. To make plots and draughts of prospect of coasts, promontories, islands, and ports, marking the bearings and distances as near as they can.
>
> 5. To sound and mark the depth of coasts and ports, and such other places near the shore as they shall think fit.

6. To take notice of the nature of the ground at the bottom of the sea, in all soundings, whether it be clay, sand, rock, &c.

7. To keep a register of all changes of wind and weather at all hours, by night and by day, showing the point the wind blows from, whether strong or weak: the rains, hail, snow, and the like; the precise times of their beginnings and continuance, especially hurricanes and spouts; but above all, to take exact care to observe the trade-winds, about what degree of latitude and longitude they first begin, where and when they cease or change, or grow stronger or weaker, and how much, as near and exact as may be.

8. To observe and record all extraordinary meteors, lightnings, thunders, ignes fatui, comets, &c. marking still the places and times of their appearing, continuance, &c.

9. To carry with them good scales, and glass vials of a pint, or so, with very narrow mouths, which are to be filled with sea-water in different degrees of latitude, as often as they please, and the weight of the vial full of water taken exactly at every time, and recorded, marking withal the degree of latitude, and the day of the month; and that as well of water near the top, as at a greater depth.[1]

To anyone familiar with Cook's voyages, the directions would sound familiar. According to Rooke, a general account of the world will arise from the accumulation of specific kinds of information from different places: temperatures, flows of water and wind, depths, heights, and extraordinary occurrences. Written down and properly organized, this information can then be duplicated and passed on to subsequent navigators who can verify, augment, or refute the descriptions. The process is communal, geometrical, and necessarily printed.

But there is an important shift from the early to the late eighteenth century, if not in the theoretical organization, then at least in how places are organized in practice. Locke's world is a world of coasts and latitudes, in which places are points located along geographical lines and open oceans are traversed in straight lines east and west, keeping to a particular latitude. This is the world of Drake, of Columbus, of Anson and, more or less, of every European navigator up until the time of Cook's voyages. But it is hardly Cook's world, and how Cook moves away from the coastline marks a profound shift in the geometrical articulation of places – a shift that changes how places are located, how travel can be carried out, and how a global system of nations and empires can be put together.

Longitude, when coupled with latitude, not only clarifies obscure claims about where things are in the world, but it also changes how places exist.

POINTS ALONG A COAST

John Locke's *The Whole History of Navigation* summarizes several key collections of earlier travel narratives. While two of his primary sources are Richard Hakluyt (published in the late sixteenth century) and Samuel Purchas (published in the early seventeenth century), he also includes many other writers, such as John de Barros's *Decads of India* and Hieronymus Osorius's *History of India,* especially when summarizing voyages that were not discussed in the primary English collections. Likewise, Locke refers to "the collection of voyages undertaken by the Dutch East India Company, printed this present year 1703."[2] The result is a summary of much of the travel writings available to the reading public up to that time.

In a very general way, Locke's narrative suggests the importance of documentation in early-eighteenth-century discussions of European exploration. Locke does not interview explorers or verify their claims himself. He is also not an explorer engaging the claims of other explorers. He is a reader who is writing an introduction to a published collection of voyages, and he is engaging with the primary books on the subject. Locke is not attempting to obtain any more facts about the world. Rather, his work offers an abbreviated accumulation of information derived from previous printed accounts, and it allows a general idea of exploration and the world to arise.

Locke explains the expansion of European activity around the world from the Middle Ages on by appealing to various technological innovations, including changes in the design of ships and rigging. The most important technological change, however, was the magnetic needle. Locke admits that, prior to the development of the magnetic needle, some nations were seafaring, such as the Normans, the Genoese, and the Venetians. However, while "they all in their turns were powerful at sea, they all ventured sometimes far from home, either to rob, conquer, or trade, but all in the same manner creeping along the shores, without daring to venture far out to sea, having no guides out of sight of land but the stars which in cloudy nights must fail them."[3] With the magnetic needle, it became possible to accurately and reliably determine north and south, regardless of where the observer was or what the conditions of observation were. By knowing the direction of the magnetic needle and how the needle was connected to the world, it then became possible to reliably sail in straight lines and determine the direction of coasts.

One of the underlying features of Locke's history of navigation is that the navigators seldom venture away from the coast, even after the discovery of the magnetic needle. They can lose sight of land from time to time without getting lost, but their paths are always tied back to the coastline, which was the fundamental reference point for locating places.

The world and Locke's narrative are both divided into general regions, which arise at different stages in European exploration. The primary division of Locke's summary is into continents – Europe, Africa, Asia, and America – and then into dates (which, given the linear progress of European navigation, generally fits into the order in which the continents were explored by Europeans). Europeans gradually extended their knowledge of the world as new navigators moved past the geographical points that earlier Europeans had reached and added to what was known. The points along the coast indicated the limits of the known world, or at least of the safe world for Europeans.

If the progress of European exploration moved along coasts, the articulation of place in this world depended on putting dots further along the line. The goal of exploration was initially India, and then China. After the coastline is traced as far as China, the thread of both the narratives and the explorations trail off. Near the end of his *Whole History of Navigation*, Locke writes of Christopher Borallo, whose voyage was "famous for several particulars, and especially for having discovered more of the north of China than was known before."[4] But no one seemed interested in extending the line much further along the northeast coastline, which offered no opportunities for either trade or plunder.

One notable exception to the dominance of coasting is in Vasco de Gama's narrative, where an oceanic line is followed from northeast Africa to India. At this point, Locke writes, "he set sail for India, and cross[ed] that great gulf of seven hundred leagues in twenty days."[5] But, as is also the case with crossings of the Atlantic and the Pacific oceans, the gulf has very little space in the narrative. The void was jumped successfully, and the articulation of places could begin again once the farther shore was sighted.

The New World is the final coastal thread that Locke discusses in his narrative. Columbus has a unique status for Locke because he was the *only* European explorer to discover a completely new coastline. The narrative of the voyage across the Atlantic is very short, and it focuses on the time that had been taken up, the mutinous character of the crew, and eventually the signs that they were approaching land. The open ocean itself is mere distance and duration, much like the Arabian Sea had been with de Gama, which helps emphasize the discontinuity of the exploration by absolutely dividing the old coastal line from the new one.

Locke's account of Columbus is very favourable. There is no mention of Columbus mistaking this part of the earth for Asia, or of his brutality towards the natives he encountered. In fact, the relationships between natives and Europeans is not part of Locke's history of navigation. As Locke writes, "Thus ended this year 1493; and here it must be observed, that all the actions done ashore must be omitted, as too great for this discourse, and in reality no way belonging to it, the design of it being only to show what advantages have been made by sea since the discovery of the magnetical needle, as has been declared before."[6] Places are located and people are sometimes referred to, especially when they are important to the exploration narrative or the subsequent economic relations. Generally, however, the spatial narrative is carried on with little concern for either the people or the qualities of the places that are included.

After the first discovery of the New World, Columbus and many others returned to following the line – the continental coast. Just as the people are uninteresting to Locke, so are the islands in the Caribbean only referred to sporadically and tersely. Their location is seldom specified. Rather, Locke's attention quickly turns to the exploration of the continent, and the narrative quickly returns to coasting, in this case north and south. In a voyage begun in 1500, for instance, Vincent Yanez Pinzon "discovered six hundred leagues along the coast lying south-east from Paria."[7] The progress of navigation in the Americas thus parallels the earlier progress along the coasts of Africa and Asia. A place acquired a location from its distance along the lines of the continental coasts, from the time when the first European discovered it, and finally from the particular European-sponsored companies that controlled the forts and garrisons dotting that section of the line.

The final section of Locke's history of navigation concerns European circumnavigations, from Ferdinand de Magellan's voyage, beginning in 1519, to John Cook's voyage, which began in 1683. With these voyages, there is a sense of the immensity of the oceans, and of the Pacific in particular. As Glyndwr Williams notes in his discussion of this period of

European exploration, "dimension is the key word, for revelation of distances rather than of new lands represented the true importance of Magellan's voyage."[8] Drake's voyage around the world also conveyed an immense space with very little description. In William's summary, "the narrative of Drake's voyage covered the unbroken navigation of more than two months from California to Palau in a half-dozen words: 'wee continued without sight of land.'"[9] These voyages added little to the European knowledge of specific places, and Locke only uses them to demonstrate with some finality the success of European technology. But the circumnavigators do not fit well into Locke's description of the world, and it is obvious that neither they nor Locke could deal with open oceans in any reliable detail or with any confidence. It was only when continents were being coasted that places could be located and made meaningful. This is how Europe articulated the world. Given the technologies of navigation and information that were available, it was the best they could do.

In general, the organization of places in Locke's world involves two primary pieces of information. The first is on which coastal line the place is located (Africa? America? and so on). The second is where that place occurs in relation to other places along the same coast. Which place comes first? How far, in miles, days, or degrees, is one place from another?

There are several implications to this way of articulating places. One is that it becomes difficult and somewhat uninteresting to relate points on different coastlines. The distance between the mouth of the Congo River and the Cape of Good Hope can be measured in terms of days or miles, and the points in between can be given. But how far is the Cape of Good Hope from a city along the coast of Brazil? An answer could be given, but it could not be derived from the information about the two separate coasts. In other words, measuring the distance between points on two different coasts requires the ability to calculate distance over an ocean that has neither landmarks nor stable ground. Typically, the number of days it normally takes to sail directly from one coast to another and the closest point on the parallel lines is the most accurate information that is given, and it is all the information that is needed.

Another implication of Locke's focus on coastlines is that islands are marginal, and they are typically positioned in the narrative in terms of the nearest point of the main line. Near the end of his history, for instance, Locke devotes several paragraphs to the islands that belong to the American continent. As he writes, "it only remains now to add a word concerning the islands belonging to this mighty continent. The first of these beginning northerly, is Newfoundland."[10] The list continues with the islands of the Caribbean:

> East of Cuba lies Hispaniola, a hundred and fifty leagues in length, and about sixty in breadth, producing the same commodities as Cuba; and both subject to Spain. Jamaica lies south of Cuba, about seventy leagues in length, and twenty in breadth, possessed by the English, and producing sugar, indigo, and cotton. The island of Puerto Rico is less than Jamaica, yields the same commodities, and belongs to Spain. The Caribbe islands are many, but small; some of them possessed by the English, French, and Dutch, others not inhabited: they produce sugar, indigo, cotton, and tobacco, and run from the coast of Paria to Puerto Rico.[11]

On one hand, Locke's account of islands parallels that of the coasts. The focus is on distances and directions, possessions and export products. But many of the islands have no specific position. There are many of them, but they are small and identified primarily in terms of which European country owns them. Unlike places on coasts, which can be described in detail in terms of before and after one another, islands are sporadic, almost accidental, and can only exist either in direct relation to the coast, or in a collection at the end of the narrative. Islands do not have coasts, and they barely have positions. To the navigators in Locke's world, therefore, islands can only be intelligible as points close to a continental line. The oceanic island can have no place at all.

For most of the eighteenth century, coasting was the primary mode of moving around the world and of locating places. Ships could traverse the open ocean, either by holding to a particular line of latitude to travel east and west or by sailing north and south along a coast until a particular latitude was reached (at which time the ships would turn east or west). Another important technique, first developed by the Portuguese and Spanish, was to sail away from the coast of West Africa into the open ocean of the South Atlantic until their ships picked up the trade winds. Then, sailing south until they reached the appropriate latitude, they could then sail back to the coast. This triangular pattern was repeated in oceans around the world. However, while this technique was an effective sailing strategy, it was only reliable where the trade winds were known. The technique was not effective for locating places in the world or, as will be the case in Cook's voyages, for zig-zagging around an open oceanic plane.

Location remained fixed on the continental coast, and places on the coast were located in terms of miles and time traversed between one place and another.

Very little changed in the sixty years following the publication of Locke's history. Among others, George Anson had circumnavigated the globe in the middle of the eighteenth century, but he added very little to the European knowledge of the world. In 1767, Captain Samuel Wallis discovered several islands in the South Pacific, including one that he called King George III's Island (which Cook would call Otaheite and now is Tahiti). In the Admiralty's account of Wallis's voyage, also edited by Hawkesworth and printed along with Cook's first voyage, the position of Port Royal Harbour, where Wallis had anchored, is given as "latitude 17° 30' S. longitude 150° W."[12] The longitude is given only to the nearest degree, which estimates the location within about 100 kilometres, but the measurement was still more accurate than what could have been made before. As Wallis wrote in his ship's journal, the purser had arrived at the longitude by "taking the Distance of the Sun from the Moon and Working it according to Dr Masculines Method which we did not understand."[13] The accuracy with which the position of the islands had been calculated allowed Otaheite to become the point in the ocean where Cook, who had never even seen the Pacific Ocean before, could arrive several years later to observe the transit of Venus. But Wallis's account of the location of Tahiti is exceptional in his narrative. As with the circumnavigators before him, Wallis spends very little time describing the location of islands. It is significant that, unlike Cook, who typically gives the coordinates at the beginning of the description, Wallis gives them at the very end, after the island and the interactions with the natives have been described. The location was given at the point of leaving, almost as an afterthought.

Wallis and other English captains such as Philip Carteret, John Byron, and Cook had all been sent to explore the South Seas, but the primary goal was to discover a southern continent, that is to say, another coastline to follow. The goal was to turn the empty spaces on the map into land. It was only during Cook's voyages that this was discovered to be impossible, that no continent was found, and that the empty map of the Pacific Ocean was filled with water and islands.

In keeping with the narrative patterns of prior navigators, Cook's voyages involve a lot of coasting. The voyages around New Zealand, for instance, are very similar in form to the earlier accounts of coasting around Africa and the Americas. The coast is a continuous line, and coasting is the articulation of trends and distances. Cook follows the contours of the coast, drawing a continuous line that turns now to the west, now to the north, and so on. Cook also divides the line into the same kinds of points and sections that were used by previous navigators, noting the distances between the capes, bays, promontories, and rivers that dot the coastline.

Paul Carter, writing of Cook's first voyage in *The Road to Botany Bay*, claims that the articulation of place in Cook's voyages is organized, in part, by the narrative structure of the voyage itself, by the movement of the ship and its crew as the voyage works its way along the coast. Carter argues that this connection can be seen in Cook's own naming practices, which tied together the organization of the world, the voyage, and the text. For Carter, "Cook's place names express the navigator's active engagement with the space of his journey."[14] The move from Poverty Bay to the Bay of Plenty, for instance, is a movement in meaning as much as a change in location. The names become part of the drama of the voyage. Thus, Carter concludes, "Cook's knowledge of the Australian coast was a product of his mobility and his active engagement with its waters, reefs and horizons; at the very least, his casual and special names represent the conditions under which he aimed to make history."[15] To support his reading, Carter notes how Cook changed several of the names he had given to places along the coasts of Australia and New Zealand once the ship had reached Batavia and Cook was able to look back on the voyage as a whole, and especially on his time spent around New Zealand. At that point, he reformulated the names he gave to the places in terms of an overall narrative. Carter writes, for instance, of how "Cook marked the culmination of the New Zealand survey by naming his point of final departure Admiralty Bay and, to underline its place in his career, its two capes were named after the signatories of his Instructions, the Secretaries of the Admiralty, Sir Philip Stephens and George Jackson."[16]

Later in the book, Carter characterizes the way that explorers in general organize their journals explicitly as narratives of exploration. To Carter, Cook is engaged in a creative articulation of the places of the world, and his narrative (including his naming) is a narrative about that encounter: "The unnaturalness of attaching ministers to mountains, secretaries to capes, the playful tautology of calling islands 'Islands of Direction', the unlikelihood of Botany Bay, as if the flora in question were marine: by all these figurative means Cook preserves the difference between the order of nature and the order of culture."[17]

In the same way, for Carter the map of New Zealand from Cook's first voyage is "not a collection of geographical objects imprisoned beneath the grid of latitude and longitude. It was closer to a picture or to the journal itself."[18] Carter argues that the grid is secondary to the linear journey; that is, to the narrated coast along which Cook travelled. Of course, this narrative organization of places works best the first time a place is explored. The next time that Cook sails along the coast of New Zealand, in the second voyage, the naming relations become much more complicated. He has to refer back to the narrative of the previous voyage to find and describe the places again, but now they do not exist along the same narrative track. Admiralty Bay is not the culmination of any part of the second voyage; it is just another place. Thus Cook cannot exactly follow the first narrative the second time, although he must appeal to the previous, now published, place names. The names stay the same, even if the narrative is new.

Carter's account of Cook's exploration is effective insofar as *The Road to Botany Bay* focuses only on the first voyage and specifically on Cook's navigation along the coasts of New Zealand and Australia. In these sections of the voyage, Cook's naming practices correspond to the earlier coastal explorations of Europeans along Africa, Asia, and the Americas.

But coasting is not the only thing that Cook does in the first voyage, and he does much less of it in the second and third voyages. Rather, for most of his time at sea he is exploring the South Seas or the Pacific Ocean, where he encountered an immense number of dispersed islands, separated by large expanses of open water. In the South Seas, the islands were no longer tied to a coast. They were points on a coordinate grid of latitude and longitude, a grid that came to dominate the narrative. During these parts of Cook's voyages, the progress of the narrative depends primarily on the articulation of changes in longitude and latitude, punctuated by the appearance of land. Where the coast is long enough, coasting may occur, but most of the islands are small, specious points, and the narrative shows little concern for coasting. At these times, the coordinate grid does not imprison Cook's narrative; it makes his particular kind of narrative possible.

THE COORDINATE SYSTEM

The directions written by Rooke and published at the behest of the Royal Society at the end of the seventeenth century urged navigators to mark "withal the latitude and longitude of the place where such observation is made." The idea, of course, was that a mathematical grid could be placed over both the world and the map, so that location could be disconnected from the presence of landmarks and the progress of exploration narratives. By connecting places to the astronomical and mathematical workings of the universe, it was in principle possible to determine location anywhere on the globe, no matter how disorienting the course of the voyage had been or how empty the place was. However, the move from the coastal line of Locke's world to the grid of Cook's world did not depend on a conceptual shift. What happened, rather, was that the coordinate system became practical as a way to determine longitude at sea reliably.

Calculating latitude, which is the position north and south, has been possible since at least the time of ancient Greece. With the proper instruments, such as a sextant, which was first developed in the 1730s, determining the latitude of a particular place is relatively simple. Latitude is calculated in the Northern Hemisphere from the angle formed by two imaginary lines originating from the observer: the first to the horizon and the second to the North Star. The nearer the observer is to the equator, the smaller the angle is between the horizon and the North Star. Conversely, as the observer approaches the North Pole, the North Star rises higher above the horizon. In the Southern Hemisphere, where the North Star cannot be seen, it is possible to substitute other stars, including the sun, although the calculations are more complicated and typically involve the use of astronomical tables.[19]

Locke provides the latitude of various places throughout his narrative. To a navigator, being able to determine latitude is very useful. For instance, when ships sailed in the Atlantic between Europe or Africa and the Americas, the crew would try to remain at a particular latitude and maintain a single direction. Then, even if they did not know how far they were away from either coast, they at least knew which way the coasts were and what direction they should be going. Likewise, ships could also sail up the middle of the Atlantic, taking advantage of wind patterns, and know when to turn eastward in order to reach a point in Europe or westward to reach a point in the Americas. When the coast was sighted, the ship could then sail along it in either direction to the desired place.

European navigation in the Pacific up until the end of the eighteenth century similarly relied on latitude; the Spaniards, pirates, and circumnavigators typically sailed along the coast when moving north and south, and then stuck to a single line of latitude, the "common track," when moving east and west. Francis Drake, for instance, crossed the Pacific at about 15° north latitude. George Anson crossed the Pacific at roughly 10° north latitude, or roughly 300 miles south of Drake's line, and discovered nothing new. This way of organizing ocean navigation is an important reason why the Spaniards, after centuries in the Pacific, had discovered, or at least integrated, so few places. They were not moving in ways that were suitable for finding oceanic islands. Theirs was a world of lines.

The limits of this approach to exploring the world were well-known at the time. At the end of the seventeenth century, for instance, the explorer William Dampier wrote that "one who rambles about a Country can give usually a better account of it, than a Carrier who jogs on to his Inn, without ever going out of his Road."[20] But the technology available up until the end of the eighteenth century meant that wandering, even if possible, could not result in reliable information that could be shared with others. Latitudes could be given with some reliability – the problem was in determining longitude.

There were many instances where knowing longitude would have been very useful. One notable example occurred during the circumnavigation undertaken by Commodore Anson. Scurvy was an ever-present danger, and the value of fresh food and water was recognized as a cure. As Anson was sailing through the Streights Le Maire, to the south of Cape Horn, on his way into the South Pacific, he encountered a storm that lasted almost two months, trapping the ships in the strait. Scurvy was killing up to ten men each day. They finally made it through the straits and sailed north until 24 May 1741, when they reached the latitude of the island of Juan Fernandez, where they could expect to find fresh food and water. The problem was that no one knew whether the island was to the east or to the west, and in the open ocean there were no landmarks to help guide them. Anson chose to head to the west, but after four days they sighted no land and so turned around and headed east. Two days later they sighted land, which turned out to be an inaccessible part of the coast of Chile. The ship had to turn around and head westward again, and finally landed on Juan Fernandez on 9 June. They had wasted two weeks trying to find an island in the open ocean. During that period, an additional eighty of Anson's men died.[21] All that Anson had to do was determine his position east and west. But in the open ocean, this could not be done.

Locke rarely provides the longitude of the places he describes, which is not surprising given that the navigators in his summary seldom gave the longitude, and when they did it was usually little more than a guess. Cook's voyages, on the other hand, contain frequent criticisms of the longitudes laid down by previous navigators, including his immediate predecessors. But Cook's criticisms had a greater strength than those of previous navigators – he could measure longitude accurately.

By the end of the eighteenth century, there were two primary methods for determining longitude, built on theoretical work done by astronomers such as Isaac Newton; they were based on information provided by timepieces or by astronomical observation.[22] The geometrical basis of longitude is relatively straightforward. The globe is divided from east to west into 360 degrees, where two places that are 180 degrees of longitude apart are on opposite sides of the world. What this means is that if it is 6:00 in the morning at one place on the globe, it would be 6:00 in the evening on the exact opposite side of the world (180 degrees of longitude away); a twelve-hour difference represented 180 degrees, six hours represented 90 degrees, and so on. As a result, longitude could be calculated if someone could determine the current time at the ship's location and the time at the prime meridian (which for Cook was at Greenwich, but this was far from standard at the time, with French explorers using Paris, Portuguese explorers using Lisbon, and so on). Calculating the current time was relatively easy, assuming that the sky could be clearly seen. The problem was knowing the time at the prime meridian. It was possible to bring a timepiece on ship that was set to the time in Greenwich, but most of the timepieces up until the late eighteenth century depended either on pendulums (and were useless on a ship that rocked at sea) or on springs (which were affected by changes in humidity and temperature). In the middle of the eighteenth century, and in time for Cook's second voyage, John Harrison developed a spring-based chronometer that could keep tolerably accurate time on a ship through a wide variety of climates. It was then possible to compare the two times, and thus calculate the longitude. The more accurate the times, the more accurately the longitude would be measured.

The second way to determine longitude, which did not depend on knowing the time at the prime meridian, was based on the position of the moon in the sky relative to the sun and other stars. In 1766, Nevil Maskelyne, Astronomer Royal, first published his *Nautical Almanac and Astronomical Ephemeris,* which provided the necessary tables for determining longitude from lunar observation. Wallis's purser had used this method to determine the longitude of Otaheite in 1767, securing a copy of Maskelyne's work before it had been printed.[23]

Among its other accomplishments, Cook's second voyage was a test of both of these techniques for determining longitude. One important implication of these techniques is that the account of place relative to the coordinate system does not depend on keeping a continuous record of the ship's movement. It became possible to determine location *sporadically*, without needing any knowledge of where the ship had been the day before, what direction it had travelled in, or how far. And with the ability to reliably calculate longitude at will, it became possible to confidently wander the open ocean in search of islands. But the changing attitude towards the ocean did not only allow new information to be collected; it changed how movements and places in the world were imagined.

The coordinates do not simply tell Cook where the places are, they also establish where he is, and they thus form a basic component of his travel narrative. In this way, Cook's voyages differ considerably from earlier voyages. Throughout the second voyage, the ship's clock was tested and found to give reliable time. Thus, he says, "Depending on the goodness of Mr. Kendall's watch, I resolved to try to make the island, by a direct course."[24] With the watch, in other words, it was possible for Cook to chart a linear course between two points, and not to have to work his way along a coast or remain in a particular latitude, for fear of getting lost in the empty space of the ocean. Cook's world became a world of points connected back to the coordinate grid rather than to the coasts of continents. The difference here is crucial. Not only can Cook move around the world in a different way, he can also narrate the location of places differently.

For Cook, knowing where the places were, even along the coast, involved a constant appeal to the coordinate system, which in turn depended on the continual access to reliable instruments and tables. The transformation of space from coastlines to oceanic grids is most evident in the first part of Cook's second voyage. The voyage began in the same way that European voyages had begun for centuries. The *Discovery* and the *Adventure* left the home port and headed south. Touching at the Canary Islands to take on supplies, the ships then proceeded along the west coast of Africa to the Cape of Good Hope, where they again took on supplies. At this point, the east coast of Africa proceeds back to the north, but Cook turned the ships to the *south,* into the open ocean towards the Antarctic. He was looking for Cape Circumcision, "which was said by Monsieur Bouvet to lie in the latitude of 54° south, and in about 11° 20' east longitude from Greenwich."[25] The cape could have belonged to a large southern continent, but Cook found neither continent nor cape.

Over the next three years, Cook spent very little time working his way along coasts. Rather, the second voyage combined exploring the open ocean in the high southern latitudes and recuperating and exploring in the island-dotted mid-southern latitudes of the Pacific Ocean. Before Cook, exploration was about lines and coasts. Cook's zig-zagging across the plane of the ocean was something very different. The line had been changed into an area, and the places of the world, wherever they existed and at whatever stage in the journey they were encountered, were located by their coordinates. The spatial organization of the narrative was no longer linear: weather permitting, Cook could move from one place to another at will.

VERIFICATION OF DETAILS

Echoing a host of other historians, J.H. Parry describes geographical exploration as the "most empirical of all forms of enquiry, and most destructive of purely *a priori* reasoning."[26] Neil Rennie likewise characterizes the seventeenth and eighteenth centuries, the age of discovery, as "an age that witnessed the beginnings of the triumph of experience over authority."[27] In narrating this shift, Cook is an important figure for both writers. Throughout the voyages, he is verifying claims made by other people, whether previous navigators, speculative philosophers, natives, or his own crew. But the age of discovery was also a time when scientific instruments of all sorts acquired increased authority. In Cook's voyages, a wide assortment of instruments, from the clocks to the dipping needles, were essential for creating an accurate account of places. Without them, Cook would not only be lost, but would be unable to provide an account to anyone else of where he had been. "Experience," then, has to be understood in terms of instruments, which often supplant direct experience in the production of facts. What mattered for the success of Cook's engagement was the ability to measure.

Cook begins measuring longitude and latitude the moment he arrives on board his ship. At this stage in the voyages, he is evaluating the precision of his instruments. They are, after all, the basis for the new science of place, so he tests the ships' instruments as often as he can. He even alters the sailing plan in order to check the accuracy of the timepieces. At one stage in the third voyage, for instance, Cook notes, "As my chief reason for putting in at this place was to give Mr. Wales an opportunity to know the error of the watch by the known longitude, and to determine anew her rate of going, the first thing we did was to land his instruments, and to erect tents for the reception of a guard and such other people as it was necessary to have on shore."[28] By comparing the instruments' results to the coordinates of well-known places, the navigator verifies the accuracy of the instruments and thus legitimates the results that they produce and that he can produce with them.

By demonstrating the watch's effectiveness for determining longitude, Cook helped to promote the geometrical division of space. Technological changes thus provided the basis for an ever more accurate, authoritative mapping of the places of the world. The founding of the Royal Geographical Society was still over fifty years away, occurring in 1830, but the image of the world as a geometrical entity runs throughout Cook's voyages. By testing his instruments, therefore, Cook was ensuring that his voyages produced a geometrically accurate account of the places in the world.

One important feature of Cook's reliance on coordinates as the primary way to articulate the location of places is that people who either cannot or do not write about place in terms of longitude are marginalized in Cook's accounts of the voyages, if not ignored. The exclusion occurs on several fronts. First, earlier published accounts of voyages are largely ignored unless they include coordinates, and then they are closely questioned and typically corrected or refuted. Second, the accounts of places that were collected from the natives who were encountered around the world were often recorded, but neither believed nor rejected. Rather, as with the earlier navigators, Cook used the information, where possible, as a way to direct his own enquiries, and he then reformulated that knowledge in terms of coordinates. Cook writes, for instance, "I think it would be pity to leave that any longer unexamined, especially as the voyage may turn to good account, besides determining the principal question, if no continent should be found, by the discovery of new islands in the tropical regions, of which there is probably a great number that no European vessel has ever yet visited. Tupia [a native of Otaheite], from time to time, gave us an account of about one hundred and thirty; and, in a chart drawn by his own hand, he actually laid down no less than seventy-four."[29]

But Tupia's claims required verification in a different system of knowledge, organized in terms of coordinates. To speak truthfully about a place in Cook's world required at the bare minimum that the coordinates were reliably determined, which in turn required the necessary instruments, tables, and skills to produce the coordinates. In other words, what Cook's voyages helped to establish was not simply the location of some islands in the South Pacific, but also the nature and methods of knowledge as such.

The voyage of George Vancouver in the 1790s continued this practice. Vancouver verified his instruments at many of the places where Cook himself had carefully calculated the coordinates. For Vancouver, one of the most important points was Nootka Sound, located on the northwest coast of the Americas, which became a local baseline in relation to which he could position points along that coast.[30]

It is little wonder that Otto von Kotzebue, a German navigator sailing under the Russian flag, stopped in London on his first voyage into the Pacific, which began in 1815, and spent a considerable amount of time and money purchasing a wide variety of instruments from reputable manufacturers.[31] The presence of these instruments turned the voyage into a modern scientific voyage, which allowed Kotzebue and his associates to participate in the scientific discourses of space carried out in early-nineteenth-century Europe. He could pinpoint places around the world, verify their location, and determine the location of previously unmapped places with an accuracy that would put him beyond the criticism of his contemporaries and give him a right to claim a discovery.

With the coordinate system, places in the world become reliable, largely geometrical spaces that can be described and verified from one person and one time to another. There is a reassurance that comes with the tables, instruments, and astronomical data that tie into the coordinate system. The reassurance is both practical and metaphysical. The coordinates create a shared, objective way to locate places, which supports an empirical, rational account of place, and the instruments also create a privileged perspective, a presumed universality. Once the instruments were tested, it became possible for Cook to engage with the descriptions of the world offered by his predecessors, and to set the world aright. The instruments that measured longitude replaced the personal experience of the navigator and dead reckoning with something that could be recorded, shared, published, and verified. Cook's demonstration of the shape of the world thus became impersonal in the same way that mathematical proofs are impersonal. As Foucault writes when characterizing an author of mathematical texts, "In a treatise on mathematics, the 'I' in 'I conclude' indicates an instance and a level of demonstration which any individual could perform provided that he accepted the same system of symbols, play of axioms, and set of previous demonstrations."[32] Cook's voice in the voyages is at times the voice of the mathematical geographer, demonstrating the shared shape of the world. In this theme, Walter Besant describes Cook as "the great sailor who had fixed on the chart all the floating and uncertain islands seen by previous voyagers, and had found so many more himself."[33] The existence of "wandering islands" became impossible. Utopias also.

For the explorers of the continental lines, summarized by Locke, the important goals of the description were the accurate account of sailing directions and the trends of the coast. The existence of the coast itself, the existence of land, was only ever in question with the first voyage of Columbus.

With Cook's voyages, on the other hand, the existence of various places became a series of empirical questions that could be tested. The relative failure of all navigators before Cook is suggested throughout the published accounts. Cook notes, "I must here observe, that amongst these low and half-drowned isles (which are numerous in this part of the ocean) Mr. Bougainville's discoveries cannot be known to that degree of accuracy which is necessary to distinguish them from others."[34] And when Cook later writes, "From hence I steered S. S. W. 1/2 W. for Otaheite, with a view of falling in with some of those isles discovered by former navigators, especially those discovered by the Dutch, whose situations are not well determined,"[35] he, on his own account, "settled the situation of some old discoveries."[36] The coordinate system thus forms the basis for a dialogue between navigators concerning the location of places in the world – it is a system in which all the questions of location can be answered. By appealing to the coordinate system, the existence, non-existence, and location of places can be established with ever-increasing authority, always depending on the reliability of instruments and conveyed in the official published results. The dialogue over location can thus be ended and other information can be organized on a firm foundation.

Travelling in a world of coordinates and books, Cook is thus able to consolidate the information that had been collected and published by past explorers into a single coordinated system in which specific claims could be checked, and inconsistencies or gaps identified. The project is ultimately totalizing. As Cook describes his attitude towards space in the first voyage, "I was determined to leave no subject for disputation which experiment could remove."[37] Given that places do not change location, that they are always there to be checked, it is possible to use the coordinate system as a ground for meticulous error-checking.

At times in the voyages, Cook is concerned with the basic question of the existence of a place. There are many examples, such as when he writes, "the next day at noon, we were in the latitude 37° 54' S., which was the same that Juan Fernandez's discovery is said to lie in. We, however, had not the least signs of any land lying in our neighbourhood."[38] At other times, Cook is concerned with settling the question of location. Sometimes he verifies past information, and other times he corrects it, suggesting that a place should be moved from one point on the grid to another. He relates near the end of the second voyage, for instance, that, "by knowing the longitude of this isle, we are able to determine that of the adjacent east coast of Brazil; which, according to the modern charts, lies about sixty or seventy leagues more to the west."[39] The location of islands is also clarified: "These must be the same islands to which Commodore Byron gave the name of George's Islands. Their situation in longitude, which was determined by lunar observations made near the shores, and still farther correct[ed] by the difference of longitude carried on by the watch to Otaheite, is 3° 54' more east than he says they lie. This correction, I apprehend, may be applied to all the islands he discovered."[40]

Given the way that claims about locations are structured, Cook is also subject to correction, even by himself. In the second voyage, he corrects mistakes that were made in the first voyage because his instruments were less reliable, or because he had less time to produce accurate measurements.

> Mr. Wales from time to time communicated to me the observations he had made in this Sound for determining the longitude, the mean results of which give 174° 25' 7" ½ E. for the bottom of Ship Cove, where the observations were made; and the latitude of it is 41° 5' 56" ½ S. In my chart, constituted in my former voyage, this place is laid down in 184° 54' 30" West, equal to 175° 5' 30" E. The error of the chart is therefore, 0° 40' 0", and nearly equal to what was found at Dusky Bay; by which it appears that the whole of Tavai-poenammoo is laid down 40' too far east in the said chart, as well as in the journal of the voyage."[41]

When Cook's biographers look back on his life, when they look back on his accomplishments, his settling of controversies is prominent. Andrew Kippis, for instance, writes, "while Captain Cook was at this country, he neglected nothing which could promote the knowledge of science and navigation. Here, as everywhere else, he settled the latitude and longitude of places; marked the variations of the compass, and recorded the nature of the tides. He corrected, likewise, an error of Captain Furneaux, with respect to the situation of Maria's Island; on which subject he hath candidly remarked, that his own idea is not the result of a more faithful, but merely of a second examination."[42] Kippis does not tell his readers what the error or the correction was; but these details do not matter by the time biographies of Cook are being written. What is more important for Kippis is how Cook engaged with prior mistakes. Cook was the one who succeeded where others had failed.

THE POSSIBILITIES OF LOCATION

In Cook's voyages, knowledge of the world is organized by first dividing the world into coordinates. Then it becomes possible to describe each point in detail, naming the points that are interesting, passing over the points that are empty. The coordinates were thus organized in terms of a table, where coordinates are placed alongside other information, as if the world had become a large filing cabinet.

Elizabeth Eisenstein argues that the printing press significantly changed how tables were created and what they were used for. Not only did printed tables help people standardize and extend information, they also helped connect people with very different areas of expertise. For instance, "Kepler's tables ... accompanied the men who went on journeys of discovery just as ... Regioniontanus' tables had accompanied Columbus ... Without themselves having moved very far out into the world, these two Germans had performed important services in the conquest of the earth's globe."[43] The table, as an ideal for organizing information, was central to Cook's account of the world. Nevil Maskelyne had already published his *British Mariner's Guide,* and the table of coordinates and places from Cook's voyages, even if it was never printed as a separate publication, was included in later tables that offered more comprehensive accounts. By the middle of the nineteenth century, the table of coordinates that would be included in nautical almanacs would be several hundred pages of small print. By that time, of course, few if any of Cook's direct measurements were included. If nothing else, the cartographic technology had advanced to such an extent that it was possible to determine coordinates with ever greater accuracy, and other, more comprehensive surveys had been undertaken.

26   A P P E N D I X.

Names of Places.	Latitud.		Longit.	
	D	M	D	M
		S		W
Los Altos de Mancord	03	43	85	39
The Point of *Plateros*	03	52	85	05
The Cape *Blanco en el Peru*	04	00	85	08
The Port of *Falara*	04	00	84	58
The Point of *Parina*	04	30	84	38
El Pueblo of *Colan*	04	46	85	46
The Port of *Paita*	05	00	84	46
La Pena de Paita	05	00	84	44
The Ifland of *Lobos de la Silla de Paita*	05	06	84	01
Le Puntilla del Tunal	05	12	84	31
The Point of *Nonera*	05	45	84	11
The Point of *Ura*	06	00	83	51
El Morro de Eten	06	20	84	19
El Morro de Requen	06	40	84	25
The Ifland of *Lobos* of *Tierra*	06	20	83	31
The Ifland of *Lobos* of *Afuera*	06	56	83	21
The Port of *Cheripe*	07	00	83	06
La Caletas de Pafo Maio	07	10	83	06
La Plaia y Morro de Malabrigo	07	32	82	49
The Ifland of *Malabrigo*	07	36	82	37
La Pa de St Tiago o balle de la Madalena	07	48	82	33
The Port of *Guanchaco*	08	00	82	19
El Morro de Carretas	08	08	82	22
Morro de Guanape	08	30	82	15
Los Farellon es de Guanape	08	33	82	02
The Ifland of *Chao*	08	40	81	58
El Porto y Corcabado de Santa	09	00	82	04
The Ifland of *Santa*	09	02	82	01
El Serro de Chambete	09	10	81	54
Les Bocas de la Ferroles	09	15	81	48
The Port of *Guanbacho*	09	25	81	45
La Caleta de la Tortugas	09	34	81	45
The Port of *Cafma*	09	40	81	38
El Serra de Mongon	09	45	81	34
La Caleta a Hondra	09	52	81	27
The Port *Bermya o di Culibra*	10	00	81	11
The Port of *Guariney*	10	10	81	08
The Port of *Gramadael*	10	20	81	08
La Tortaliza de Paramenga	10	34	80	55
The Port of *Barranca*	10	40	80	48
The high Land of the Port of *Supe*	10	50	80	38

The

A page from the table of coordinates reprinted in Pascoe Thomas's account of George Anson's voyage, first published in 1745.

Tables of coordinates existed well before Cook's voyages. A table that had been captured from the Spaniards during Anson's voyage into the Pacific, for instance, was reprinted in the appendix to Pascoe Thomas's 1745 account of that voyage. This particular table, however, is limited to a small section of the west coast of south and central America, and the sense of space remains coastal. Partly, the close connection between coasts and coordinates arose for the practical reason that navigators were the ones who needed that information.

The table of coordinates arising from Cook's voyages, on the other hand, included cities, points, islands, and rivers throughout the Atlantic and the Pacific. More than just information for coastal pilots, the coordinates in Cook's voyages provided information for a table in which the places described could be specified and differentiated in the narrative itself. The table of coordinates became a surface on which places could be located, specified, described, and analyzed. The table acquired a comprehensiveness and a geographical presence – it became closely tied to the map, which itself became a table of coordinated points. The map offered an image, a mapping, of the table. For instance, Sydney Parkinson's journal, from Cook's first voyage, reads, "as we have, in plate XXV, given a map of the coast of New Zealand, in which the latitudes and longitudes, of the several places we explored, are correctly set down, we shall, in our account of that island, omit mentioning the situation of places in that respect, and, once for all, refer the reader to the map."[44]

While Cook is concerned with narrating where the places of the world are, Parkinson could refer the reader to a copy of Cook's map and treat the issue as settled. Nonetheless, the map is still appealed to in Cook's voyages, if only as a way to avoid describing tedious details that would overcrowd more important aspects of the narrative. In the first voyage, for instance, Cook writes, "Our latitude, by observation, was 11° 23' S., and our longitude 217° 46' W., our soundings were from fourteen to twenty-three fathom; but these, as well as the shoals and islands, which are too numerous to be particularly mentioned, will be best seen upon the chart."[45] With the map, the reader is able to view a large amount of information in a single statement. The map is not only a collection of points or a list of place names; it also shows the geometric relationships between those points. The map summarizes coordinates and links those coordinates to the specific contours of a map.

Organizing a map of the world by the grid of longitude and latitude also creates a sense of the possibilities of place. The map includes unknown regions, which helps travellers avoid surprises, or at least makes it clear where surprises could be expected. The narrative of exploration, then, becomes an attempt to fill in blank places rather than to move further along a line.

An important use of the table of possible locations, a table that included all possible coordinates, is Cook's attempt to demonstrate the non-existence of a large southern continent, whose existence had been theorized and that had reputedly been sighted for several centuries before Cook. To demonstrate that a large continent did *not* exist, Cook's ships had to criss-cross a vast and largely empty body of water. The ships tended to avoid the tracks that had already been reported, whether by Cook or previous navigators. Cook thus says, "had the wind continued favourable, I intended to have run 15 or 20 degrees of longitude more to the west, in the latitude we were then in, and back again to the east in the latitude of 50°. This route would have so intersected the space above-mentioned, as hardly to have left room for the bare supposition of any land lying there."[46]

At this point in the second voyage, Cook is searching for emptiness, and, for his demonstrations to be successful, he needs to organize his movement in terms of the tracks of previous navigators. In the first voyage, Cook claims that his "navigation has certainly been unfavourable to the notion of a southern continent, for it has swept away at least three-fourths of the positions upon which it has been founded."[47] The demonstration, which became decisive in the second voyage, depended on a general table of locations, organized by coordinates, that indicated whether a particular point was land or ocean. Not only could Cook then avoid the course taken by former explorers, he could also combine the information from the tracks of different ships into a single table and then divide the ocean into sections, cutting away possible locations. The coordinate grid thus creates a plane on which the tracks of different navigators can interact in a single account of the world. These tracks are not the well-worn trenches of coastal navigators or oceanic crossings; they cut across the plane of possible locations, ideally only once. Cook's strategy was still linear, in a sense, but the line did not follow a coast. It was not restricted by the presence of land, and it tended to wander.

Cook thus surveyed large areas of open ocean, always with an eye to his tables, his instruments, and the points on the grid that were still empty. Cook's triumph over space, in other words, did not depend on how far he explored along a particular line. Rather than distance, Cook's success depended on the amount of area he surveyed.

All knowledge about the world was built on geometrical and verifiable points. The image of the point, supported by mathematical certainty, is important for Cook's voyages. Even though the account of space is clearly geometrical, Cook's engagement with space is far from indifferent. Points are everywhere; they are the basic unit with which Cook pieces together his account of the world, demonstrating the existence of small islands and the non-existence of a large southern continent. But the points are not merely abstracted or dispassionate. The search for points is the deepest engagement that Cook has with the world. Kippis writes that many of the islands in the South Pacific "are mere points, when compared with the vast ocean by which they are surrounded."[48] But it is these "mere" points that form the backbone of Cook's world. It is on these islands, as much as on the vast ocean, that his sense of the world and of his own success as an explorer relies. There is a subjective, perhaps even poetic, aspect to coordinates in Cook's voyages. Their pervasiveness may help form Cook's objectivity, but they also help form his desires. When Cook is verifying the claims of prior navigators, he is *hunting* for points, because it is by capturing them that the places of the world can be known.

TWO

Shapes

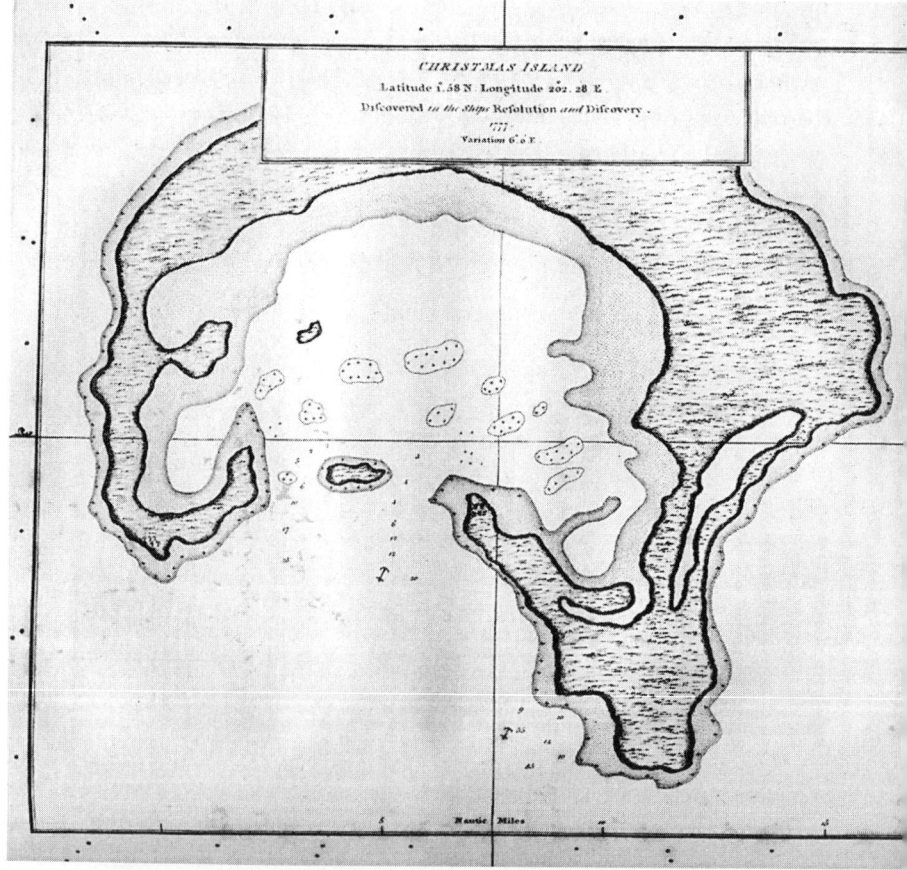

CHRISTMAS ISLAND
Latitude 1.58 N. Longitude 202. 28 E.
Discovered in the Ships Resolution and Discovery.
1777
Variation 6°. o E.

Nautic Miles

A map of Christmas Island from Cook's third voyage. Christmas Island,
now called Kiritimati, is a coral atoll in Micronesia. The *Resolution* and the
Discovery arrived at the island on Christmas day in 1777.

By moving away from the coast, and by accurately locating places in the open ocean, Cook's voyages refigure the world. Not only do the voyages change a world of lines into areas, they also allow an exact accounting of location, where location exists at the intersection of the printed narrative and the coordinate system. Longitude and latitude, functioning as mathematical place names, form a structure of possible names well before the human names are narrated – establishing the coordinate point is an act of pure referencing. But the coordinate points contain no area. The coordinates offer an account of location, but not of shape; in the end they contain nothing.

Cook's accounting of places is based on a geometrical measurement of shapes, in which the grid is tied to the boundary of the place and points are joined together in the mathematical area. In the mapping of shapes, Cook's voyages are again differentiated from accounts of prior navigators. Not only does he produce a large number of maps, but his ability to measure longitude gives his maps a geometrical accuracy that was unequalled at the time. The maps also become part of a general collection, where one map is placed alongside another, or many maps are brought together into a larger area, such as the Pacific Ocean as a complete place.

In the account of the world in Cook's voyages, the appeal to shapes and areas in a Cartesian plane accomplishes two things: it frames the world in very broad terms, and it divides the world into static, two-dimensional chunks that can be arranged, first in terms of coordinates, and then in terms of other attributes. By expressing the map and the world in terms of geometrical objects and verifiable measurements, social and political identities can be organized. By mapping the shape of Otaheite, Cook is mapping the home of the Otaheiteans and the dominion of the Otaheitean king.

GRAND DIVISIONS

As is the case for most terrestrial navigators, the largest spaces in Cook's voyages are created with the division between the Earth and the rest of the universe. Not only does the shape of the world ground the image of circumnavigation, it also allows the navigator to approach places in the world as if the world were not moving. Aristotle claimed centuries ago that the place, understood as a container, should be considered stationary. A boat is thus in the river because it is "the whole river that is place, because as a whole it is motionless."[1] Immanuel Kant likewise notes in *The Metaphysics of Morals* how "nature has enclosed [everyone] together within determinate limits (by the spherical shape of the place they live in, a *globus terraqueus*)."[2] For Kant, this is a key condition for the possibility of morality, because without this absolute border, people would simply wander away from each other and make morality unnecessary. Cook, of course, appeals to the stars and the planets to determine the coordinates of both ships and places, but through the use of measurements and astronomical tables, the places are ultimately related to each other on the fixed terrestrial sphere rather than to the transient, albeit predictable, location of the stars and the planets. This finitude, and its division into fixed coordinates and a single map, framed the projects of eighteenth- and nineteenth-century exploration. There are only so many places on the earth, and the goal is to find them all, locate them, and produce an account of them. Exploration is a project that will one day come to an end, and it is towards that end that Cook's voyages are directed.

While the sphere helps contain the navigation on the curved plane of a single object, the sphere also helps Cook express the idea of absolute distance. On 3 December 1773, for instance, Cook notes how he and his crew "reckoned ourselves antipodes to our friends in London; consequently, as far removed from them as possible."[3] In this passage, "removed" refers to the distance measured in terms of geometrical length, either through the sphere or as the crow flies. Such a sense of place does not consider the time or hardship necessary to traverse the distance. At that point, the ship was near the southern parts of New Zealand, and the journey back to London would have been relatively routine. The voyage from the northern Pacific, which is much closer on a featureless sphere, would have been much more arduous and time-consuming, but by taking the world as a single geometrical object, distance can be abstracted from movement. Location no longer depends on narratives of travel.

Cook's emphasis on his distance from England also helps emphasize the finitude of the earth. This is an important feature of the voyages, insofar as it encourages the reader to understand the world as a single accessible area. The world map is the complete map of possible human activities.

One of the more important general divisions on the sphere is between the land and the sea. Rivers and lakes play a role in the articulation of places on land, especially between different sections of the coast. But it is through the division of land and sea that oceans, continents, and islands can be specified and named, and out of this division arises a general outline of the world.

To navigators who were primarily interested in coasting, the division between land and sea was also the division between knowledge and confusion, or between geographical civilization and geographical savagery. The ocean was wild. In *New Atlantis*, a utopian novel from the early seventeenth century, Francis Bacon marks the separation from land in the following terms: "Finding ourselves in the midst of the greatest wilderness of waters in the world, without victual ... [we] gave ourselves for lost men, and prepared for death."[4]

John Rickman's account of Cook's second voyage likewise adopts a sense of the ocean as a wild, uncivilized, and hostile place. When the ships land on Anamooka, one of the Friendly Islands, he notes how the "tents were now carried on shore; the astronomers observatory erected; wooders and waterers appointed; and all the artificers on board employed in the reparations of the ships; not a few being wanting after a voyage of two months, through a tempestuous sea, during which the elements of fire, air, and water, might be said to be in perpetual conflict."[5]

But "wilderness" is not a term that is typically used by Cook to describe the open ocean. Rather than being lost, Cook thrives in the absence of landmarks. Just as changes in nutrition solved the problem of scurvy and made every kind of navigation less dangerous, the development of the instruments needed to accurately determine coordinates reduced the dangers of being lost. Instead of detailing the outline of the continent, Cook's goal was to fill in an ocean, whether with land or water, to demonstrate that it was always possible to know where you are. And when you always know where you are, it becomes possible to accurately describe the geographical divisions of the world.

EXTREME PLACES

In addition to the division of the world into continents and oceans, another key division of the globe in Cook's voyages is narrated during his time in the high latitudes, and the high southern latitudes during the second voyage in particular. The extreme places had never been so extensively described, in part because no ship had tried to spend so much time so far south and because Cook's were the first ships to do so at a leisurely pace. After spending over a year in his second voyage sailing in and out of the Antarctic Circle and finally running into pack ice, Cook writes this much-quoted passage: "I, who had ambition not only to go farther than any one had been before, but as far as it was possible for man to go, was not sorry at meeting with this interruption; as it, in some measure, relieved us; at least shortened the dangers and hardships inseparable from the navigation of the southern polar regions. Since, therefore, we could not proceed one inch farther to the south, no other reason need be assigned for my tacking, and standing back to the north; being at this time in the latitude of 71° 10' S., longitude, 106° 54' W."[6] There is obviously an element of self-promotion here, both for Cook and his superiors. Cook knows that his journals are going to be published and that his status as a navigator depends in part on the dangers and the successes that have occurred during the voyage. The Antarctic, which is the epitome of the extreme place in his world, provides both the dangers and the successes that are necessary to constitute Cook as the explorer who pushed exploration to its limits.

In the second voyage, Cook pushes into the high southern latitudes twice, first in late 1773 and then in late 1774, wintering in the South Pacific (primarily at New Zealand and Otaheite) from March to November 1774. The map included with the second voyage, which is centred on the South Pole, shows the ships encircling the extreme. The Northern Hemisphere is not included at all, except as the implied source of the track of Cook's ships. Instead, the voyage alternates between the field ice and the islands of the South Pacific. Just as earlier navigators moved between the ocean and the coast, marking the existence of land, Cook's second voyage moves between mundane or tropical places and extreme places, tracing the limits of what is humanly possible.

The narrative of the voyage emphasizes Cook's existence at the edge of the world. There are several persistent themes, the first of which is the suffering of the crew. On leaving the Cape of Good Hope, Cook notes how the "sudden transition from warm mild weather, to extreme cold and wet, made every man in the ship feel its effects."[7] Not only did the weather kill a large portion of the livestock on board, it foreshadowed the dangers faced when the ships were to enter the Antarctic Circle. Some precautions were taken, such as lengthening the sleeves on the crew's jackets, but the suffering of the crew continued. Scurvy began to occur and was controlled by various antiscorbutics, such as lemon and malt extracts. The crew also faced bitter cold, not only on deck, but also in their cabins and when they were sent out in the longboats to collect chunks of floating ice for fresh water.

Cook's ship itself also suffered from the extreme cold. The weather threatened to damage the ship's equipment and thus their ability to function. Cook notes how the "rigging were all hung with icicles," an image that will come to have strong appeal to the European readership.[8] Cook continues with this theme by saying that "the worst was, the ice so clogged the rigging, sails, and blocks, as to make them exceedingly bad to handle. Our people however surmounted those difficulties with a steady perseverance, and withstood this intense cold much better than I expected."[9]

During the second time in the voyage that the ships entered the high latitudes, the same themes are used. "The sheaves also were frozen so fast in the blocks, that it required our utmost efforts to get a top-sail down and up; the cold so intense as hardly to be endured; the whole sea, in a manner, covered with ice; a hard gale, and a thick fog."[10] The weather suggested the severity of their situation. On 29 January 1773, Cook notes how the weather during the night was "very dark and stormy."[11] During the day, the weather was often hazy and gloomy, which, coupled with the cold winds and the frequent rain, sleet, and snow, helps the reader imagine the ships sailing at the edge of the world. But this is not wilderness, it is adversity. A sense of horror pervades the voyages at these times, and Cook is very concerned that the reader participates in that horror.

While the weather and the degeneration of the ships and crew are important for describing the horror of these extreme places, by far the most powerful images in the voyages are those of the islands of ice:

> On the 12th, we had still thick hazy weather, with sleet and snow; so that we were obliged to proceed with great caution on account of the ice islands: six of these we passed this day; some of them near two miles in circuit, and 60 feet high. And yet, such was the force and height of the waves, that the sea broke quite over them. This exhibited a view, which for a few moments was pleasing to the eye; but when we reflected on the danger, the mind was filled with horror; for, were a ship to get against the weather-side of one of these islands when the sea runs high, she would be dashed to pieces in a moment.[12]

The danger of quick destruction existed alongside the danger of being trapped by a field of ice, where the destruction would have been painfully slow, but equally inevitable: "Dangerous as it is to sail among these floating rocks (if I may be allowed to call them so) in a thick fog, this, however, is preferable to being entangled with immense fields of ice under the same circumstances. The great danger to be apprehended in this latter case, is the getting fast in the ice; a situation which would be exceedingly alarming."[13] There is no safety in this part of the world. At the limits of human existence, the Antarctic becomes the place where the adventure of open ocean navigation occurs in its purest form. Without the possibility of either help or survival if the ships were severely damaged or sunk, the narrative offers an ideal image of the extreme place, in which life is always and absolutely at risk. But Cook and his crew survive; they even adapt as much as is humanly possible:

> These dangers were, however, now become so familiar to us, that the apprehensions they caused, were never of long duration; and were, in some measure, compensated, both by the seasonable supplies of fresh water these ice islands afforded us, (without which we must have been greatly distressed,) and also, by their very romantic appearance, greatly heightened by the foaming and dashing of the waves into the curious holes and caverns which are formed in many of them; the whole exhibiting a view which at once filled the mind with admiration and horror, and can only be described by the hand of an able painter.[14]

The extreme areas to which Cook and his crew are able to navigate thus take on a cosmic tone. The ice fields do not simply represent a wall beyond which further navigation is impossible; they represent the limits of human existence and representation as such. At the edge of the world, words fail, and only the best painting can hope to convey an appropriate image to people who have not been there.

The associations that are invoked also acquire an explicitly gothic tone. Near the beginning of the second voyage, Marra, the gunner's mate on the *Resolution*, writes, "some of these islands appeared to be three or four miles in circumference, some more; but by far the greatest number appeared like the ruins of ancient towns, or the fragments of gothic castles."[15] Later in his journal, Marra continues the theme: "Here the ice islands presented a most romantic prospect of ruined castles, churches, arches, steeples, wrecks of ships, and a thousand wild and grotesque forms

The Ice Islands from the second voyage. The crew faced bitter cold and constant fear of running into icebergs. There was plenty of water, but only if the crew went out in the long boat to haul ice onto the ship to be melted.

of monsters, dragons, and all the hideous shapes that the most fertile imagination can possibly conceive. About these islands the penguins are heard continually screaming, and add to the horror of the scene, which cannot be beheld by the most intrepid without some emotions of fear."[16] The romantic, gothic appearance of these ice islands again helps Cook and his fellow narrators mark the edge of the world. But even surrounded by horror, these islands are still accounted for. Cook even gives their temporary coordinates and discusses how they could have been created.

At the end of December 1773, Cook considers moving away from the Antarctic ice into the South Pacific: "Under all these unfavourable circumstances, it was natural for me to think of returning more to the north, seeing no probability of finding any land here, nor a possibility of getting farther south." On 22 December 1773, Cook turns to the north for two weeks to run through an empty space he found on the map. He finds nothing interesting, and so, on 11 January 1774, the ship is turned to the south again to continue sailing among the fields and islands of ice. Soon after this point, however, Cook finally turns his ship away from the ice: "I will not say it was impossible any where to get farther to the south; but the attempting it would have been a dangerous and rash enterprise; and what, I believe, no man in my situation would have thought of."[17]

Cook had taken his ship as far south as humanly possible to demonstrate that there was no accessible land at the edges of the world, and by turning away at the extremes of both navigation and his own ambition, Cook marked the edge of the possibilities of navigation. Cook showed how far it was possible for human beings to go, and by journeying to the edge of the world and back, he proved his ship to be aptly named and himself to be as heroic and resolute as any adventurer. The demonstration, mixing geometry and danger, was complete.

Having survived the extremes of the Antarctic and demonstrated that a southern continent cannot exist in the navigable ocean, Cook moves on to the next stage: "since now nothing had happened to prevent me from carrying these views into execution, my intention was first to go in search of the land, said to have been discovered by Juan Fernandez, above a century ago, in about the latitude of 38°; if I should fail in finding this land, then to go in search of Easter Island or Davis's Land, whose situation was known with so little certainty that the attempts lately made to find it had miscarried."[18] Cook also lists other possible places that require verification, and empty places that require a first survey.

There is an excitement here that may strike some people as strange. Typically, the sea, much like grasslands, offers very little of interest. As Paul Carter notes in his discussion of the spatial organization of Australia, "if at times the sea promises an ease of passage impossible on land, at other times it seems disastrously flat, depressed, pointless."[19] And "as Tristram Shandy pointed out, however it might appeal to the traveller, a spacious plain made dreary reading."[20] But for Cook, the undifferentiated, pointless space *was* interesting. *Every* point on the grid was interesting, at least the first time. In his three voyages, Cook is not only looking for land but also for ocean, and accounting for empty places in the open ocean is a key element of his success. Of course, Cook is worried about the narrative possibilities of the open ocean. He notes at one stage in the second voyage that "I never made a passage any where of such length, or even much shorter, where so few interesting circumstances occurred. For, if I except the variation of the compass, I know of nothing else worth notice."[21]

But just as when exploring the extreme places, the underlying assumption is that after Cook this kind of exploration will no longer be necessary, and people will be able to focus on the useful and remarkable places of the world. On leaving the southern extremes, Cook becomes a surveyor, verifying the claims found in the accounts offered by other voyagers. Once again, the *Resolution* is appropriately named. But at this point, Cook is not pushing into extreme places, forcing the question of how far it is possible for human beings to go. He is forcing the question of what description of the world should be accepted. These attempts at resolving descriptions dominate the remainder of the second voyage and a good part of the third.

The move away from the ice fields in Cook's voyages does not simply create the field of possible navigation in abstraction. The move also helps demonstrate the possibilities of travelling anywhere else. Human beings cannot survive beyond the line that Cook has drawn. At the end of the second voyage, Cook summarizes the health of his crew: "Having been absent from England three years and eighteen days, in which time, and under all changes of climate, I lost but four men, and only one of them by sickness, it may not be amiss, at the conclusion of this journal, to enumerate the several causes to which, under the care of Providence, I conceive, this uncommon good state of health experienced by my people was owing."[22]

Rather than the narratives of pervasive death (such as Anson's account of how scurvy destroyed his crew), in the second voyage, Cook makes travel look easy, or at least safe. Near the end of the second voyage, for instance, the Admiralty's edition has Cook note "That our rigging, sails, &c. should be worn out, will not be wondered at, when it is known, that, during this circumnavigation of the globe, that is, from our leaving this place, to our return to it again, we had sailed no less than twenty thousand leagues; an extent of voyage, nearly equal to three times the equatorial circumference of the earth, and which, I apprehend, was never sailed by any ship in the same space of time before."[23]

The voyages also present that world as something that is accessible to others. Cook has not only gone farther south than anyone either has or probably could go, he has also gone farther in total distance. The second voyage, moving well beyond a simple circumnavigation, was the longest single voyage undertaken by anyone up to Cook's time. Previous European navigators had taken close to the same amount of time,[24] and many other Europeans had spent much more time in total sailing in the Pacific (Dampier and Thomas Cavendish being the most notable English examples). But Cook's success, in both the space covered and the lives preserved, was exceptional. After Cook turned from the ice, the narrative continues:

> We undoubtedly might have reached the Cape of Good Hope by April, and so have put an end to the expedition, so far as it related to the finding a continent; which indeed was the first object of the voyage. But for me at this time to have quitted this Southern Pacific Ocean, with a good ship expressly sent out on discoveries, a healthy crew, and not in want either of stores or of provisions, would have been betraying not only a want of perseverance, but of judgment, in supposing the South Pacific Ocean to have been so well explored, that nothing remained to be done in it. This, however, was not my opinion; for, although I had proved there was no continent but what must lie far to the south, there remained, nevertheless, room for very large islands in places wholly unexamined: and many of those which were formerly discovered, are but imperfectly explored, and their situations as imperfectly known. I was besides of opinion, that my remaining in this sea some time longer, would be productive of improvements in navigation and geography, as well as other sciences.[25]

Here, one of the implied reasons that Cook gives for remaining in the South Pacific is that the ship and crew were too fit and healthy to consider returning home. The ships would return home only when destruction was imminent and recovery unlikely, the dangers no longer being ice islands and fields, but much less extreme dangers to be found on much more mediocre, mundane points.

Having survived the extremes, Cook and his readers are left with the ocean and the accessible places that are walled in by the ice and the penguins. The geographical distinction between the wilderness and the coast has thus been turned into the distinction between the possible and the impossible, and the possible is all that remains interesting. With the second voyage, Cook unfolds his account of the world by framing it with the description of extreme places, but he also creates it by his movement through the mundane world of the open ocean. After turning away from the extreme, the focus of the voyage becomes the world that is accessible, and the goal is to turn what is geometrically possible into what is real; that is to say, to create a full and accurate account of the world.

THE OCEANIC PLANE

As has been suggested already, Cook's voyages changed the understanding of the ocean. Travellers move from a fear of open ocean to a desire to discover and describe points in an expansive field. The ocean is not just a grid divided into abstract points and lines, but an experienced plane that is narrated and illustrated in many different ways. For the oceanic navigator, the water is a plane of fixed points surrounded by coastal lines. The ocean does not simply disconnect the island from the mainland, it creates the possibilities for distinguishing oceans, islands, and continents as different *kinds* of spaces. The world, once mathematically featureless, begins to take shape.

Touching on this image, Joseph Conrad once asked whether Balboa, the first European to see the Pacific, "perhaps, like a man touched with grace, [had] a moment of exalted vision, the awed feeling that what he was looking at was an abyss of waters comparable in its extent to the view of the unfathomable firmament, and sown all over with groups of islands resembling the constellations of the sky?"[26] The mysticism of the Pacific would last for centuries. But near the end of the eighteenth century, the specific image of the Pacific changed. The ability to determine position in the open ocean created an expansive textualized space that allowed Cook to detail the minutiae of travel: the birds sighted, the fish caught, the weather, the water temperature, and so on, for any and all locations.

The narratives of Cook's voyages thus offer a sense of motion unlike anything that could be offered by previous navigators. With the help of his instruments and his tables, Cook could move from one point to any other point in the plane. He could cross the tracks laid down by others and traverse the Pacific in any direction, weather and supplies permitting. It is thus not surprising that Cook's voyages were the first to include an account of what he called the Sandwich Islands, insofar as Cook was likely the first European to intentionally sail up the middle of the Pacific. He was the first one who could do so without fear of getting lost.

To put this more emphatically, Cook's voyages *create* the Pacific. Of course, the Pacific had existed well before Cook and had been travelled by others. But in Cook's voyages, the ocean came to exist as a single entity, comprehended in a single travel narrative, with a relatively clear sense of what it was. For Drake, oceanic travel meant that there would be nothing to write about. With the military adventures of the buccaneers and Commodore Anson, the ocean became tracks of conflict in which the descriptions of places was secondary. Cook's voyages are something different. Through the narration of oceanic travel, especially in the last two voyages, the ocean becomes an extended, narrated plane, where fact and fiction could be distinguished once and for all.

More than relating his own discoveries, which are, in the end, not very numerous, the importance of Cook's voyages rests on the way that they settle the problems that were either posed or created by the discoveries of previous navigators. Jacob Roggeveen may have been the first European to land on Easter Island, in 1722, but Cook was the first one to fix the location of the island reliably on the map of the Pacific. The same can be said for each of Cook's predecessors, who discovered land in an ocean that they could not comprehend.

And so, soon after moving away from the Antarctic ice, Cook and his crew go in search of some land described by Juan Fernandez. The ship wanders in the area, and after failing to see land, Cook notes, "I was now well assured that the discovery of Juan Fernandez, if any such was ever made, can be nothing but a small island; there being hardly room for a large land, as will fully appear by the tracks of Captain Wallis, Bougainville, of the *Endeavour,* and this of the *Resolution.*"[27]

The high southern latitudes were empty of reliable places, and Cook had to look elsewhere for islands that could be known. From the point where Cook turns away from the extremes of the Antarctic ice, therefore, he is engaged in rectifying places. Fact is divided from fiction, estimations are replaced with definitive accounts, and places are located and mapped with as much accuracy as his instruments and skill allow. The result is an edited and verified summation of the places of the Pacific, whose situations are articulated in terms of coordinates and geometrical shapes on maps.

COOK'S TURN TO ISLANDS

It is only after leaving the fields of ice that the map of the world begins to freeze. In Cook's second voyage, the move away from the extreme edge of the world is a move towards islands. This is Cook at his most triumphant. He may have been looking for a southern continent, but the world described through the voyage ends up being far from continental. The focus on islands in Cook's voyages is somewhat accidental. As he writes near the middle of the second voyage, "all hopes of discovering a continent vanished. Islands were all we were to expect to find."[28] The manuscript version of the same passage reads, "having now crossed or got to the north of Captain Carteret's Track, no discovery of importance can be made, some few Islands is all that can be expected while I remain within the Tropical Seas."[29]

Disappointment is evident in the manuscript passage, which was muted in the official account. In the published version, the islands became more important and more valuable.[30] Discovering a continent might have established Cook's place in European history alongside Columbus, but Cook would not have been the one who discovered the continent, its existence having been suggested for centuries. At best, he would have been confirming and expanding on the discoveries of previous navigators. As it happened, however, he does confirm previous discoveries, but these discoveries were only islands and, taken as a whole, what Cook discovers is the true order of the Pacific Ocean.

With the shift from continents to islands, something important happens to the way that places are characterized. Not only does coasting become secondary, not only does the coordinate grid ground the progress through space, but the places become things that are easy to identify and differentiate. The ocean is punctuated by suddenness, and with these sudden islands, Cook's readers are offered clear and distinct places.

Each place is brought into the narrative by a standard series of stages: first of sighting, then of landing, and then of describing. The place becomes an obvious object, and the map becomes a still life. Islands become discrete entities, in part because they are described as geometrical objects. Cook is obsessed with working his way around each island to determine its shape, to prove that it is in fact an island, to set one island off from another and all islands off from the mainland. In describing an island near the Isle of Pines, which Cook's ship was unable to explore in detail, he can at least claim that "we pretty well know the extent of the land, by having it confined within certain limits."[31] For Cook, this is the beginning of knowledge about a place. A general outline is followed by a detailed map. When Cook demonstrated to his readers that New Zealand was not connected to a southern continent, and that it was in fact two islands, he said, "about this time, the weather happening to clear up, we saw Cape Turnagain, bearing N. by E. 1/2 E. at the distance of about seven leagues: I then called the officers upon deck, and asked them, whether they were not now satisfied that Eahienomauwe was an island: they readily answered in the affirmative; and all doubts being now removed, we hauled our wind to the eastward."[32] Once geometry has been combined with the agreement of all the worthy men on the voyage, the two main islands of New Zealand reliably exist as clear and distinct shapes that can be confidently placed on maps.

A key aspect of Cook's voyages is the way that areas in the world are mapped and located in a mathematically pure way. That Cook is exploring an ocean of islands helps to promote the clarity and distinction of places. Islands have edges, the distance between which can be measured. Inside, this gives each island a breadth; outside, it gives each island distance from other islands. By distinguishing "this" island from both the ocean and from "that" island, Cook is not only separating one set of coordinates from another. He is marking a physical division in which the open ocean is separated from the specific places that can and will be described in greater detail. *The* island, *this* island, *these* islands, all become the basis on which the rest of the descriptions in the voyages depend.

In addition to having distinct shapes on a map, islands are also associated with objects of everyday experience. For instance, one common way of describing the figure of an island is to compare it with a sugarloaf. The association is not new with Cook. Other comparisons between islands and everyday objects occur throughout the voyages. Leper Isle, for instance, is "of an egg-like figure, very high, and eighteen or twenty leagues in circuit."[33] During the second voyage, Cook writes that he "can say no more of this island [Paoom] than that it towers up to a great height, in the form of a round hay-stack; and the extent of it."[34] With these comparisons, Cook does not give enough information for later navigators to reliably identify the places, but he does bring each place into the voyages as

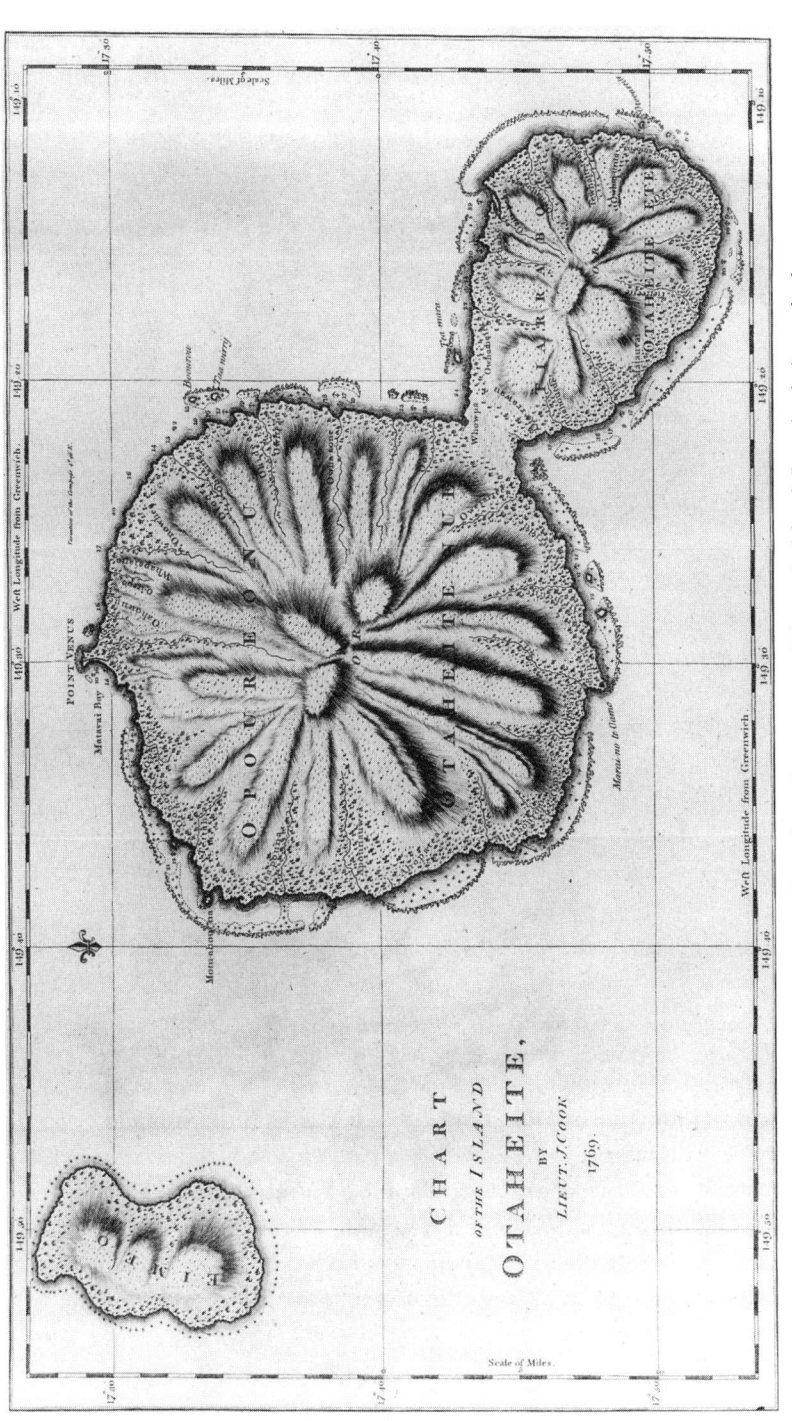

CHART
OF THE ISLAND
OTAHEITE,
BY
LIEUT. J. COOK.
1769.

Cook's map of Otaheite from the first voyage. Point Venus is at the very top of the main island. Longitude is marked to the nearest 10 seconds and referenced to Greenwich.

Sketch of Samganooda Harbour from Cook's third voyage. The harbour and the island both became containers where natives and supplies could be found.

a tangible, distinct object, which can be located, imagined, analyzed, represented, and discussed. The geometrical clarity of islands infects the clarity of places and of all the information organized around them.

As a distinct object, the island also acquires a proper name. Naming goes hand in hand with fixing shapes on a coordinate grid, but these names are not applied to the coordinates, they are applied to the shapes that are distinguished on the map.

Islands are also like bodies – they are given features and personalities. Cook frequently promises to "give some account of the face of the country."[35] Islands are "friendly," "inhospitable," or "savage." Often, the island becomes a complete person that Cook can relate to as an equal. During the third voyage, for instance, Cook describes how "a young bull and a cow, and some sheep and goats, were also, at first, intended to have been left by me, as an additional present to Van Diemen's Land."[36] The land thus enters into the narrative in specific, often human ways. Cook establishes a dialogue with the places and includes them in the voyages as he would a character in a narrative.

We have already considered how naming is tied to the narrative of the voyage itself, such as how Cape Farewell was named because that is where Cook finally left New Zealand in the first voyage. But there are many other kinds of names that Cook gives. One common theme connects the place to a person, such as Point Hicks, which was named after Zachary Hicks, one of the sailors on the *Endeavour*. Sometimes, as Carter points out, these names are given to honour people who were connected to Cook's career, such as Hugh Palliser, one of Cook's early patrons, or the Earl of Sandwich, or to people of considerable status in England, such as members of the royal family or of the House of Commons. Other names are more circumstantial. While the ships are in the high southern latitudes during the second voyage, for instance, Cook notes, "the northern extreme [of Staten Island, near Cape Horn] was the same that we first discovered, and it proved to be an island which obtained the name of Willis's Island, after the person who first saw it."[37] Likewise, "to the S.E. the coast seemed to terminate in a high promontory, which I named Cape Colnett, after one of my midshipmen, who first discovered this land."[38]

Other names in Cook's voyages associate newly identified places with other places, just as the Dutch used "New Holland" to designate what came to be called Australia. While this kind of naming tends to emphasize the connection between the navigator's home country and the areas that are being explored, such as the New Hebrides, there are others that depend on a grander sense of space. For instance, in the second voyage Cook names an island Southern Thule "because it is the most southern land that has ever yet been discovered."[39] Thule was a name found in ancient Roman texts, such as Polybius's account of the voyage of Pytheus, where it referred to an island that was six days' journey north of Britain – the island was probably either Iceland or the Hebrides. By the middle of the eighteenth century, Thule came to refer to any extreme limit of travel. Whether Cook is referring to one of the islands or to the general idea of an extreme place, the name is a good indication of the global perspective that his naming practices are trying to create. All the places of the world, while distinct, are part of a single, coordinated system no matter how extreme their position.

Cook's description of the world in terms of tangible shapes results in a world of identifiable containers on a map. The shapes are not only tangible, they are also empty. Places become containers *in* which other objects exist, whether people, geological formations, plants, or animals. Cook described one small island as "no more than a few detached rocks, receptacles for birds."[40]

While the representation of places as containers works well when the places are islands, when Cook is coasting, such as along New Zealand or the northwest coast of North America, other geographical features such as bays and headlands themselves become containers, understood in terms of islands. Bays have shapes that can be mapped and positioned in relation to other places around the globe. They are also distinct containers – so long as Cook can obscure the difference between "in" and "near," people can live in bays as they do in islands. Comparing the map of Samganooda Harbour with maps of the islands, the same organization of space is evident and, unless the viewer is paying attention, it would be easy to mistake a harbour for an island. Even when faced with a continental coast, then, the features of the coast become a series of containers, well diversified and almost as hermetic as islands.

For Cook and other European thinkers, the island is an image of clarity that is used when describing the organization of knowledge. For Thomas Hobbes, for example, the mind divides in order to understand: "men divide a body in their thought, by numbering parts of it, and, in numbering those parts, number also the parts of the place it filled; it cannot be, but in making many parts, we make also many places of those parts; whereby there cannot be conceived in the mind of any man, more, or fewer parts, than there are places for."[41] In the eighteenth and nineteenth centuries, the island became a specific image, an epistemological principle, for these ideals.

In *The Critique of Pure Reason*, first published in 1781, Kant describes the progress of his philosophical text in terms of exploration: "We have now not merely explored the territory of pure understanding, and carefully surveyed every part of it, but have also measured its extent, and assigned to everything in it its rightful place. This domain is an island, enclosed by nature itself within unalterable limits. It is the land of truth – enchanting name! – surrounded by a wide and stormy ocean, the native home of

Map of New Zealand from Cook's first voyage. Cook was the first European to circumnavigate the island, and the accuracy and detail of his map became an ideal for subsequent cartography.

illusion, where many a fog bank and many a swiftly melting iceberg give the deceptive appearance of farther shores, deluding the adventurous seafarer ever anew with empty hopes."[42] While Kant's often-quoted image echoes some of the images that permeate Cook's voyages, specifically in the contrast between ice islands and regular islands, there is a marked difference between the two. In Kant, there are many ice islands, but only one "territory of pure understanding." In Cook, there are many islands, and it is their discovery and proper description that constitutes a true understanding of the world. In Kant, the island of truth is divided from the ocean of confusion. In Cook, a grid of truth is placed over both ocean and island, while confusion is left no place to go. Islands are more interesting, but everything is known.

LANDSCAPES AND MAPS

In Cook's voyages, the shapes of places are also described through engravings, whether of maps or "views," as they are referred to in the voyages. Like the narratives in the voyages, the engravings contribute to the imagination of places as separate and distinct. But unlike the map, landscapes take several significant forms, and not all of them affirm borders.

Traditionally, one way that places are represented in travel journals is in views taken from off the coast. Abel Tasman, the early Dutch explorer of Australia, includes many coastal profiles to illustrate the published account of his voyage of 1642 to 1643. Anson's account of his voyage also contains several cross-sections, including one of the Strait of Le Maire. These pictures, which offered only the rough outline of the land, represented landscapes in a specific way for a specific audience. The cross-sections were important because they offered navigators a way to identify coastlines by sight. The first volume of Hawkesworth's collection likewise included a chart and four views of Pitcairn Island, which were connected to Carteret's voyage. Together, the chart and the views provided a relatively detailed, if plain, image of the island.[43]

In the Admiralty edition of Cook's three voyages, however, coastal views were replaced by landscapes and maps, where the maps could be used to identify location and the landscapes could be used to create a sense of place.

The landscape engravings from the first voyage, however, were far from faithful representations of either the people or the places in the South Pacific. Rather, the images conformed to the standards of classical landscape painting, with Otaheiteans appearing more like Greeks, and the

A view of the Streights Le Maire from Anson's voyage into the Pacific, showing little geographic or ethnographic detail. The picture's effect is primarily dramatic, showing Anson's ships heading towards a storm. Of the seven ships under Anson's command, only the *Centurion* returned to England. The rest had been lost to storms and most of Anson's crew had died from scurvy.

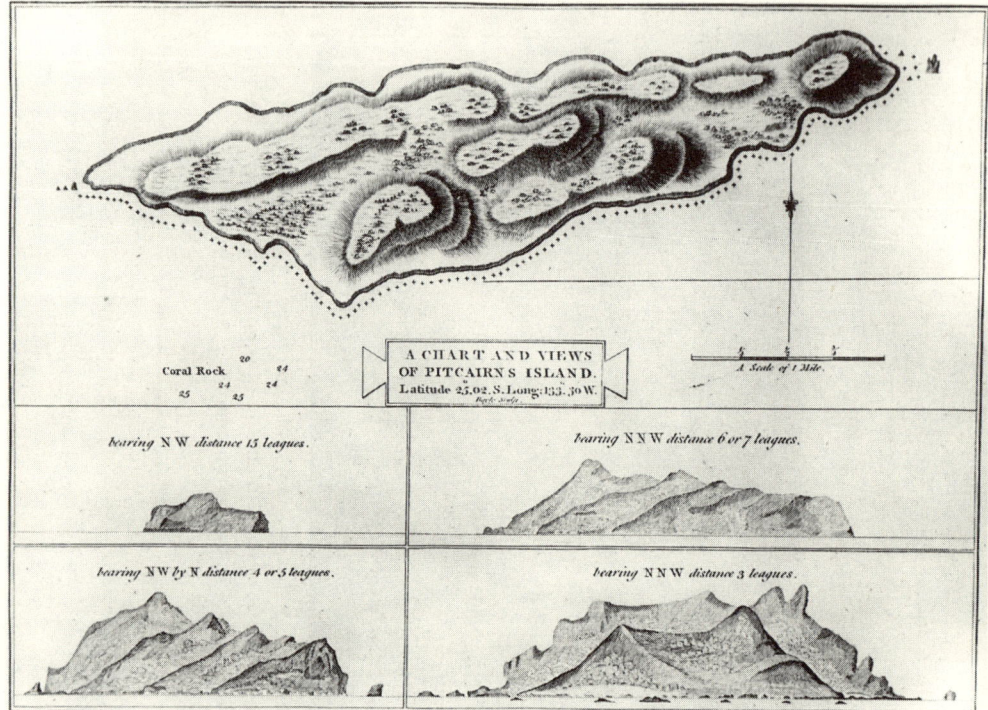

Chart and four views of Pitcairn Island from the published account of Philip
Carteret's voyage to the South Pacific. During his second voyage, Captain Cook
searched for the island to verify its location, but his crew was suffering from scurvy,
and so the search was brief and unsuccessful. While Carteret's views have some
detail, the map is poorly defined and, when compared to later maps of the island,
appears to be quite distorted.

physical landscape reworked towards Mediterranean ideals. The engravings had been produced by classically trained artists who had never been
to the South Pacific and had no real desire to represent the world in
anything but classical style.

A shift is evident in the cross-sections that were produced for Stanley
Parkinson's journal from the first voyage, as Bernard Smith has pointed
out. Parkinson, who became the de facto landscape artist on the *Endeavour* once Alexander Buchan had died in Otahcitc, offered views of the
coast that were much more accurate and aesthetic than the coastal profiles typically produced by prior naval artists. Smith draws attention, for
instance, to the reflection of light on the water and the use of shading to

Landscape engraving from Cook's first voyage. The picture, ostensibly of the "Indians" of Tierra del Fuego, was designed by Giovanni Battista Cipriani, a classical painter who showed little concern for the ethnographic or biological accuracy of the painting.

enhance the detailed profile of the hills. While earlier accounts of voyages, such as Samuel Wallis's voyage to the South Pacific a few years before Cook's, offer a general coastal outline, Parkinson draws the coast with the accuracy of a botanical draughtsman. His goal was not simply to identify the coastline, but to represent it as a biologist would a species.

During the second voyage, the primary artist on the *Discovery* was William Hodges. According to Smith, Hodges was influenced by Joseph Priestley's 1772 *History of the Present State and Discoveries Relating to Vision, Light and Colours*. Among other things, Hodges is much more interested in representing the play of "atmospheric phenomena" on the landscape. Hodges's landscapes also emphasize details from the leaves of the plants to the dress of the natives, which would be unnecessary for travellers but desirable for people who want to see how the place would appear to them. The production of landscapes, then, became animated by the

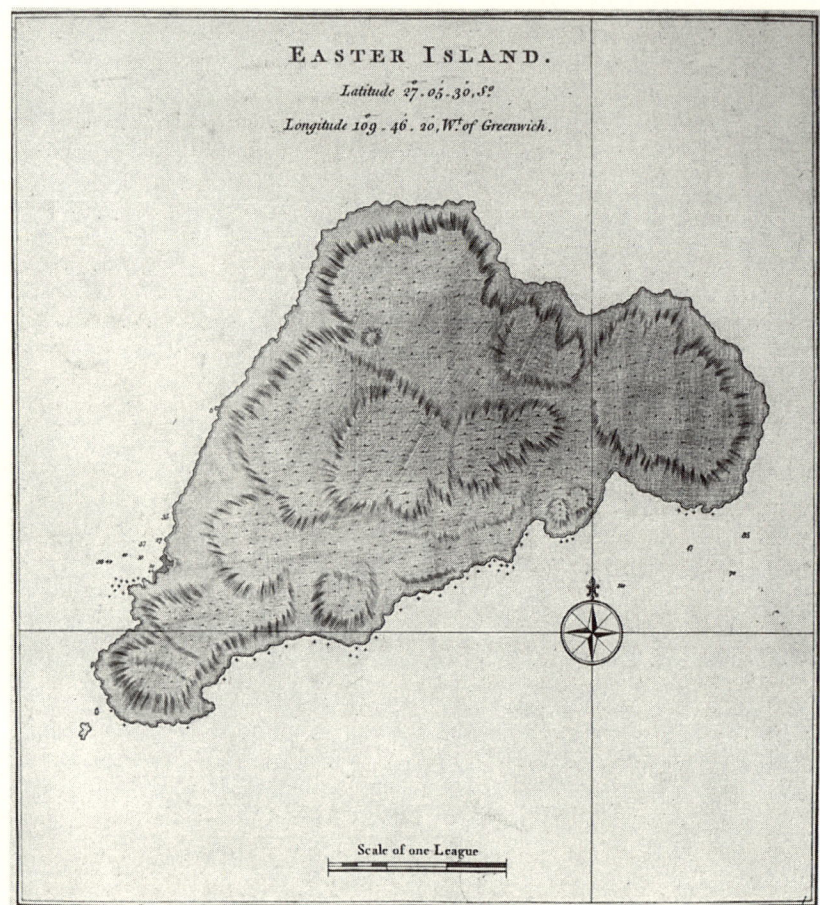

Map of Easter Island from the second voyage. When comparing this to Carteret's map of Pitcairn Island (p. 68), one can note the general accuracy of the coastline, including the details of the smaller rocks along the shore.

same desire for accuracy that already animated the production of maps and botanical illustrations.

John Webber, the primary artist on Cook's third voyage, continued Hodges's attention to accuracy and detail. The only significant differences, for Smith, were the quantity of illustrations that were produced and the range of places and peoples that were included. As Smith notes, with Webber "the people and the landscapes of all the five oceans of the globe came, as the eighteenth century put it, under his pencil."[44] Whereas the move from the first to the second voyage was a change in quality, the move from the second to the third voyage was a move in quantity.

Landscape of Easter Island from the second voyage. Although clearly romantic, the landscape also includes ethnographic and biological detail connected to the island.

While the cross-sections were organized around the basic principles of perspective, the paintings, sketches, and engravings were seldom composed of sharp lines. The goal was to capture light and life; it was not to provide location or shape. Whereas the geographer's world is built upon complete shapes, and especially circles, the landscape artist's world is built upon the horizon. Unlike the maps, the landscapes typically continue off the page, often with mountains or trees framing the picture. The result is a sense of place beyond identification and geometry. Managed spaces of containers and the sublime nature of the universe thus coexist on the printed pages of the voyages. The result is an often romantic and almost always exotic sense of place, couched within the geometrical guarantee of location.

If the landscapes become less geometrical in successive voyages, the maps, which also permeate Cook's voyages, become more so. There are significant differences between the maps created by Cook and those created earlier by Wallis and Carteret. Compare, for instance, Carteret's map of Pitcairn Island (p. 68) with the map of Otaheite that is included in

Portraits of a man and a
woman of Easter Island,
from Cook's second
voyage. These portraits
are at the intersection of
maps and characters,
providing a generalized
ethnographic image tied
unambiguously to a clear
and distinct place.

Cook's first voyage (p. 61). The first thing to note is that there are no cross-sections in Cook's voyages. One reason, presumably, is that cross-sections were no longer needed for navigators to identify islands. Instead, navigators could rely on measuring their coordinates. And the coordinates are the other significant change in Cook's map. In Wallis's map of Pitcairn Island, the coordinates are given in the title panel. In Cook's map the grid extends over the water.

Surveying and mapping were important aspects of Cook's early training, and they were important reasons for his being chosen as the captain. Cook's map of New Zealand was the highest achievement of mapping in the voyages. Given the technological advances in surveying and mapping that occurred just before Cook's voyages, the coast of New Zealand was likely the most accurately mapped coast in the world. It is important to note that it is only after Cook's voyages that large-scale surveys of European coasts were carried out using the new techniques.

One important aspect of Cook's mapping is the relationship between the two different scales in which the maps are presented. Small-scale maps provide the detailed articulation of specific places. An entire island or chain of islands is shown, framed by the white of the ocean. Places are identified in these maps by the absence of other places: the place stands alone, identified as an object that is subject to detailed analysis. For this reason, the only detailed maps that are included in the voyages are maps of places that have not been clearly mapped before. Otaheite is included, but Teneriffe is not. The Society Islands are included, but the Cape of Good Hope is not. The detailed maps of the other places are located in other published works, and the readers can refer to those works as needed.

The large-scale maps, on the other hand, provide a general picture of the world and of Cook's voyages within it. The map may still be framed, but the frame indicates something very different. The map of the world is a complete picture whose edges fold together. For these maps, places are identified by the *presence* of other places. The identity of a place arises more from its coordinates and from its spatial relationship to other places. While the detailed maps provide new information, the only new information on the large-scale maps is the path of the voyage and any newly discovered places that can be added. Cook's voyages not only fill in empty spaces, but also help produce an updated edition of the world.

Cook's voyages represent places as unproblematic entities that can be reliably located on the global grid. As has been suggested already, the places are also containers in which further descriptions of the world can be organized. Having geometrically and physically identified a place, its area takes up a position in the table of identities, where the place is lined up with its geological, biological, and human attributes. Having located the containers in the world, the written account puts them together, first one chapter at a time, and then collected together as a complete series. Cook thus constructs a global grid of coordinates and a table of places based on the ideal of the island. The time of the narrative is replaced by the space of the table. The places of the world all have positions in the table – a one-to-one correspondence between the shape, the name, and the place.

These tables of places, in turn, are used to construct a large-scale view of the world. At the end of the second voyage, Cook has completed the account of the places of the Pacific, offering his successors very little significant work to do in this ocean. But Cook's voyages do not offer a complete view of the world. The outline is given, but only a limited number of places are described in any detail. To achieve a complete view, it is necessary to combine the information that was collected on Cook's voyages with information from other voyages.

The process of remapping the world begins immediately. Mr. Henry Roberts, a mate on the *Resolution* in the third voyage, notes, "soon after our departure from England, I was instructed by Captain Cook to complete a map of the world as a general chart, from the best materials he was in possession of for that purpose; and before his death this business was in a great measure accomplished: That is, the grand outline of the whole was arranged, leaving only those parts vacant or unfinished, which he expected to fall in with and explore."[45]

On the ship's return, Roberts was given the task of creating the official map of the world on which Cook's three voyages were to be drawn, to "give a general idea of the whole," which meant, of course, to produce an exemplary map that could be printed and distributed throughout the reading community. At the time, the information collected by Cook was not only the newest, but also the most accurate. The task that remained was to remap the rest of the world in the same way that Cook had done in the South Pacific. Even the maps of the English, Scottish, and Irish coasts included in this new global map were published within a few years after the *Resolution* and *Adventure* returned to England following Cook's death. The process had begun again, as it would from time to time, with new details from different areas and new equipment producing more accurate information for already-included places.

THE MOVE TO INTERIORS

From 1780 to 1830, many other voyages had been undertaken by Britain, France, Russia, and the United States. George Vancouver had sailed around the world and surveyed the Sandwich Islands and the northwest coast of North America from 1791 to 1795. Charles Wilkes sailed throughout the Pacific under an American flag between 1838 and 1842. He used more ships and better instruments to produce more accurate measurements of places and more detailed searches of the empty space. And then the project was more or less over. There were no new places of any significance to be discovered in the ocean, and there was a general shift towards the exploration, and sometimes re-exploration, of continental interiors. In her discussion of the exploration of South America in *Imperial Eyes,* Mary Louise Pratt discusses how travel narratives, such as those of Charles-Marie de la Condamine's expedition in the middle of the eighteenth century, mark the shift from the ocean to the interior. As she notes, there is "a new orientation toward exploring and documenting continental interiors, in contrast with the maritime paradigm that had held center stage for three hundred years. By the last years of the eighteenth century, interior exploration had become the major object of expansionist energies and imaginings."[46]

While navigators can comprehend an island from a single point or several days' coasting, comprehending a continent is a much more extensive and essentially different project. A similar argument was made in 1822, when Alexander von Humboldt wrote, "It is not by sailing along a coast that we can discover the direction of chains of mountains and their geological constitution, the climate of each zone, and its influence on the forms and habits of organized beings."[47] But in turning towards the continental interiors, it is also evident that the explorers brought their epistemological longing for islands. In the interior, places are more likely to be landmarks, such as rivers, mountains, and geological curiosities, but the metaphorical space in which they operated often remained oceanic. In Africa, the jungle acquires the same status as the desert, as a substitute for the sea. Likewise, Carter summarizes how the early explorers of the interiors of Australia understood the land: "What unites their narratives is their unusual ambitiousness in attempting to constitute their journeys under the aegis of a single, unifying metaphor: that of the sea."[48]

To Charles Sturt, "isolated hills remind him of islands; he himself is a navigator." Just as descriptions of the ocean appealed to images of the wilderness, "marine imagery often characterizes wilderness descriptions,"[49] Carter points out. "But the likeness in difference felt in contemplating the sea as land-like, the land as sea-like, goes deeper than this. It is rooted phenomenologically in our most primitive sensations of earth and water and of their common heritage in the wind filled sky."[50]

Carter wants to equate water and earth, but this is too abstract to be completely true. Rather, water should be equated with desert, and mountains should be equated with islands. They are the points of identity on a table that constitutes distance and difference. The division between earth and water is thus transposed to a division within the earth itself, between rock and sand.

The division of the land into islands was a persistent theme in the European settling of Australia; it was a key feature in the reorganization and acquisition of the land. In *The Songlines,* Bruce Chatwin relates a conversation about European imperialism that he had with a Russian living in Australia:

> "Pity we didn't get here first," he said.
> "We the Russians?"
> "Not only Russians," he shook his head. "Slavs, Hungarians, Germans even. Any people who could cope with wide horizons. Too much of this country went to islanders. They never understood it. They're afraid of space."[51]

The solution to the fear of space, as it emerges in Cook's voyages and as it develops through the history of British expansion throughout the nineteenth century, is to turn space into islands, to find or create shapes on the otherwise unnerving grid of continental space in the case of Australia, and global space in the case of the British empire.

As the culmination of global exploration, Cook became the ideal, and it was through Cook that Britain (and Europe) looked again to the world, regrouped their knowledge, and turned inland to a different kind of ocean. The importance of the South Pacific, as an ideal account of explored space, lies not only in the amount of energy and popular interest that it generated as an area of the globe, but also in the way that it became an idealized image of the organization of knowledge about space. The Pacific Ocean was a test case for a new way of knowing the world. In Cook's case, it is the obviousness of the island that grounds his description. Sturt does not move from island to island, but he travels on a terrain where hills and islands coincide.

The spaces in Cook's voyages were generally self-evident, natural, and unproblematic. If they are unclear, he clarifies them. The places in the idealized world of maps and shapes are like objects found in a field, and it is this idealized world that forms the ground on which the material world is described. In Cook's voyages, the maps became more accurate, but they also acquired additional functions. The shapes came to represent, in detail, the border of biological, social, and political space. The coast became a natural, self-evident border between peoples, and the shapes of the islands became the shapes of the territorial nation-state. The island thus became one of the key principles through which information was organized.

THREE

Nations

Drawn from Nature by W.Hodges.   Engrav'd by J Bafire
                                                              № XXVI.

Portrait of a man of Tanna, from the second voyage. One of the many
engravings of nations in Cook's voyages.

The readers of Cook's voyages are presented with a series of printed books in which places from around the world are located through coordinates and shapes, all described in a voice cloaked with the captain's authority. The geographical articulation of places, idealized as islands in an ocean, is the basis of a global accounting of space. The abstracted progress of the narrative moves from determining location to tracing the outlines of a container and then to placing all the containers on a single tabulated globe. This is how Cook organizes his voyages, and as readers, we are encouraged to follow him. But this is only the beginning. The movement from one place to another, in both the world and the table, demarcates the social, biological, and physical divisions of the world. The narrative is always tied back to the ever more accurate coordinates and maps, and all that remains is to fill these oceanic containers, to populate the places with minerals, trees, birds, fish, quadrupeds, peoples, and artifacts.

THE ORIENT, THE SAVAGE, AND EUROPE

Of course, describing and dividing human groups in terms of space was not new with Cook's voyages. Appeals to various sharp spatial and human dichotomies, such as between Greeks and barbarians, between Christians and heathens, or between Europe and the Orient, had been a persistent theme in European thought. In his discussion of Orientalism, Edward Said focuses on a particular, but pervasive, motif in European accounts of the world. Orientalism, for Said, is not simply an idiosyncratic opinion, it is also part of a large social process in which Europeans came to understand and dominate other parts of the world. Orientalism is an epistemological, metaphysical, and political category, a basic intellectual theme. Said traces the continuity of Western political thought, suggesting, for instance, that Aristotle's attitudes towards the barbarians parallels the current attitudes of some towards Arabs in the Middle East.

By the late eighteenth century and throughout the nineteenth, the global division between Europe and the Orient (and by extension the savage) was augmented, if not supplanted, by a much finer and more detailed division of the world into specific places and nations. To Europeans, the Orient became a list of well-known place names: Egypt, India, China, Japan, Palestine, and so on. While Said recognizes that the grand division between Europe and the Orient was reworked into a global system of distinct nations, he does not explain that change beyond making a general appeal to the scientific attitudes current in Europe in the eighteenth and nineteenth centuries. These changes, however, can be connected to the reorganization of space that first appears in Cook's voyages. This rearticulation of the world was first idealized in Europe's studied analysis of the South Pacific. Not only were places such as New Zealand and Otaheite for a time the best-mapped places in the world, the accounts of them were also the model of a new way of giving an account of peoples and places.

In eighteenth-century discussions of the South Pacific, the generally equivalent idea of primitivism or savagery was applied instead of Orientalism, but the same general dichotomy persisted. To someone approaching the world expecting a strict geographical and moral division between Europe and everything else, Cook's voyages have very little that could be interesting because they offer details where details are not wanted. In a passage from 1784 in Boswell's *Life of Johnson*, for instance, Boswell reports how Johnson complained that "a book may be good for nothing; or there may be only one thing in it worth knowing; are we to read it all through? These *Voyages*, (pointing to the three large volumes of *Voyages to the South Sea* [Cook's third voyage], which were just come out) who will read them through? A man had better work his way before the mast than read them though; they will be eaten by rats and mice, before they are read through. There can be little entertainment in such books; one set of savages is like another."[1]

The other, and more valuable, places in Johnson's world are the classic origins of European history and the source of its quality. In 1776, for instance, Boswell reports Johnson saying, "The grand object of travelling is to see the shores of the Mediterranean. On those shores were the four great empires of the world; the Assyrian, the Persian, the Grecian, and the Roman. All our religion, almost all our law, almost all our arts, almost all that sets us above savages, has come to us from the shores of the Mediterranean."[2] The Mediterranean is not simply a moral ideal, it exists literally at the middle of the world as a space to be contrasted or connected with other spaces. The dispersion of savagery and civilization in a morality that is largely indifferent to space existed alongside another, which reinforced the large spatial divisions between a Mediterranean-focused Europe and the outside, the other.

For Johnson, the key relationship is between the individual and the universally valid civilizations that were created in the Mediterranean. Spatial and national divisions fade into the background, if they are ever recognized at all, and the key concern is the connection between individual characters and universal sources of evaluation (culture, civilization, wisdom, virtue, and so on). Thus, it is not surprising that Johnson praises the manners of Omai, as an individual, even as he roundly rejects "the savages." Boswell reports that in 1776, Johnson

> had been in company with Omai, a native of one of the South Sea Islands, after he had been some time in this country. He was struck with the elegance of his behaviour, and accounted for it thus: "Sir, he had passed his time, while in England, only in the best company; so that all that he had acquired of our manners was genteel. As a proof of this, Sir, Lord Mulgrave and he dined one day at Streatham; they sat with their backs to the light fronting me, so that I could not see distinctly; and there was so little of the savage in Omai, that I was afraid to speak to either, lest I should mistake one for the other.[3]

All civilized people are also alike. In Johnson's world, a sharp distinction between civilization and savagery is coupled with the ability of individuals to move from one side of the division to the other. Some groups, like the English, may have more advanced individuals than other groups, but the focus on individuals means that there could be as much variation in character within groups as between them. As a result, the key issue for Johnson is the extent to which people have been influenced by the best aspects of the Mediterranean civilization. Savages can be found as easily in the North Atlantic as in the South Pacific.

On the other hand, whereas primitivism is a pejorative for Johnson, primitivism had been an ideal for some Europeans in the eighteenth century – an ideal that remained sharply contrasted to the ideals of the classical world, but that acquired a higher value. Whereas writers such as Jean-Jacques Rousseau used examples associated with the islands in the Caribbean and other regions in the Americas, one dominant image of primitivism for Europe, beginning with Wallis's voyage, was Otaheite. Here was an entire society where life was easy and people lived according to nature, in contrast to the frivolity and violence of Europe. In the words of Beaglehole, "so almost suddenly, so overwhelmingly, was the idea of the Pacific at last to enter into the consciousness, not of seamen alone but of literate Europe, in the form of this remarkable, this – as it were – symbolic island ... Wallis had not merely come to a convenient port of call. He had stumbled on a foundation stone of the Romantic Movement."[4] The South Pacific was thus used by some people in Europe to verify Rousseau's arguments. The island, at least while it remained only partially described, began to function as a utopian ideal.

Throughout the published accounts of Cook's voyages, there are passages that explicitly echo this characterization of the South Pacific. During the second voyage, for instance, Cook reflects on one of his crew who attempted to escape from the *Resolution* and remain on Otaheite: "Where then could such a man be more happy than at one of these isles? Where, in one of the finest climates in the world, he could enjoy not only the necessaries, but the luxuries of life, in ease and plenty."[5]

In a letter to John Walker dated 13 September 1771, Cook discusses the natives of the "East Coast of new Holland" in a similar way: "These people may truly be said to be in the pure state of Nature, and may appear to some to be the most wretched upon Earth: but in reality they are far more happier than that [sic] we Europeans, being wholy unacquinted not only with the superfluous but [? also] of the necessary Conveniencies so much sought after in Europe they are happy in not knowing the use of them."[6] Here, Cook is not claiming that people in the state of nature are virtuous, pious, or civilized, but they are undeniably happy, at least in a physical sort of way. As in Rousseau's writings, the happy life is the one that lacks complicated and degrading economic and social relations.

While there is an obvious moral dimension to these competing visions of savagery, accounts of facts and events were also very important for these debates. As would be expected, events such as the death of Furneaux's away team in New Zealand during the second voyage were of particular interest. Tobias Furneaux, the captain of the *Adventure* during Cook's second voyage, had been separated from Cook and the *Resolution* while they were both in the high southern latitudes. While the *Adventure* was at Queen Charlotte's Sound, ten members of the ship's crew were killed by natives. Anders Sparrman, in his journal from the second voyage, reports that "when he [Crozet] dined with Cook and his officers aboard the *Resolution* at the Cape of Good Hope in March 1775, Lieutenant Julien-Marie Crozet told them of the massacre at New Zealand and of Rousseau's response: 'Is it possible that the good Children of Nature can really be so wicked?'"[7] Given the intellectual terrain of late-eighteenth-century Europe, there were several plausible answers to Rousseau's question, which, when considered together, suggest the effect that Cook's voyages had on the debate.

One response is to claim that the natives were provoked, perhaps by the brutality of the English sailors. In this case, the idealization of the natural, primitive state can continue, and the guilt can be placed on the so-called civilized people. In keeping with this line of reasoning, Cook reflects on his own encounter with natives in that bay after hearing of the deaths:

> We found these people hospitable, civil, and good-natured, when not prompted to a contrary conduct by jealousy; a conduct I cannot tell how to blame them for, especially when I consider the light in which they must view us. It was impossible for them to know our real design; we enter their ports without their daring to oppose; we endeavour to land in their country as friends, and it is well if this succeeds; we land, nevertheless, and maintain the footing we have got, by the superiority of our fire-arms. Under such circumstances, what opinion are they to form of us? Is it not as reasonable for them to think that we come to invade their country, as to pay them a friendly visit? Time, and some acquaintance with us, can only convince them of the latter.[8]

In this interpretation, the innocent or the virtuous are able to do terrible things, but only in reaction to the flawed actions or characters of others. The blame for the atrocities, in other words, rests with the Europeans who, whether from impatience, misunderstanding, or brutality, forced the "children of nature," who were not themselves wicked, to react in wicked ways.

Another possible response to Rousseau's question is to distinguish individual natives from the general characterization of the primitive. For instance, Anna Seward, a contemporary of Cook's, responded to a similar challenge created by the death of Cook in the Sandwich Islands on the third voyage. Bernard Smith summarizes Seward's argument: "the islanders are still people endowed with natural sensibility and a freedom of emotional expression which they have derived from the simplicity of the 'natural' life. For her the death of Cook resulted from the treachery of individual natives."[9] The general qualities of the primitive, natural life are thus maintained by appealing to the exceptional (and degraded) characters of individuals – Seward thus offers an account of the spatial and moral world that exactly parallels the one evident in Johnson, although she takes the non-European as the ideal. The South Pacific replaces the empires of the Mediterranean in this interpretation, but it is still necessary (and possible) to explain the Catalines and Caligulas by their individual characters and leave the general qualities of the ideal intact.

A third response to Rousseau's question, adopted by the missionaries, among others, is to argue that, in fact, the "children of nature" were not noble: civilization was morally superior to savagery. Here the emphasis is on the negative qualities of non-Europeans. This understanding, of course, directly challenges the idealization of primitive life that was connected to Rousseau's writings. Nature is not the source of virtue or goodness, civilization is. Such responses also echo Johnson's attitudes. For instance, Boswell recounts Johnson's belief that "pity is not natural to man. Children are always cruel. Savages are always cruel. Pity is acquired and improved by the cultivation of reason."[10] For Johnson, if natives were like children, it was because they could also "grow up" into the civilized and Christian adult world that arose out of the Mediterranean empires. But we should never expect them to behave well without having been provided with a significant civilizing influence.

In all three of these responses, opposition between the civilized and the primitive is central. The terms designated not only two groups but also two ideals. The responses differ in which state – civilized or primitive – was seen as the ideal, and on whether (and how) individuals could move from one state to the other.

THE PRIMACY OF PLACE

As the debates over civilization and primitivism were carried on from Cook's voyages into the early nineteenth century, the terms of the discussion changed. Rather than discussing the character of "the savages" as a single group, the question, "which natives?" began to be asked. This shift creates a fourth response to Rousseau's question, which is to claim that some non-European nations are wicked and others are peaceful. As a result, Cook's voyages help mark an important shift in how human beings are described, first in relation to their environment, and then in relation to national identities.

One of the important aspects of late-eighteenth-century discussions of primitivism, as Smith and others have noted, is that the natives, just like plants and animals, begin to be closely associated with their natural settings. For instance, Smith comments on a short piece written by M. Taitbout and published in 1779: "Taitbout's pamphlet is of interest, not for the originality of its ideas, but because it reveals how notions of geographical control deriving from Montesquieu and applied by the Forsters to the islands of the Pacific, could provide a rational explanation for the soft primitivism with which Bougainville, Hawkesworth, Banks, Denis Diderot, and others, had endowed the peoples of the Society Islands."[11] Eighteenth-century European ideas of primitivism thus combined an idealized image of a place (Otaheite) with a similarly idealized image of the people who lived there (Otaheiteans), and suggested that there was a close, causal connection between the places and the inhabitants. The question of "which natives," therefore, becomes intimately tied to the account of where the natives came from. And specifying where people come from is something that Cook's coordinates and maps could do with triumphant ease.

The importance of place began, for Smith, with the penguin, or specifically with how penguins were portrayed in relation to a detailed and appropriate landscape. In Thomas Pennant's painting, which was included as an illustration of his article on the penguin for the *Philosophical Transactions,* the birds are shown in their natural settings: "There lay an incipient programme for the landscape-painting radically different from the neo-classicism predominant in British landscape-painting during the 1760's."[12] The accurate connection between places and animals became a general way to organize descriptions about the world, where the relationship between a species and its habitat was extended to include human groups. People were treated like penguins.

The close association between human groups and their habitats in Cook's voyages, which grouped the natives of the South Pacific islands according to their geographical locations, was becoming increasingly important, but it was somewhat accidental and did not occur in the first voyage. There the landscapes were idealized classical images or devoid of inhabitants. Alexander Buchan, the landscape painter in the first voyage, had died days after the ship landed at Otaheite so most of the landscapes were sketched by Sydney Parkinson, who had been trained to draw and paint biological specimens. Parkinson's physiological and ethnographical approach to the representations of human beings, with little concern for the habitat of the specimen, is in sharp contrast to the discourses offered by both Johnson and Rousseau, insofar as the general categories of primitive and European are not as important in the representations of specific human groups. The approach in the portraits also contrasts with discourses that take the whole of human existence as their domain and use abstract moral categories to sift individuals into types that are scattered everywhere (the virtuous, the lazy, and so on). Rather, the pattern of representation in Parkinson's journal, building on a geographical division of places, divides human beings into physiological and ethnic groups, as if these island-nations were distinct species. Not all savages are alike.

Parkinson's approach to representing native populations is not exceptional, although it is not until the second voyage that Cook combines a sharp, detailed, and geometrical articulation of places on the map with a deep association between places and their inhabitants.

The profound changes in the relationship between places and peoples can be noticed through the shifts in the basic vocabulary that is used in the voyages. Whether one looks at the Admiralty's edition of the voyages or Cook's manuscript journal, the people who are encountered are referred to as "Indians." There are many examples. Near the beginning of the voyage, the Admiralty version reads, "this day we learnt the Indian name of the island, which is OTAHEITE, and by that name I shall hereafter distinguish it: but after great pains taken we found it utterly impossible to teach the Indians to pronounce our names."[13] At this point, the native name of the island is known, but the natives remain "Indians," an indiscriminate category referring to any and all of the non-Europeans that are encountered.

At some stage in the production of the account of the second voyage, however, the terms change. In the manuscript journals from the second and third voyages, Cook still uses "Indian" throughout. In the version published by the Admiralty, however, "Indian" has almost always been changed to terms such as "inhabitant" and "native." For instance, Cook's entry in his journal for 17 January 1779 reads, "the Ships were much Crouded with Indians and surrounded by a multitude of Canoes."[14] The published version, on the other hand, reads, "the ships continued to be much crowded with natives, and were surrounded by a multitude of canoes."[15] When "native" is used in its geographical sense, it implies that human beings are connected to (and are perhaps, therefore, explained by) the land in which they live. The native or inhabitant is connected to the place, existing in relation to a place that is itself a natural entity. Phrases such as "this island and its people" thus pervade the voyages. And it is here, in opposition to the dichotomy of "savages" or "Indians" and the Mediterranean, that the nation acquires a natural character as well as an epistemological edge, which cuts at the broad generalizations of Europe and its Orientalist or primitive other.

The basic terms of Cook's narrative thus return to some core images in *Robinson Crusoe* and specifically the image of isolation, but it is now the native *nation* that is isolated rather than Crusoe. The island, as a natural entity, exists prior to the people, surrounds them, and collects them into a single unit. Like the flora and fauna of the island, the nation becomes an object of extensive analysis. Cook's voyages thus offer an image of social coherence based largely on geographical shapes. The island is no longer considered to be lacking society and politics; it is a container for the society and politics of the island's nation. The island collects together a group of people who can be described both in general terms and by using specific samples (such as Tupia and Omai). The island thus naturalizes the borders of a native people and attempts to determine their attributes (habits, customs, physical characteristics, and beliefs) by first connecting them to a bounded and distinct physical space that has already been located and mapped.

We should note, however, that "native" becomes equivocal in Cook's voyages and afterwards, referring both to the specific group – "the nation of," "the inhabitants of" – and to the general group of non-Europeans taken together. When "Indian" drops out of use and "native" becomes the dominant generic term for referring to non-European, "primitive" groups, "native" comes to mean both "inhabitant" *and* "primitive."

We have already discussed some of Cook's naming practices, in particular those that are connected to the narrative of the voyage itself, such as when he names Cape Farewell. The voyage is not the only source of names, though. Sometimes Cook names places as a way to emphasize the connection between peoples and their places. In the first voyage, Cook changes the name of King George III's Island to Otaheite. According to Paul Carter's analysis, "when, on the *Endeavour* voyage, Cook restored St. George's Island to its native name of Tahiti, he was not so much exhibiting his interest in Tahitian sovereignty as his self-interest in establishing his precedence there over the island's earlier English visitor, Samuel Wallis."[16]

Even if Cook is establishing his precedence over Wallis, however, it is important to note how the new name also underlines the connection between people and places, which also marks one of the most significant differences between Cook and his predecessors. If the natives are connected to their places, the use of native names becomes one more way to trace the connections, however sovereignty is determined. As a result, Cook is not simply establishing his status over Wallis as a navigator; he is also promoting a different way of articulating and explaining human groups in relation to space. The change in name, therefore, is a way to establish Cook's claim to being someone who can provide reliable accounts of particular native nations. Not only can he find the place, but he also knows what the natives call it; and by accepting that name he affirms a world view that closely ties a nation to its place.

A similar naming strategy in Cook's voyages connects the place to other characteristics. In the second voyage, for instance, Cook writes that "the skirts of this island were covered with the elevations more than once mentioned. They had much the appearance of tall pines, which occasioned my giving that name to the island."[17] Later in the same voyage, Cook writes that "the other isle, which obtained the name of Bird Isle, on account of the vast number that were upon it, is not so high, but of greater extent."[18] The connection between names and characteristics is extended to the attributes of the human inhabitants. Again, in the second voyage, Cook writes, "the conduct and aspect of these islanders occasioned my naming it Savage Island,"[19] and "the promontory, or peninsula, which disjoins these two bays, I named Traitor's Head, from the treacherous behaviour of its inhabitants."[20] These kinds of names, which are created throughout the three voyages, persistently emphasize the connection between places and the things that can be found there.

Nevertheless, an important feature of this articulation of geographical and national space is that the world must be mapped into areas that can support clear and distinct national identities. One problem that Cook faces, as a result, is the existence of "adjoining parts," where one place is not clearly divided from another. This problem does not typically arise with Cook's descriptions of islands, but it does become a concern when the ideal of the island is applied to other areas, such as coasts or larger islands that have distinct groups of inhabitants. In the third voyage, for instance, as the ships are coasting along the northeast shore of the Pacific, that is to say, the Pacific northwest coast of North America, Cook writes:

> On the 18th a party of strangers, in six or eight canoes, came into the cove, where they remained, looking at us, for some time; and then retired, without coming alongside either ship. We supposed that our old friends, who were more numerous at this time about us than these new visitors, would not permit

them to have an intercourse with us. It was evident, upon this and several other occasions, that the inhabitants of the adjoining parts of the Sound engrossed us entirely to themselves; or if, at any time, they did not hinder strangers from trading with us, they contrived to manage the trade for them in such a manner that the price of their commodities was always kept up, while the value of ours was lessening every day.[21]

Along the coast of America, which always threatens to become an indistinct continuity, Cook's account of islands turns into one of sounds and villages, but the place remains a container. Phrases such as "the inhabitants of the sound" occur throughout the voyages, in more or less the same context that phrases such as "the inhabitants of the island" would. Along the coast of what is now British Columbia, for instance, Cook reflects, "were I to affix a name to the people of Nootka, as a distinct nation, I would call them Wakashians, from the word wakash, which was very frequently in their mouths. It seemed to express applause, approbation, and friendship; for when they appeared to be satisfied, or well pleased with any thing they saw, or any incident that happened, they would, with one voice, call out, Wakash! wakash!"[22] The phrase "the people of Nootka" suggests that the land possesses the people. In voyages after Cook, and especially when English imperial control was exerted over the area, "the people of Nootka" simply become "the Nootka." But what these people share, in Cook's account, is neither a physical characteristic nor a disposition. They may not even share a language, as far as Cook knows. In Cook's voyages, the primary groups are identified spatially, and then the narrative turns to consider what "they" are like and what, if anything, they name their places and themselves. Characteristics, dispositions, beliefs, and lifestyles are all tied to the national groups that are contained in the first instance by their place.

If the problem of adjoining places and peoples is resolved by using the model and terminology of the island to represent places on the coast, ocean communication *between* islands also presents a problem for the account of distinct places. How can Cook assume that islands are so clearly separated from each other? The answer, implied throughout, is that the distance between them is a barrier that isolates them and helps preserve their identities. What Cook's account must do, in other words, is ensure that the islands have long been isolated from each other. For the South Pacific to work as an ideal source of knowledge, Cook must assume that no one else (specifically natives from other islands) could move from

Portrait of a man "in Christmas Sound." Emphasizing place as a container, even when it was a sound or a harbour, became increasingly important for Cook's account of national identities.

island to island the way he can. If islands can communicate in any sustained way, the system of clear and distinct national descriptions does not work.

STUDYING NATIONS
Having fixed the places of the world through geometry, navigational instruments, and naming practices, the nations (the people, the inhabit-

ants, the natives) became important objects of study. A seventeenth-century navigator like Dampier might have offered a narrative of his time spent in various nations in the South Pacific, but Cook also offers an analysis following the scientific principles then promulgated by core intellectual institutions in Europe.

How were these nations to be approached? It was not enough to collect whatever information came to hand – it was also important to pay attention to where and from whom the information is collected. Otherwise the description of specific native nations would fade once again into a general account of primitive Indians. The enquiry involved a variety of different considerations of the island, from viewing behaviour, to collecting artifacts, to testing reactions, to asking questions. Cook's voyages are epistemological as well as navigational narratives. The differences between geographical, biological, and anthropological studies were reduced as all of the objects of study were approached as attributes of geometrical containers (the islands). From time to time, Cook describes these geographical, biological, and social forays in terms of exploration, using words such as "soundings" and "examinations."[23]

The goal of the voyages, then, was not only to create a complete description of the places and the peoples, but also to show how such descriptions should be produced. As a result, Cook's voyages have often been placed at the beginning of modern European anthropological discourse, as one of the first and one of the best of the early accounts of the South Pacific. As Besant writes in his late-nineteenth-century biography of Cook, "in many respects the methods recommended by modern students of anthropology might have been based upon those followed by Cook and his sagacious assistant [Lieutenant William Anderson]."[24] It is from his voyages that knowledge of the South Pacific begins. But the voyages discuss *how* places and people should be known. Having been separated from the inhabitants of other places, the nation became an object of study. Once "Indian" was no longer used as the primary category, more information could become interesting, and much more information was required to complete a description.

Cook had to somehow secure access to the artifacts of the nation, just as he had to somehow secure access to the resources of the place. Most of the time, collecting data depended on creating some level of interaction – there is some information that can be collected at a distance or by force, but very little. In the introduction to the second voyage, for instance, Cook represents the will to knowledge that animates much of his activity:

"I was also directed to observe the genius, temper, disposition, and number, of the inhabitants, if there were any, and endeavour, by all proper means, to cultivate a friendship and alliance with them."[25]

One incident from the first voyage, at a place Cook named Poverty Bay, suggests Cook's overriding commitments. Not being able to gain access to the beach due to high surf, Cook attempts to "get some of the people into my possession without mischief." The natives in the canoe attempted to escape to the shore, but Cook "ordered a musket to be fired over their heads, as the least exceptionable expedient to accomplish my design, hoping it would either make them surrender, or leap into the water."[26] The natives in the canoes, however, decided to fight. They were throwing stones so vigorously, again according to Cook's account, "that we were obliged to fire upon them in our own defence; four were unhappily killed, and the other three, who were boys, the eldest about nineteen, and the youngest about eleven, instantly leaped into the water; the eldest swam with great vigour, and resisted the attempts of our people to take him into the boat by every effort that he could make: he was however at last overpowered, and the other two were taken up with less difficulty."[27]

In his calmer reflections on this episode, Cook admits to his readers that these deaths were "unfortunate." However, he affirms, "the nature of my service required me to obtain a knowledge of their country, which I could no otherwise effect than by forcing my way into it in a hostile manner, or gaining admission through the confidence and good-will of the people."[28] Having taken the boys on board, Cook attempts to gain their confidence by giving them presents and convincing them that they were safe in his custody. Once they were secure as sources of knowledge and access, the three boys then became the basis for establishing a broader peace, allowing Cook access to the people on the shore, and thus to the nation as such.

Smith discusses how important it was for the artists, in particular, to cultivate peaceful relationships with their subjects in order to produce portraits.[29] When the explorers and the natives were on good terms, the Europeans were given extensive access to the people and the place. In the first voyage, for instance, Cook recounts how, "in their walk, they [a group from Cook's ship] visited several houses of the natives, and saw something of their manner of life; for they showed, without any reserve, every thing which the gentlemen desired to see."[30]

Sometimes, however, the natives did not show the gentlemen every-thing, and either resisted attempts to land or organized the interaction in specific ways and turned the attention of the visitors away from certain things. There are many examples of Cook or his fellow travellers being guided to unexplored parts of an island, only to be brought to already-familiar places. For Cook, these attempts to reorient the European intrusions are often understood in terms of native deceitfulness, jealousy, or fear. After all, Cook, by his own admission, is keen to show the natives whatever they want to see on the ship. As a result, the voyages are permeated with an ethics of scientific exchange in which those who resist the relationship are judged harshly. Disclosure, voluntary for one nation, becomes mandatory for the other.

One important aspect of a nation that Cook records is its physical appearance, including its height, build, and hair colour. Cook's descriptions tend to combine mechanical and aesthetic categories. Some nations are "well-made," others are "ugly" or ill-proportioned. Cook writes during the third voyage, for instance, that the inhabitants of New Caledonia "are nearly of the same colour as the natives of Tanna, but have better features, more agreeable countenances, and are a much stouter race; a few being seen who measured six feet four inches."[31]

In addition to the textual descriptions, the artists on the voyages produced portraits. In the first voyage, the fate of the portraits paralleled the fate of the landscapes: details in the sketches were transformed into stereotypical classical images. On the other hand, in the second and third voyages, and in Parkinson's work during the first voyage, there was a greater attempt to represent individual, or at least national, characteristics.

As the portraits became more realistic, they became the basis of scientific debates, even between people who had never travelled outside of Europe. The drawings executed by Hodges during the second voyage, for instance, are part of later debates between two other members of the second voyage: William Wales, the astronomer, and Georg Forster, the naturalist. In his response to Forster's criticism of a specific portrait that had been produced by Hodges, the ship's artist, Wales writes, "for my part, I will not flatter Mr. Hodges so far, as to say I think his drawing either a national or particular likeness. It could not be the former, because Tinamai differed from every one else of her countrywomen in the circumstance of wearing her hair long; and, with all due deference to Doctor Forster's opinion, I cannot help thinking that he has rather flattered her."[32]

The specifics of the controversy between Wales and Forster are less important here than that such a controversy took place at all. There are,

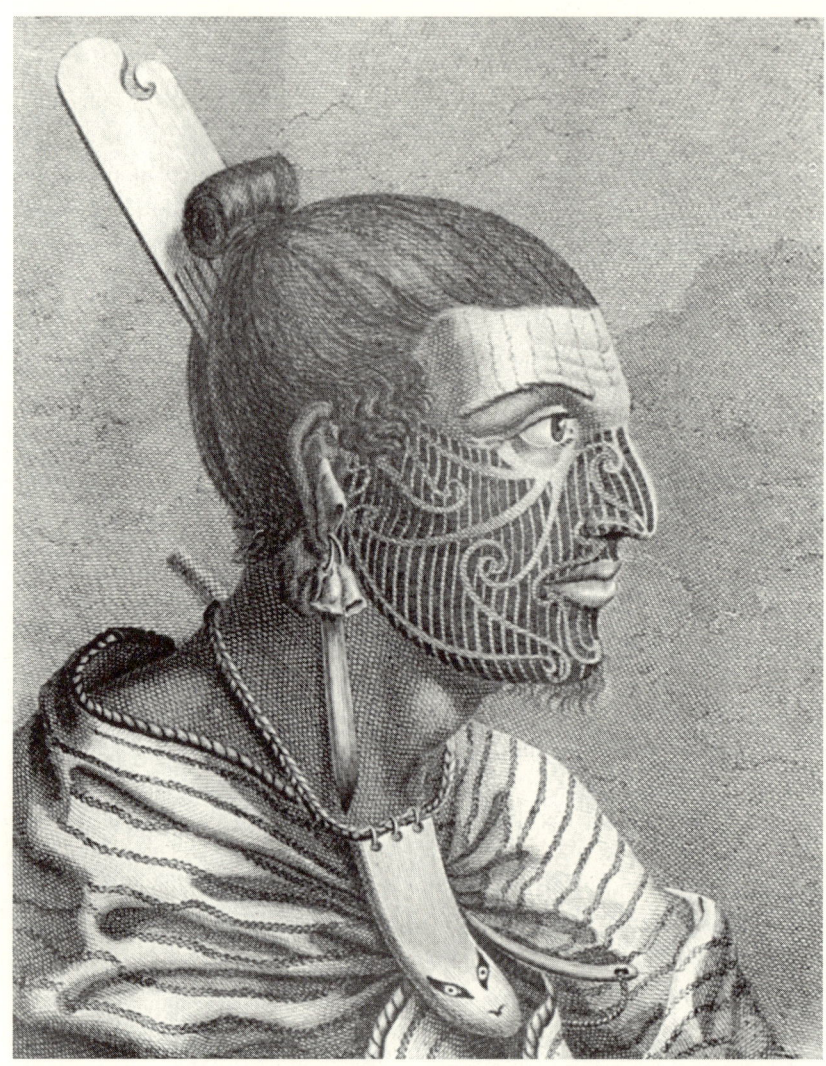

Portrait of a man of New Zealand from Sydney Parkinson's account of Cook's first voyage. The detail and techniques of the portrait prefigure the portraits that would come to dominate the engravings from Cook's second and third voyage.

in fact, two controversies: the first revolving around the portrait as a representation of a specific individual, and the second concerning the portrait as a representation of a specific nation. Along the same lines, George Mortimer, a lieutenant on a later voyage to the Pacific Northwest, writes in 1789 of how "in this and every other particular [the natives of

Oonalashka] exactly resemble the prints of them in Captain Cook's last voyage, taken from the elegant drawings of Mr. Webber."[33] The national portrait, in other words, becomes a statement about the world, which can be verified or challenged. If the portraits are done well, if they accurately represent the nation as such, they become the basis of a new discussion of human nature, not understood in terms of civilization and savagery but rather in terms of physiology and diversity.

The importance of portraits is related to the importance of bringing back a live specimen. Dampier had done so at the end of the seventeenth century, when he brought Giolo back to England. Giolo, also known as "Prince Joely" and the "painted prince" because of his tattoos, was a native of Meangis Island, an island that is now part of Indonesia.[34] In Europe, however, he became much more of an exotic novelty than an object of scientific study. According to Rennie, on returning to England, Dampier "soon sold his painted Prince, who was advertised by his new owners as 'exposed to publick view every day' and privately by appointment to 'Persons of Quality.'"[35]

In his first voyage, Cook also tried to bring back two natives from the South Pacific, although as part of a larger scientific enterprise – an institutional rather than a personal possession. Tupia and Tayeto, both natives of Otaheite, died in Batavia on the way back to England, and Cook returned to England without living human specimens. In the second voyage, Captain Furneaux brought back Omai, "a native of Ulietea." Cook notes, "I at first rather wondered that Captain Furneaux would encumber himself with this man, who, in my opinion, was not a proper sample of the inhabitants of these happy islands, not having any advantage of birth, or acquired rank, nor being eminent in shape, figure, or complexion. For their people of the first rank are much fairer, and usually better behaved, and more intelligent, than the middling class of people, among whom Omai is to be ranked."[36]

According to Cook, there are two primary reasons why Omai was not an appropriate example of the natives of Ulietea. First, Omai was not a valuable source of information. The second and more important criticism, however, is that Omai was too average, too unremarkable, and from too middling a class to be appropriate. The goal, it would seem, was to bring the *best* example, not a typical example. The class biases of the collecting process are obvious: the upper classes of Europe are looking for specimens of the upper classes of other nations. What would European aristocrats want with lower-class natives? But even before questioning the political assumptions that conditioned the choice of who counts as the best specimen, there is a prior question concerning the identities created by sampling. Allowing one person or one portrait to stand for a group of people assumes that the group of people share attributes that are not shared by any other group. This kind of generalization occurs throughout the voyages and, supported by the unquestioned identity of the place, is itself unquestioned.

Individual national portraits can also be taken up into larger collections of portraits from a variety of places. In *Ideas on the Philosophy of the History of Mankind,* first published in 1785, Herder calls for "a collection of new ethnographical illustrations, the basis of which has already been laid by Niebuhr, Parkinson, Cook, Höst, Georgi, and others."[37] The parallel between biological and human groups continued, as did the importance of the printing press as a basic condition for the overall process: as Eisenstein notes, "diverse names for flora and fauna became less confusing when placed beneath identical pictures."[38] Cook's voyages do the same thing with people. Cook attempts to determine the character or customs of nations on the same scale. Can this nation be trusted? Are these people violent? The assumption is that every member of the nation is more or less the same and that a well-chosen, idealized character can stand in the place of a larger group.

Another important feature of a nation is its language. Up until the eighteenth century, language was often the central criterion for distinguishing one nation from another. In Cook's voyages, language became secondary to space as the defining attribute of a nation. It nonetheless remained an important aspect of national identity, not only for practical reasons, such as helping the crew relate to the natives, but also for descriptive reasons, helping Cook and others sort out the customs and beliefs of the people with whom they were interacting.

By closely studying different languages, it is possible to determine which nations originated from the same source. As Johnson says, "there is no tracing the connection of ancient nations, but by language; and therefore I am always sorry when any language is lost, because languages are the pedigree of nations. If you find the same language in distant countries, you may be sure that the inhabitants of each have been the same people; that is to say, if you find the languages a good deal the same; for a word here and there being the same, will not do."[39] This assumption is carried into the Pacific – Cook and his companions create lists of words and phrases from as many places as they can. Cook realizes that the process is not easy, and the narratives reflect on the best ways to construct such lists. In the first voyage, he says, "this method, though it was the best we could contrive, might certainly lead us into many mistakes; for if an Indian was to take up a stone, and ask us the name of it, we might answer a pebble or a flint; ... however, as much as possible to avoid mistakes of this kind, several of us contrived, at different times, to get from them as many words as we could, and having noted them down, compared our lists."[40]

The primary goal was to create a reliable, standardized written list of words and their English equivalents. These lists of words also changed the way that Europeans could interact with the world, because they could reference words that had been collected by previous explorers. When Cook first arrived at Point Jackson, for instance, he recounts an encounter: "Having a catalogue of words in their language, we called several things by name, which surprised them greatly."[41]

It is also possible to use these word lists from many different places to compare which people use which words. In the third voyage, Cook writes about a list of words that Anderson collected from Adventure Bay, in New Zealand. Cook notes that "his specimen of their language, however short, will be thought worth attending to, by those who wish to collect materials for tracing the origin of nations."[42] But for Cook, lists of words collected from places around the world are not the primary criteria for distinguishing one nation from another, as Johnson argues. People on different islands, hundreds or thousands of miles away, often speak very similar languages and may have a common ancestry. It is not so much that people who share the same language are members of the same nation, but that different nations can share the same (or a similar) language, and so be traced back to a shared pre-national origin. Cook thus inverts the order of precedence.

In addition to the physical and linguistic aspects of each nation, Cook's voyages also provide an account of each nation's character. Here, for instance, is Cook's description of the Otaheiteans during the first voyage: "In their motions there is at once vigour and ease; their walk is graceful, their deportment liberal, and their behaviour to strangers and to each other affable and courteous. In their dispositions, also, they seemed to be brave, open, and candid, without either suspicion or treachery, cruelty or revenge."[43] In writing of the people of New Caledonia, Cook notes that they are "not in the least addicted to pilfering, which is more than can be said of any other nation in this sea."[44] Some nations are peaceful, others

are vicious; some are curious about the English, and others are indifferent or fearful. Throughout, what arises is the reaffirmation of typical
humanistic concerns for character (virtues and vices), but these attributes
are now connected directly to nations and only indirectly to individuals.
It is the *nation* that has the character.

As with the descriptions of physical appearance, language, and character, the descriptions of social practices, habits, and technologies are important attributes of nations, and Cook attempts to study them
systematically. When Cook and his companions are collecting specimens
from the different nation-places, their activities are formed by a system of
epistemological obligations. They do not simply collect objects that appeal to their fancy; they collect objects that expand and eventually complete their acquisition of the nation's productions. They need to acquire
certain kinds of things – handicrafts, tools, weapons, clothing – because
whatever other appeal the objects may have, they are needed to create a
full account of the place, just as samples of all the rocks, plants, and animals are needed. Rickman gives a sense of the scope of this process: "Besides the natural productions of the country, we purchased in these islands
many tons of salt; much of their cordage and cloth; and a great variety of
artificial curiosities, such as their weapons of war, their instruments for
fishing; their cloaks and coverlids; their caps, masks, nets, instruments of
music; their needles, thread, working-tools, bracelets, ear-jewels, and, in
short, almost every thing that was new to us, or which was peculiar to
them."[45] The goal, in other words, is to collect one of everything, and to
determine what is typical and what is rare. While the rare objects might
be more valuable to some collectors, however, the typical objects are more
important for creating the general account of the nation and for comparing one nation to another.

One of the key experiments that Cook and his companions pursued
throughout the Pacific was to determine which nations were cannibals.
Although they seldom claim to have directly seen natives eating human
flesh, Cook and his crew discover what they take to be indirect evidence
of the practice. In the first voyage, for instance, Cook claims, "this day,
some of our people found in the skirts of the wood, near a hole or oven,
three human hipbones, which they brought on board; a farther proof
that these people eat human flesh."[46] Just before this discovery, Cook had
been interviewing a native to determine the question of cannibalism.
Describing this interview, Cook notes that, "to convince us that the flesh
had been eaten, he took hold of his own arm with his teeth, and made

show of eating: he also bit and gnawed the bone which Mr. Banks had taken, drawing it through his mouth, and showing, by signs, that it had afforded a delicious repast; the bone was then returned to Mr. Banks, and he brought it away with him."[47] Banks takes the bone away as a memento, or as evidence, of cannibalism. Here, as elsewhere, the desire to collect evidence is coupled with the desire to collect curiosities. Curiosities are evidence of human possibilities. Soon after finding the human hipbones, Cook says, "the people here brought us out several human bones, the flesh of which they had eaten, and offered them to sale; for the curiosity of those among us who had purchased them as memorials of the horrid practice which many, notwithstanding the reports of travellers, have professed not to believe, had rendered them a kind of article of trade."[48]

While the English did not eat human meat, they were obviously quite happy collecting body parts. And collecting appendages and other mementoes did not end with the first voyage or with the question of cannibalism. When a native brings a tattooed head on the ship during the second voyage, Cook says, "the sight of the head, and the relation of the above circumstances [that a piece of human flesh was "broiled and eaten by one of the natives"], struck me with horror, and filled my mind with indignation against these cannibals. Curiosity, however, got the better of my indignation, especially when I considered that it would avail but little, and being desirous of becoming an eye-witness of a fact which many doubted, I ordered a piece of the flesh to be broiled and brought to the quarter-deck, where one of these cannibals ate it with surprising avidity."[49]

The discussion of cannibalism in Cook's voyages may have recreated the sharp dichotomy between Europe and its savage other, and it is not as if the dichotomies suddenly evaporated once national distinctions were described. Rather, the analysis of nations was carried out partly within the dichotomy, but with a considerable amount of detail. If Cook's voyages offered an account of savagery, they did so by first offering detailed accounts of a diverse array of savage nations, some more and some less savage. By unfolding a world of diversity, in other words, the voyages ended up challenging the terms of Rousseau's question, which glorified native purity, just as they challenged the terms of Johnson's dismissal of everything that was not derived from classical Rome and Greece. What was created, instead, was an image of national diversity, grounded on reliable experiences and located in a single global table and map where each nation had its own place. Nevertheless, savagery remained a powerful way of evaluating natives, where some savages were less savage than others.

To appreciate better the value of geographical and national clarity in Cook's voyages, consider a typical description of the inhabitants of the Americas. James Adair published *The History of the American Indians* in 1775, while Cook was on his second voyage. Based in part on over thirty years of direct experience, Adair's book contains over four hundred pages of ethnographic details of Indian customs and culture and, in keeping with his Mosaical account of the peopling of the world, extends the comparison of these nations to biblical accounts of the tribes of Israel. One of the nations that Adair discusses is the Cheerake, as he spells it. To describe where they live, he writes, "the country lies in about 34 degrees north latitude, at the distance of 340 computed miles to the north-west of Charlestown, – 140 miles west-south-west from the Katahba nation, – and almost 200 miles to the north of the Muskohge or Creek country."[50] The location is essentially relational. If you know where Charlestown is and how to get there, then you have a rough idea of where the Cheerake can be found. On the other hand, if you do not know where you are, you do not know where they are either. Several pages are then taken up describing the physical and biological elements of the area – the "best herbage," the general location of rivers, and so on. The greatest botanical detail in the description is a reference to "hemp, and wine-grapes" that grow in the area.[51] The rest of the discussion, roughly twenty-five pages, details the historical relationship between the Cheerake and the Europeans. What ethnographical information is offered is contained in the first part of the book, which focuses on the Indians as a general category, haphazardly using examples from different Indian nations to illustrate different points.

Cook's account of a South Pacific nation differs in several key ways. First, the map that accompanied Adair's book runs from Florida to the Great Lakes and from Maryland in the east to well past the Mississippi in the west. The Cheerake are located simply with a word on the map, with no borders at all. Second, there is a greater connection between the nation and the space in Cook's voyage. In Adair's terms, the Cheerake are "settled" in the country. They are not natives in any strong way, and they have no significant historical connection to the area prior to entering European history. Cook, on the other hand, operating with the luxury of natural borders, would have offered a detailed account of the area, intimately connecting the map, the place name, the environment, and the natives into a single entity. For Cook, it is as if the natives had always been there. For any particular, Adair's account contains as much information as Cook's, but his descriptions become bogged down by continental ambiguity, where there are no sharp geographical boundaries, and Adair rarely offers the reader the sharp descriptions and comparisons that characterize Cook's voyages. Rituals are described, but where they took place and who was doing them is not mentioned. The details are lost or, more accurately, they were never collected in sufficient detail. And how could the rituals of one nation (or one group, or tribe) be compared with another group if the groups are so indistinct? Adair offers few comparisons, partly because he is more concerned with offering a general account of the American Indian, and partly because he is more concerned with connecting the American Indian to a theological story rather than to a geographical or a social one. Adair is not collecting species for further study; he is telling the story of humanity's fall into savagery in a savage land.

CLASSIFYING NATIONS

Cook, on the other hand, is a geographical Linnaeus. Separate places acquire the status of separate species: here is a place, here are its characteristics, and here is how its parts function as a whole. Thus customs, people, weather, geology, flora, and fauna are all parts of a single entity, both static and changeable. One implication of this approach is that the concept of the nation establishes a way of distinguishing two kinds of difference, one between and the other within nations. The differences between nations are like the differences between species, which can be collected together into various genera but which are nonetheless necessarily separate. The differences within nations, on the other hand, are like the differences between parts of a body or a machine. Not only are the members of a nation functionally different, but they *have* to be different in functional terms because they are too geographically close to develop different national identities.

These oceanic nation-places are not the only kind of human identity that Cook describes. There are also systems of identity that do not arise from space, such as gender, race, and class. In Cook's voyages, however, these systems remain connected to the nation-space, and their specific organizations are described as aspects of a place, much as tools and climate are. The description of diversity is thus ceaselessly tied back to a sense of the normal nation-place. Thus, when Cook notes in the first voyage that "the women, contrary to the custom of the sex in general, seemed to affect dress rather less than the men,"[52] the exception is explained by how different parts of the nation function. The way that Cook handles exceptions is important, if only because the account of the world in the voyages could have proceeded in very different ways. For Cook, diversity exists between nations, but the account of any particular nation turns to a functional account in which the parts, such as certain classes of women, are described in terms of an idealized coherent national identity. As a result, not only does the account minimize the importance of idiosyncrasies within a nation, it also minimizes any significantly different national organization by focusing on what functions are normally performed and by what kinds of people. Although Cook's voyages move away from the broad generalization of the savage, they do not thereby assert individuality. Rather, individuals are generalized in a new way.

Compare, for instance, the manuscript and print versions of the second voyage, focusing in particular on an encounter in Dusky Bay, New Zealand, in April 1773. In the manuscript version, Cook writes that he and his men presented a group of natives "with fish and Wild fowl which we had in our boat, which the young Woman afterwards took up one by one and threw them into the Boat again giving us to understand that such things they wanted not."[53] In the Admiralty's version, on the other hand, the woman does not appear as an active agent in the exchange. Rather, the passage reads, "we presented them with fish and fowl which we had in our boat; but these they threw into the boat again, giving us to understand that such things they wanted not."[54] The result is that the woman is changed from an active agent to an almost absent part of a collective entity, which helps to confirm and naturalize what Ruth Dawson refers to as a "male monopoly on leadership."[55] More generally, the account affirms a monopoly on leadership as such. Men are also subsumed by the group. Cook, after all, refers to the English in the first person – the royal we, as it were – during the exchange. And this episode is not unique. Throughout the voyages, human beings exist in groups, and individuals, if they survive the shift from manuscript to book at all, exist because they have a specific and important relationship to the national body.

In general, natives who retain their names in the published narrative are those who have either power or prestige, as do Cook's ship and England itself. This pattern cuts in two directions. First, it means that many people lose their individuality, including most women, natives, and regular sailors. On the other hand, when women have prestige, such as Oberea, who was ruler in Otaheite during Cook's first voyage, they retain their names from one voyage (and one edition) to the next. Here, again, the aristocratic values that permeate the voyages are evident: the lower-class people are anonymous and the upper-class members have personalities. The upper class is worth mentioning.

The functional relationships between parts of a nation connects to the debate over which natives should have been brought back to Europe. The belief that the nobles are the best part of the nation would be equivalent to the belief that the flower is the best part of the plant. The nobles are important, not because they are quantitatively common, but because they are qualitatively the most important, the most honourable, and thus the most representative. Cook is always trying to locate people of "consequence" and spends little time with anyone else. There is, as a result, an assumption in Cook's voyages that the nations of the South Pacific are more or less organized like the nations of Europe: there are divisions in terms of class and gender, there are specific groups that serve specific, typical functions (such as priests, monarchs, and warriors) and there are problems that are faced by every nation, such as the problems of resource management and of the afterlife. Different nations, as species, are organized differently, but they are all part of the same genus.

It may be objected that Cook's voyages do not approach classification in the same way that Linnaeus did, insofar as the voyages are concerned with the location of things rather than with their physiological organization. Where a specimen was discovered is not an immediate concern for Linnaeus, and that information plays no role in its place in the classification system. As Paul Carter writes, "unlike the various branches of eighteenth century natural history, whose classificatory system derived from Linnaeus and wholly ignored the circumstance of discovery, exploration was a spatial discourse. It was attentive to the where and how of objects, and its strategic deployment of names was integral to its transformation of the natural world into an object of knowledge."[56] For Carter, the epistemological difference is best personified in the relationship between Cook and Joseph Banks: "Where Banks was preoccupied with the typical, Cook was concerned with the singular; where Banks tended to generalize, Cook tended to specify. And this, indeed, was the difference between botany and geography as they were practiced in the eighteenth century."[57]

The singular, in Carter's account, is the geographical place that arises through the travel narrative and the system of coordinates. Whereas Banks is concerned with the genera and the species of what he collects, Cook is interested in unique individuals. Carter continues: "Once specimens of all that came immediately to hand had been collected, the botany of the place held no further interest. As Banks wrote, 'The Plants were now intirely compleated and nothing new to be found, so that sailing is all we wish for if the wind would but allow us.'"[58] While this characterization is true to a point, Carter's discussion of Cook's voyages misses an important feature of the narrative, which occurs after Cook has located, named, and mapped the singular place; Cook then describes the place in genera-creating terms: its climate, character, produce, and so on. As a result, the nation-place becomes the boundary of a self-reproducing singular species.

On the other hand, nations are not exactly the same as biological species. They are related to the world differently because they are neither dispersed nor mobile. Instead, nations are like singular plants that relate to each other in the system of classifications. Thus, rather than a new place offering the possibility of finding already-collected species, the place guarantees that a new nation, and only one nation, will be found.

EXPLAINING NATIONS

In addition to dividing nations in terms of their respective places and classifying them in terms of their attributes, they are also connected back to the physical and biological character of their places. Places not only become objects of analysis, but also sources of explanations. During the second voyage, for instance, Cook notes, "In short, of all the nations I have seen, the Pecheras are the most wretched. They are doomed to live in one of the most inhospitable climates in the world, without having sagacity enough to provide themselves with such conveniences as may render life in some measure more comfortable."[59]

To discuss the impact of place on national identity in Cook's voyages, Bernard Smith adopts the term "typical landscape," which he defines as "a form of landscape the component parts of which were carefully selected in order to express the essential qualities of a particular kind of geographical environment."[60] Typical landscapes, in other words, are geographical species that more or less line up with, and support, the national species.

The effects of climate are pervasive and are one of the key variables for explaining the differences between one nation and another. In the third voyage, Cook reflects, "I am persuaded that distance of place, entire separation, diversity of climate, and length of time, all concurring to operate, will account for greater differences, both as to their persons and as to

A landscape of the island of New Caledonia from the second voyage. As with the landscape of Easter Island, the engraving includes typical features of that particular island, including plants, birds, artifacts, and natives.

The landscapes in Cook's voyages brought together places from around the Pacific into a single account of the world. Here is a view of Bolcheretzkoi from the third voyage, also including typical features of a place, which in this case is not as well defined as either the islands or the harbours.

their customs."[61] For instance, accounts of the voyages emphasize the importance of the fertility or the infertility of the land. As a result, population will vary in "proportion to the extent of their ground [being] capable of cultivation."[62] Thus, "the superior fertility of their [the Friendly Islanders'] country enables the inhabitants to lead a more indolent life; and its place is supplied by a plumpness and smoothness of the skin."[63]

In Cook's voyages, the interaction between human nature and customs is constant, where customs tend to arise from the opportunities and imperatives of the nation-place. Throughout, the voyages turn on the question of the relevance of human will or activity in relation to the inexorable influence of climate. During the second voyage, for instance, Cook says,

"What the natives brought them here was real salt water; but they observed that some of them drank pretty plentifully of it; so far will necessity
and custom get the better of nature!"[64]

Significant metaphysical points are at stake in the increased emphasis on the ecological connection between nations and places. For late-
eighteenth-century Europe, Cook's voyages offered a wide range of
examples that spoke to debates over human nature, but always in a way
that affirmed the basic interaction between nature and climate. Natural
imperatives may be more pronounced in some places than others, but the
basic causal pattern remains intact. The account of nations in Cook's voyages can thus account for a large amount of variation, if properly understood, without challenging a general account of human nature, so long
as human nature is causally tied to the varieties of climate and situation.

THE SAVAGE, THE NOBLE SAVAGE, AND THE NATION
The shift to islands and national identities is central to understanding
why Cook's voyages mark a significant shift in the way that the world is
understood. A contrast between the civilized and the savage remains in
the voyages, but the contrast exists within a much more complicated system of identities and locations. Consider again the description of Otaheite
that was offered by Beaglehole in his account of the impact of Wallis's
discovery on European ideas: "So almost suddenly, so overwhelmingly,
was the idea of the Pacific at last to enter into the consciousness, not of
seamen alone but of literate Europe, in the form of this remarkable, this
– as it were – symbolic island ... Wallis had not merely come to a convenient port of call. He had stumbled on a foundation stone of the Romantic
Movement."[65] There is a troublesome shift in this passage from the Pacific to Otaheite, or, abstractly, from the ocean to the island. The difference between islands and oceans is crucial. Wallis did not present "the
idea of the Pacific." Wallis was responsible for presenting Otaheite to
Europe. It was *Cook* who presented the idea of the Pacific, who collected
together a world of fixed containers, filled them with specimens, set them
in relation to each other, and wandered throughout the watery areas that
separated them. Otaheite was simply one of many points.

Bernard Smith argues that the idealization of the primitive changed
during Cook's three voyages, and that the change continued through the
works of later Europeans who travelled through the Pacific in the middle
of the nineteenth century:

There was, for example, the growing insistence by scientists and philosophers that particularized and factual accounts of native peoples must be assembled. There was, too, the wide publicity given to massacres and atrocities perpetrated upon navigators by hostile natives. And there was, above all, the austere religious temper of evangelical thought growing more powerful among all classes of English society year by year, a temper that was disposed to take neither a lenient view of cannibalism, infanticide, and what appeared to be the licentious dances and sexual orgies of native savages, nor of the parodies of such things which pamphleteers and popular versifiers had made capital use of during the 1770's.[66]

While these responses to the ideal of the noble savage were all significant in the eighteenth and nineteenth centuries, Smith does not consider that the responses were actually quite distinct and at times incompatible. On the one hand, there was what he calls the "particularized and factual accounts of native peoples," which led to more detailed and extensive descriptions of the world. On the other hand, there was the "austere religious temper of evangelical thought," which cared little for the differences between nations and reaffirmed the division between the savage and the civilized.

Smith also overstates the defeat suffered by those offering the noble savage as an ideal. Rather than one evaluation of primitivism supplanting another, as if new information demonstrated the truth of one account and refuted its opponent, the debates continued as new information was printed and already-published information was reworked. And if, at some point, the noble savages of the South Pacific were no longer popular, or available, in the debates, the noble savages of ancient Britain became increasingly so.

Cook's voyages were thus connected in various ways to a three-way debate. The first two positions were based on the positive and negative evaluations of savagery, while the third was based on the move away from savagery to the detailed descriptions of nations. Cook's voyages offered the first example of an expansive account of different nations that were more or less "savage." Thus, by focusing on how Cook's voyages move away from a basic division between civilization and savagery, a more complicated system of identities emerges, which connects many nations to many places throughout the South Pacific. Cook does not demonstrate the truth of either Johnson or Rousseau so much as he shows why they both can be true, depending on the nature of the material container in which the group exists, or at least on the shared nature of the group that is being contained. For Cook, the natives of Otaheite were welcoming, and the natives of the Marquesas were not. One result of this move is to challenge a tendency to reduce all articulations of difference to a binary opposition between the self and the other.

FOUR

States

Cook's landing at Mallicollo during the second voyage. The series of engravings depicting landings typically mix images of political authority, physical threat, and national character. Cook is always looking for natives who can maintain order, and the landing is one of the first points where that search begins.

Specific attention should be paid to the political order of the island and the nation because Cook's voyages inadvertently reworked the conceptual foundations of European political thought. There is a particular logic to Cook's narrative. The voyages not only offer detailed measurements and descriptions; they also create a conceptual series – points, coordinates, shapes, islands, and nations – that forms the basic framework in which fragments of the world are identified. To articulate who people are, Cook starts by describing the places where they are from, and then follows the implications of how he began. Where we exist determines where we have come from, what group we belong to, what we believe, how we act, and to whom we are obligated.

When Cook's voyages are placed alongside typical European political philosophies, they offer a significantly different account of the relationship between the nation, the state, and the territory. In Cook's voyages, the island-territory is identified and described first, as a natural, fixed entity, and the nation or society and the state or government are accounted for later if they are accounted for at all. One significant implication is that the political state, far from being either a fluid creation of political power, an artifact of conscious human intentions and agreements, or a divine gift, is thought of as a natural entity, just one more attribute of the singular territorial national species.

The claim that Cook's voyages changed the understanding of sovereignty in European thought may at first appear strange. He is not a political theorist and likely knew very little about the concepts of sovereignty, power, or government, at least beyond the specific rituals that would be known to a naval captain. He also does not become a political theorist after the fact. If we consider the passages from the voyages that are explicitly about sovereignty, we will find them to be well-worn repetitions of political categories that were typical of his time, with their talk of monarchs, ministers, and policy. But something important happens in Cook's voyages, specifically in the way sovereignty is connected to the geographical and national spaces that have been discussed in previous chapters – the voyages contain a somewhat innovative account of the sovereign state. Rather than states creating territory, territory created states. But these states are not the states of Europe, they are the islands and the bays that are found throughout the Pacific.

HOBBES

In early modern European images of political order, such as those offered by Thomas Hobbes and John Locke, the political order is understood as a territorial dominion connected both to a government and a group of people. The discussions are concerned primarily with the relationships between people – representation, obedience, constitutionalism, common law, and so on. *Where* these relationships occurred was both secondary and necessarily a human creation. Hobbes's account of the origins of the political order begins with an account of sovereignty, and then moves to an account of the society (or the nation), and then finally to territory. In *Leviathan,* building on an image of the violent chaos of the state of nature, Hobbes discusses how a multitude can become a single entity with a single coherent will: "A multitude of men, are made one person, when they are by one man, or one person, represented; so that it be done with the consent of every one of that multitude in particular. For it is the unity of the representer, not the unity of the represented, that maketh the person one. And it is the representer that beareth the person, and but one person: and unity, cannot otherwise be understood in multitude."[1]

The commonwealth is created by collecting obedient bodies together through contract and force. The commonwealth is thus based on the maintenance of a legal and political jurisdiction, and in particular on the ability to enforce decisions, to command internal parts, and to resist external threats: "For jurisdiction is the power of hearing and determining causes between man and man; and can belong to none but him that hath the power to prescribe the rules of right and wrong; that is, to make laws; and with the sword of justice to compel men to obey his decisions, pronounced either by himself, or by the judges he ordaineth thereunto; which none can lawfully do but the civil sovereign."[2] The basic requirement for membership in the political order is the willingness to obey. Other personal characteristics, including religion, language, and nationality, are secondary, and can easily be subsumed by the systems of representation and dominion that form the political body. An English king need not be the king of the English.

Once the political body exists, it can then conquer and consolidate a place. This is an important feature of Hobbes's account of both sovereign territory and private property. In the state of nature, there is a division between mine and thine, but "onely that to be every mans that he can get; and for so long, as he can keep it."[3] For Hobbes, therefore, the division between mine and thine has very little relevance in the state of nature. As Hobbes writes in *Leviathan,* "hence it comes to passe, that where an Invader hath no more to feare, than an other mans single power; if one plant, sow, build, or possesse a convenient Seat, others may probably be expected to come prepared with forces united, to dispossesse, and deprive him, not only of the fruit of his labour, but also of his life, or liberty. And the Invader again is in the like danger of another."[4] It is only after people have become part of a political body that their possessions can be secured. When space is finally organized, the territory comes into existence first, and then private property, which is really the distribution of the spoils of war, comes second.

In Hobbes's account of the political order, warfare is a constant threat, and the size and shape of the commonwealth are always contested. Political orders are always pushing up against each other, sometimes taking land and other times losing it. Thus Hobbes, relying on the classical period for examples, writes of how the Athenians and the Romans "live in the condition of a perpetual war, and upon the confines of battle, with their frontiers armed, and cannons planted against their neighbours round about. The Athenians, and Romans were free; that is, free commonwealths: not that any particular men had the liberty to resist their own representative; but that their representative had the liberty to resist, or invade other people."[5]

To dominate an area is not to directly dominate a border, but rather to dominate a city from which a frontier can be patrolled. And so, in his account of the English civil war, Hobbes focuses on the acquisition and loss of cities: "In pursuit of this victory the English marched to Edinburgh (quitted by the Scots), fortified Leith, and took in all the strength and castles they thought fit on this side the Frith, which now has become the bound betwixt the two nations."[6]

Relevant to our discussion here is the physics of sovereignty that Hobbes offers. Castles and fortified cities are key to creating the kinds of pressure necessary for maintaining dominion or obedience. One aspect of Hobbes's account of political space is that the spatial distinctions between sovereignties, rather than being single, thin lines, have depth, much like the Roman frontiers or the Athenian farmlands. Points on the terrain have a military value – rivers, hills, and cities are places where one side may gain an advantage over the other – but that is all. In other words, war creates territory, defining it through the activities and the results of warfare itself. The primary goal of warfare, on the other hand, is to maintain sovereignty, not territory.

In Hobbes's works, there is no sense that the terrain has an impact on national identity, either in the sense that the place gives rise to identity or that the identity extends horizontally throughout a fixed place. For Hobbes, for instance, the English civil war was between factions who were fighting for control over cities, people, and resources. The factions were not attempting to unite the island, as if the island were an already-existing natural goal. The island existed, of course, but the space was understood as a terrain where forces would move from one strategic point to another.

While Hobbes almost never discusses the political relevance of the island, at one point in *Behemoth*, he mentions the potential significance of the island that is shared by the nations of England and Scotland. He notes how "it is strange to me, that England and Scotland being but one island, and their language almost the same, and being governed by one King, should be thought foreigners to one another."[7] While language and geographical proximity are important, however, the overriding basis for the island-wide political identity is the existence of a shared sovereign power. Even on an island, it is the king who keeps everyone together.

LOCKE

In contrast to Hobbes, John Locke grounds the territorial nation-state on an account of pre-social, pre-political private property. Locke accepts that

God "has given the earth to the children of men; given it to mankind in common." However, Locke then offers a way of dividing the common world into private property without having to appeal to any larger political power or "any express compact of all the commoners."[8] Even if people initially shared the world, they were able to acquire private property by mixing their labour with the objects that could be found in the state of nature: "Whatsoever then he removes out of the state that nature hath provided, and left it in, he hath mixed his labour with, and joined to it something that is his own, and thereby makes it his property."[9] Thus "he that is nourished by ... the apples he gathered from the trees in the wood has certainly appropriated them to himself."[10] Locke then moves from the fruits of the earth to the earth itself. How can people legitimately claim to possess land? Locke again appeals to labour as the deciding factor: "As much land as a man tills, plants, improves, cultivates, and can use the product of, so much is his property."[11] Thus, Locke concludes, "he that in obedience to this command of God, subdued, tilled and sowed any part of it, thereby annexed to it something that was his property, which another had no title to, nor could without injury take from him."[12]

Unlike Hobbes, whose state of nature is composed of isolated and generally hostile individuals, Locke's state of nature contains all the trappings of an extended bourgeois estate, in which the head of the household can be said to own other people's labour and therefore the products of that labour.

For Locke, the contiguity of the territory that is connected to a specific state arises from joining together individual plots of land. Territory, in other words, is created by the accumulation of smaller pieces of clearly bordered private land. However, Locke does not discuss the patchwork of sovereignties that could result from such a contractual arrangement. Why should people who live near each other join the same political body? Why did everyone in England happen to agree to join the same government? Locke fails to address these questions, and it is not clear that he could do so in an adequate way, given the centrality of private property and the non-coercive origins of the legitimate state in his theory. And just as Locke cannot appeal to the coercive power of the sovereign, as Hobbes could, he also does not explicitly appeal to the prior existence of a national identity. There is society insofar as there are persistent relations between proximate property owners, but there is no sense of a politically relevant national identity in the state of nature – the English, for instance – that plays a relevant political role.

ROUSSEAU

Jean-Jacques Rousseau reacted against writers such as Hobbes and Locke and published *On the Social Contract* six years before Cook began his first voyage to the Pacific. In Rousseau's discussion, geographical places acquire a new status – the nation and the state are tied back into a natural system of separations and unions among people. As a result, the nation acquires a presence beyond and prior to the creation of the political order. For Rousseau, the people of the world are divided into different nations, each with specific characteristics and possible futures: "For nations, as for men, there is a time of maturity that must be awaited before subjecting them to the laws. But the maturity of a people is not always easily recognized; and if it is foreseen, the work is ruined. One people lends itself to discipline at its inception; another, not even after ten centuries."[13]

Throughout Rousseau's political writings there is a tendency to idealize a pure, uncontaminated society, in part through the organization of geographical space. His examples frequently return to ancient Greece and Rome and the idealized Geneva of his own time. The autonomous nation, with a coherent social identity, exists within the confines of a walled city, large enough to defend itself but not large enough to distance its inhabitants from each other: "The Romans? But they became conquerors out of necessity and, so to speak, in spite of themselves. War was a corrective measure forced on them by the peculiar vice of their constitution. They were an island of discipline in the midst of a sea of barbarism, always attacked and always victorious, and they became masters of the world by constantly defending themselves."[14]

The island is an image of political purity that Rousseau uses in various places in his arguments. In *On the Social Contract,* after discussing what conditions are necessary for a proper social contract to be established, Rousseau offers a vision of what could happen: "In Europe there is still one country capable of receiving legislation. It is the island of Corsica. The valor and constancy with which this brave people has regained and defended its liberty would merit having some wise man teaching them how to preserve it. I have a feeling that some day this little island will astonish Europe."[15] The fact that Corsica is an island may be circumstantial. However, given the importance of natural boundaries, shared climate, and national isolation in Rousseau's account of politics, islands offer the ideal conditions for the creation and maintenance of a people. They are natural city-states without the cities.

In *The Government of Poland,* Rousseau argues that the size of the country should be reduced for the sake of its own internal coherence. He recommends to the Polish reformers that, because the Polish have become spatially incoherent, "if you wish to reform your government, then, begin by narrowing your frontiers, though perhaps your neighbors intend to do that for you. It would certainly be a great misfortune for the dismembered parts, but a great blessing for the body of the nation."[16]

As with Locke and Hobbes, there is an overwhelming need for spatial coherence. In *On the Social Contract,* Rousseau argues that "once the state is instituted, residency implies consent. To inhabit the territory is to submit to sovereignty."[17] But submitting to sovereignty is not the same for Rousseau as it is for Hobbes or Locke, who both understand this submission in terms of simple conformity to sovereignty and its laws. For Rousseau, submitting to sovereignty is tied to being assimilated into the nation, which is understood as a single social, cultural, and political unit. Being English or Scottish or Polish thus becomes one of the key starting points for describing and explaining the origins and character of sovereignty.

The island becomes the daydream of the nation-state. But for Rousseau, the daydream also ends up casting a cynical shadow over the possibilities of legitimate political order. There are few islands in Europe, metaphorical or real, and most nations are beyond hope. Thus, while Rousseau rails against the bloated states of western Europe and the confusion that can be found everywhere else, the appeal to the natural limits created by national identity and permeable geography make workable alternatives all but impossible to imagine.

THE SCOTTISH ENLIGHTENMENT

At roughly the same time as Rousseau was imagining the island nation, several thinkers, later joined as the Scottish Enlightenment, were also working with similar issues (many of which can be traced back to some of Montaigne's essays). In Adam Ferguson's 1767 publication, *An Essay on the History of Civil Society,* for instance, there is a constant appeal to national identities. In the third part of the book in particular, he offers an account of the history of nations from their original rude state to more advanced and civilized states. Ferguson argues that geography helps to protect and improve nations: while the shores of the Pacific and Atlantic oceans contain "thriving and independent nations ... there is scarcely a people in the vast continent of Asia who deserves the name of a nation."[18] However, while geography helps to explain why some rude and feeble nations survive, the primary explanation for why a nation develops is the history of the conflicts that it has with other nations.

If we situate him alongside the thinkers already discussed, Ferguson agrees with Rousseau's claim that human history begins as a system of nations, some of which survive while others are assimilated or dissolved. However, whereas Rousseau submerges all European nations into a generalized decadence called civilization, Ferguson maintains the national divisions in Europe and argues for their continued development. Some nations have survived, and those should be praised. Thus Ferguson's account of the progression moves from the nation (as a natural creation that is barely different from other nations) to the territory (as an incubator of national identity), to the state (as the means to develop the nation through conflict). Ferguson, in other words, begins with Rousseau, but ends with Hobbes; he begins with naturalized nations, but ends with conflict and competition as the driving force of human existence and development. The relationship of territory to the political order, then, changes from one of passive protection to one of conflict and transformation.

THE NATIVE STATE IN COOK'S VOYAGES

Cook's voyages offered a significant alternative to the seventeenth- and eighteenth-century European understanding of politics. In Cook's voyages, the relationship between territory, nation, and state is reworked, both in terms of the order in which they are described in the narrative, but also in the relative importance they each have in constituting the identity of the whole. Territory, far from being secondary and always contested, is naturalized and given priority over the nation and the state. The territory is the first thing that existed and the first thing that is described. By constantly connecting natives to their islands, by relying on the ideal of fixed boundaries describing an internally undifferentiated container, as discussed in the last chapter, Cook's voyages naturalize the relationship between a specific kind of social group and a specific articulation of areas. For this reason, the articulation of sovereignty in Cook's voyages is more in line with Rousseau's writings. While Rousseau's *On the Social Contract* offered an unattained and almost unattainable ideal, however, Cook, travelling in a world of islands and coordinates, found that ideal in an almost natural form almost everywhere he went.

The order of precedence changes: the king rules everyone within the territory, while the territory pre-exists both sovereigns and subjects. On this theme, Rousseau notes that where kings once claimed to rule people, they now claim to rule places, even if those places are artificial:

> One can imagine how the combined and continuous lands of private individuals became public territory; and how the right of sovereignty, extending from subjects to the land they occupied, becomes at once real and personal. This places its owners in a greater dependence, turning their very own forces into guarantees of their loyalty. This advantage does not seem to have been fully appreciated by the ancient monarchs, who, calling themselves merely King of the Persians, the Scythians, and the Macedonians, appeared to regard themselves merely as the leaders of men rather than the masters of the country. Today's monarchs more shrewdly call themselves King of France, Spain, England, and so on. In holding the land thus, they are quite sure of holding the inhabitants.[19]

In Cook's descriptions of nations and states, something similar to this political strategy becomes the natural order. First, there were island-territories, which existed before humans arrived, and it was in these containers that nation-states were formed. One example of many is from the second voyage, where Cook emphasizes not only the spatial separation of islands, but even the way that some islands were naturally fortified:

> This island, and also that of Eaoowe, is guarded from the sea by a reef of coral rocks extending out from the shore one hundred fathoms more or less. On this reef the force of the sea is spent before it reaches the land or shore. Indeed, this is, in some measure, the situation of all the Tropical Isles in this sea that I have seen; and thus nature has effectually secured them from the encroachment of the sea, though many of them are mere points when compared to this vast ocean.[20]

It becomes possible to locate nation-states, even if they are mere points, on maps, which not only places one nation in relationship to others but also clearly and distinctly separates each nation. The geographical and mathematical separation between points in the ocean thus becomes the foundation for the political and national divisions between people. There is neither overlap nor mixture.

To someone who is interested in presenting a complete and accurate account of the world – geographical, biological, and political – the islands and other physical divisions are a godsend. Rather than having to investigate where one place begins and another ends, Cook can take those borders for granted and focus on describing the character of the nation and the identity of the sovereign thus contained.

By coming to the description of the state so late in his articulation of places, however, Cook faces a problem that is opposite to the one faced by Hobbes. In Hobbes, the sovereign is obvious: it is a spectacular entity whose presence in the body politic must be pervasive and visible. A hidden sovereign makes no sense in Hobbes's account of political order. The problem for Hobbes's sovereign is in securing the territory. In Cook's voyages, on the other hand, one of the key problems is finding out who the sovereign is.

Typically, Cook tries to identify the king by noting how the natives treat one another. Can some people command or at least influence others? Are some people more respected than others? In the second voyage, Cook writes, "I was told by the officers who were on shore, that a far greater man than any we had yet seen was come to pay us a visit. Mr. Pickersgill informed me that he had seen him in the country, and found that he was a man of some consequence, by the extraordinary respect paid him by the people."[21]

Cook also tries to determine who the monarch is by asking the natives themselves. How this is achieved varies from episode to episode, and it tends to be relied upon only after the Europeans have gained some acquaintance with the people and the language. Cook notes in the second voyage, "I have frequently mentioned a king, which implies the government being in a single person, without knowing for certain whether it is so or not. Such a one was, however, pointed out to us; and we had no reason to doubt it."[22]

Readers may wonder whether Cook's questions were understood clearly by people who were not thinking in his categories. There are certainly times when the answers given were later found to be wrong, such as when a more powerful or more respected person comes onto the scene, and the prior king is relocated as a secondary figure. At other times, however, the answers seem to be accurate, but the results are confusing in terms of the European images of sovereignty. For instance, William Ellis writes during the third voyage that "this circumstance appeared very strange to us, no less than three people having been pointed out to us as king."[23]

Behind these interactions is a sense of confusion, and, more than confusion, a sense that western political categories may not be appropriate for the South Pacific. But Cook does not pursue this question. Instead, the possible complexity of the political system is turned into a question of intensity. If there are three kings on the island, it is because there are no kings, only three people with limited power over the nation and a series of confused or deceitful natives.

At times, Cook finds native nations who seem to live without any kind of sovereignty. For instance, during the narrative of the second voyage he writes, "I am satisfied that the people in this Sound, who are, upon the whole, pretty numerous, are under no regular form of government, or so united as to form one body politic."[24]

In a Hobbesian world, this situation is all but unthinkable. The lack of government implies the war of all against all. In Locke's theory, on the other hand, the situation is at least possible, but only within an already-existing system of private property. However, in Cook's voyages, the people in this sound are not individual property owners tolerating the inconveniences that arise from no central government. There are customs, interactions, and a shared language. What is evidently lacking, however, is a sovereign power to enforce a legal and moral order, and to mediate the relationship between that nation and the outside. But the nation still seems to maintain itself.

While Cook is often unable to describe the specific character of the government, he is able to offer, to the highest degree of accuracy, the outline of the territory. There is thus an interesting inversion in what Cook can confidently describe when compared with thinkers like Hobbes, Locke, and Rousseau. Cook's account of sovereignty moves very quickly from absolute certainty to almost complete confusion, as the territory, the nation, and the state are described and related. The state, even if poorly understood, thus exists in the shadow of certainty, because it is always connected back to cartographical and astronomical measurements that can be verified and made ever more accurate. To those who might be suspicious of Cook's account of the sovereign dominion, Cook can describe the identity of the nation. To those who wonder about the coherence of the nation, Cook can respond with the clear and distinct shapes on his maps. And to those who question the reliability of his maps, Cook can offer a table of coordinates, a description of his instruments and methods, and he can challenge the skeptics to verify the measurements for themselves.

The coherence of the island-nation-states is connected to Cook's own ships, which exist throughout the voyages as clear national, monarchical spaces. Throughout the narrative, the ships become very clear, determinate, and ritualized images of the mature, rational European state. Cook's crew, whatever their origin, are intimately connected to each other, to the point where the ship, like the island, becomes a physical container for the group. The ships were microcosms of the European social order. However, far from portraying the political struggles for power that characterized the narratives of the buccaneers, Cook's voyages narrate the political order of a modern rational monarchy, as contained on the ships of the Royal Navy.[25] Everyone knew (or should have known) their place and function, and the role of the captain was to ensure that everyone understood and performed their duty.

The ships were also organized in terms of social class. Not only was the chain of command clear, it was also tied to a system of social classes in which the officers and the gentlemen were intermediaries between the king and the peasant sailors. Cook writes in the second voyage, for instance, that his crew, "throughout the whole voyage, merited every indulgence which it was in my power to give them. Animated by the conduct of the officers, they showed themselves capable of surmounting every difficulty and danger which came in their way, and never once looked either upon the one or the other, as being at all heightened by our separation from our consort the *Adventure*."[26]

Throughout Cook's three voyages, the ship remained the most coherent social unit, with the possible exception of England itself. Cook was a benevolent sovereign, but he was unquestionably the one who was sovereign. He was interested in the general wishes of his crew, but not in obliging himself to follow the general will. There were diseases and deaths, but no one in the group escaped either Cook's ship or his authority.

The social and political order on Cook's ship parallels the order that he tries to find on the islands. The interaction between ship and island is thus understood as the interaction between two nations, where the identity of the ship helps constitute the identity of the island and vice versa. While no chiefs are referred to as "captains" of their islands, Cook is frequently described as the "chief" of his ship.[27] When John Marra relates an episode in which Cook is responding to the theft of a water cask, he writes, "to this remonstrance, menaces were added, and the whole island threatened if the [water] cask was not produced, and the thief delivered up."[28]

The triad of the ship, the crew, and the captain is placed in opposition to the triad of the island, the natives, and the king. Throughout the voyages, Cook threatens islands as if they, their inhabitants, and their kings shared a collective responsibility and were thus subject to a collective punishment. The dialogues between the English and the native nations are thus telescoped through the principles of sovereignty and the consolidation of voices into a single exchange.

One important difference between the ship and the island is that the ship does not have a fixed location in the table of places. The island never moves, but while Cook's ship always has a location, its identity is based on its ability to move from place to place, to transcend the particular identities on the table (the islands) as it gradually comprehends the table as such (the ocean). This difference cannot be emphasized enough. At any given point in the interaction, the ship and the island are equals: they are both nations with states. But then Cook moves, the island is lost over the horizon, and it is eventually replaced by another one, inhabited by different people and ruled by someone else.

The tone of Cook's description of native political systems is important insofar as it reinforces several significant themes. Specifically, Cook's voyages adopt a tone of paternalism, persistently emphasizing the immaturity and underdevelopment of the political systems of the South Pacific. In the third voyage, for instance, Cook notes how the sovereign authority along the coast of North America has not developed beyond the extended family: "But, I should guess, the authority of each of these great men extends no farther than the family to which he belongs, and who own him as their head."[29] Severe criticisms of uncivilized nations are implied by this account, although different nations will be judged more or less severely. Cook does not simply describe the authority structures; he is also constantly tying those descriptions back to an ideal in which sovereignty not only extends beyond the family, but also controls human life beyond immediate physical threats. The sovereign allows for the existence and policing of promises.

While Hobbes's account begins with the creation of the sovereign, then of the people, and then of the territory, and Locke's account begins with the creation of the people, then of the sovereign, and then of the territory, Cook's account begins with discussing the territory, then the nation, and finally the sovereign. These three narrative sequences have significantly different implications, specifically in terms of the modes of justification and the overall character of the political system. Of course, it is not that people suddenly recognized a relationship between geography and politics, as if it were only in the late eighteenth century that the British realized that they lived on an island, or that the English Channel suddenly became an important site of demarcation. Rather, the identification of the British with a fixed area of the globe, the sentiments of nationalism, and the statistics of the nation became the object of a diverse set of political and social projects that were related to changes in navigation, mapping, and description. The character of the nation, as a standardized and knowable entity, became a core political concern once the geographical borders became clear and distinct. In other words, geography became the foundation of a scientific method in terms of which everything ought to be understood.

The value that is placed on the spatial order of islands and ships in Cook's voyages creates a political ideal that is significantly different from those of Hobbes, Locke, and to a lesser extent Rousseau. Cook is not a political theorist, but the implications of the voyages for political philosophy can nonetheless be traced. What happens is that the ideal native-state in Cook's voyages becomes a generalized ideal. The islands of the South Pacific become a good model, if not the dominant model, for how the world ought to be organized.

KANT

Immanuel Kant does not write about Cook's voyages directly in any of his main work. The conceptual connections are our main concern here. To consider the connection between the nation, the state, and territory in Kant's writings, it is necessary to work against the tendencies of the commentators. There is ample concern in the secondary literature for Kant's republicanism and cosmopolitanism. There is widespread discussion of how Kant articulates politics as a system of rights or as a kingdom of ends, and for how Kant connects those rights both to the enlightenment and to the intersection of law and ethics. But when it comes to considering Kant's account of space, the commentators focus on the discussion of space as a form of sensory intuition in *The Critique of Pure Reason,* and when it comes to considering Kant's discussion of nations, the commentators are largely silent.

Kant and Cook were contemporaries. Kant was born in 1724, while Cook was born in 1728. The Admiralty's edition of Cook's first voyage was published in German in 1774 and the second voyage in 1778, the year before Cook's death. Kant published his first major philosophical work, *The Critique of Pure Reason*, in 1781, and he continued to write until the year of his death, in 1804. Kant's political works, which focus on how human beings are manifested "in the world of phenomena,"[30] were published primarily in the 1770s and 1780s, at the time when Cook's voyages were a common currency in European intellectual communities. Also, Georg Forster, the naturalist on Cook's second voyage, returned to his native Germany in the 1780s and frequently appealed to Cook's voyages throughout his writings. Kant and Forster engaged in an extended debate over the status of race as a descriptive category,[31] and Forster's influence on Kant and his contemporaries, such as Herder and Humboldt, can be noticed.[32] But there are also conceptual connections between Kant's writings and Cook's voyages.

Like Rousseau, Kant articulates a global vision of humanity based on national divisions that frequently depend on natural, or at least naturalized, geographical divisions. One relevant text here is Kant's *Anthropology from a Pragmatic Point of View*, a book published in 1797 based on notes from a course that Kant had taught from the late 1760s.[33] The first section of the work is devoted to distinguishing and describing the nations of Europe. In this discussion, the exemplary nations are England and France. Kant writes, "since the coastlines of England and France are close to each other and separated only by a channel (which could well be called a sea), the rivalry of these two people nevertheless produces in each of them a different turn of political character in their conflict: on one side apprehension, and on the other hatred."[34] Kant's account is fixated on the coast while the channel is used to mark the distinction between France and England. As the discussion moves away from the channel, the clarity begins to dissolve. He does not mention the Germans. The other peoples of Europe he considers, such as the Italians, the Spaniards, and the Poles, are not pure nations, but are instead the result of mixtures: "The Spaniard, born of the mixture of European with Arabic (Moorish) blood, shows a certain solemnity in his bearing, both in public and in private, and even the peasant shows an awareness of his dignity in the presence of his betters, to whom he is obedient."[35] "The Spaniard," then, while still a recognizable national identity, is nonetheless the result of a combination of two prior, purer identities. Kant's categories here are a bit equivocal: is "the European" a national identity contrasted to the Arabic nation, or is it something more general that is shared by nations such as England and France? Unfortunately, Kant does not consider how the different scales of group identity interact.

Kant continues his list of national identities, gradually moving to the south and to the east. While "the Spaniard" still has a coherent character, other countries farther away from the English Channel fare worse: "Russia has not yet reached the stage where we could form a definite concept of what natural tendencies lie ready to develop. Poland is no longer at this stage. But the nationals of European Turkey never have attained and never will attain what is necessary to acquire a specific popular character. So we are properly excused from sketching these peoples."[36] As an epistemological ideal, it is only clear and distinct nations that can be well described, so as Kant's account moves from England and France to Turkey, it also moves from being the most intelligible and interesting to the least.

In his *Anthropology from a Pragmatic Point of View,* Turkey is as far as Kant takes the discussion, as if anthropology were an essentially European concern. In other texts, however, he considers the various South Pacific nations, and in particular the New Zealander and the Tahitian. Here, however, the move from clear identities to mixed identities is reversed. The nations of the South Pacific are primitive, but they are not mixed; rather, they are unproblematically and naturally pure. In his review of Herder's *Ideas on the Philosophy of the History of Mankind,* for instance, Kant refers to the "happy inhabitants of Tahiti," while in *The Critique of Judgment* he refers to the "Greenlander, the Lapp, the Samoyed, and Yakut."[37] Far from lacking a specific national character, these groups are brought into the discussion as unproblematic and unmixed identities. Nations do not come into existence through historical progress but exist primordially.

In Kant's account of the origins of political order, the nation becomes a civil society through a social contract that establishes a republican government. But how does the nation relate to its territory? Hobbes had territorial wars occurring after the social contract had taken place, where the commonwealth would consolidate an area and establish boundaries. Locke had private property already existing before the people entered into the social contract. For both writers, the contract (or submission) is an essential condition for the creation of sovereign territory. There are times when Kant's account echoes those offered by Hobbes and Locke, appealing sometimes to warfare and sometimes to the social contracts that consolidated individuals and their private property. However, at other times, Kant's discussion organizes the relationship between nations and places in geographical and anthropological terms that are much closer to those that pervade Cook's voyages. But Kant's analysis is far from consistent, mixing together different accounts in sometimes incoherent ways.

In the opening sections of *The Metaphysics of Morals,* Kant considers how it is possible for someone to possess external objects, that is to say, how private property is to be understood. Kant's account of the acquisition of land here parallels, to some extent, the one offered by Locke in the *Second Treatise on Government.* Both writers begin with individuals acquiring private property. The key difference is that Locke focuses on cultivation as the key for translating common property into private property, whereas Kant focuses on the much more Hobbesian idea of protection. As Kant writes, "the question arises, how far does authorization to take possession of a piece of land extend? As far as the capacity for controlling it extends, that is, as far as whoever wants to appropriate it can defend it – as if the land were to say, if you cannot protect me you cannot command me."[38] The personification of the land in this passage is important, not only because it helps establish something like a legal and moral relationship between people and places, but also because it reinforces the material separation of one place from another.

Different lands have different mythical voices, making agreements with different individuals. Kant continues, "My possession extends as far as I have the mechanical ability, from where I reside, to secure my land against encroachment by others."[39] The original distribution of land thus apparently arose from individual warfare, or at least the threat of warfare, centred on an already-established residence. Forgetting for a moment whether this historical narrative is even plausible (given Hobbes's concern for how protection and residence are even possible in the state of nature), one thing that Kant establishes with this image is a specific sense of bordered space and an individual's relationship to that space.

There are times in Kant's discussion when the territory of the nation-state is not simply the accumulation of private property, but rather the nation exists in its own right and owns territory in the same way that individuals do in other parts of Kant's discussion. In *The Metaphysics of Morals,* for instance, Kant claims that the principle of control "is how the dispute over whether the sea is free or closed also has to be decided; for example, as far as a cannon shot can reach no one may fish, haul up amber from the ocean floor, and so forth, along the coast of a territory that already belongs to a certain state."[40] Here, cannons and territories belong to specific groups. The shift to nation-states as the agents of protection resolves the problem of protection that arose in Hobbes's state of nature. The acquisition that is carried out by groups offers Kant a much more plausible narrative to respond to Hobbes's challenge. Individuals are incapable of protecting anything for any length of time, but nations can.

In addition to narrating the creation of the territorial nation-state by combining elements of Hobbes and Locke, therefore, Kant's account also echoes Rousseau's focus on the nation as the ground of political identity. But where did the nation come from? In *The Metaphysics of Morals,* Kant defines a nation as "a multitude of human beings living in proximity to one another."[41] While this definition may seem trivial, it relies on the assumption that proximity is something that occurs naturally – what Kant calls "a necessary result of [people's] existence on the earth." If, on the other hand, the earth's surface were an unbounded plane, "people could be so dispersed on it that they would not come into any community with one another"[42] and so would never be formed into nationalities. But the world is, in fact, bounded, and therefore human beings are organized into nations. Proximity must therefore join some people together and also separate that group from groups farther away. Of course, this image is easy to establish with islands, or by pointing to channels, but its application to continents is rather more awkward. Yet if the nation and the state are connected to territory, and if territory is what creates the proximity necessary for the nation and the state to arise, then the separation of one territory from another – the existence of a territory as a thing that is divided from other territories even before people exist as a nation – is essential.

The value of geographical separation as the ground for national divisions connects to the idea of spatial insularity. National identity is best formed in enclosed areas. As Kant argues in *Perpetual Peace,* "thus nature wisely separates the nations, although the will of each individual state, even basing its arguments on international right, would gladly unite them under its own sway by force or by cunning."[43] Kant points to the natural geographical separation of nations, which are connected to specific and different tracts of land, to articulate a universalized principle of natural and national ownership. Here, an individual's activity has a secondary importance at best. What matters is the agreement, which is completed before nations start to interact, between a nation and a place. In *The Metaphysics of Morals*, Kant asks, "can two neighboring peoples (or families) resist each other in adopting a certain use of land, for example, can a hunting people resist a pasturing people or a farming people, or the latter resist a people that wants to plant orchards, and so forth?" His optimistic answer, which assumes the natural existence of both peoples and places, is "certainly, since as long as they keep within their boundaries the way they want to live on their land is up to their own discretion."[44] In other words, so long as the lands do not overlap, it is possible for national diversity and for peace to exist. The more awkward issues, such as whether people can share land, or not connect to any specific land, or connect to the same land in different ways are not raised here. All that Kant establishes is that different nations can coexist as neighbours, so long as they keep to themselves.

It is significant that in these sections Kant discusses the relationship between peoples in terms of whether "they keep within their boundaries" and not in terms of their ability to continue to protect those boundaries. In other words, while Kant narrates the origins of private property in terms of protection, when he turns to consider the relations between groups of people, he argues that there are natural boundaries that separate nations from each other. Thus, in *The Metaphysics of Morals*, Kant claims that the victors in a just war "are not called upon to divide its territory among themselves and to make the state, as it were, disappear from the earth, since that would be an injustice against its people."[45] Kant extends this argument to say that it is wrong for Europeans to take land from natives, however savage:

> It can still be asked whether, when neither nature nor chance but just our own will brings us into the neighborhood of a people that holds out no prospect of a civil union with it, we should not be authorized to found colonies, by force if need be, in order to establish a civil union with them and bring these human beings (savages) into a rightful condition (as with the American Indians, the Hottentots, and the inhabitants of New Holland); or (which is not much better), to found colonies by fraudulent purchase of their land, and so become owners of their land, making use of our superiority without regard for their first possession.[46]

Kant is not attacking the desire to enlighten other peoples or the moralizing despotism that could and probably ought to result. Instead, what he is establishing here is the division between enlightened control and colonialism. European powers can and in fact ought to control savage nations, but it is wrong for those European powers to send out European colonies to take over the land of those savage nations. Rather, the task is to improve the nations that need it, much like one should improve a child. Kant's cosmopolitan vision, grounded in a sense of the world divided into fixed nation-places, thus conforms very well to Cook's ideals.

In Kant's view, the progress of human history, the rise of a cosmopolitan order, is the progress of ever-increasing connections between nations. Sometimes these connections are brought about through warfare, and sometimes through economic exchange: "The peoples of the earth have thus entered in varying degrees into a universal community, and it has developed to the point where a violation of rights in one part of the world is felt everywhere."[47] The result, for Kant, is a repetition of the civil contract at the level of nations, "abandoning a lawless state of savagery and entering a federation of peoples in which every state, even the smallest, could expect to derive its security and rights not from its own power or its own legal judgement, but solely from this great federation."[48]

As may be evident by now, to label Kant a cosmopolitan thinker is inaccurate. He is rather a cosmo-nationalist thinker. When describing the human world, he rarely writes about cities, and these are never the primary political units. Rather, the primary relationship is between the cosmos and the territorialized nation. And while the move to a global organization of nations may shift some political power beyond the nation-state, the nation itself continues to exist as the fundamental building block of a global system of identities. The image of the cosmopolitan world thus parallels the image of the collected world, in which each of the isolated, coherent political entities are brought together in a single table of relations.

FINDING AND CREATING THE TERRITORIAL NATION-STATE

Cook is searching for strong sovereigns, not only because his description is incomplete without them, but also because the world is imperfect until they exist. Throughout his voyages, Cook maps an area, labels the nation, finds its rulers, and positions his ships, his crew, and himself in relation to the island, the natives, and the monarch. His confidence is infectious, while his claims to know a place, apparently so certain and complete, become the epitome of what it means to know any place at all. As the ideal of the nation-state extends through the nineteenth century, the basic epistemological and political categories of Cook's voyages extend as well.

In the late eighteenth century and on into the nineteenth century, "government" was being established around the Pacific, not only through direct European rule, but also through the cultivation of native authority. Roughly ten years after Cook, George Vancouver was the captain of the next ships sent by the British Admiralty into the northern Pacific. Vancouver's impact on the Sandwich Islands was far more profound than Cook's had been, especially because Vancouver intervened to a much greater extent in domestic politics. Vancouver's actions in the Sandwich Islands are comparable to the situation in south Asia in the nineteenth century. Edward Said has claimed that "as imperialists the British felt their task in India was to solve 'the problem of sovereignty in Bengal' in favor, naturally enough, of the British crown."[49] By helping to solve "the problem of sovereignty" in the Sandwich Islands, Vancouver was helping to transform Hawaiian social and political relations into western ideals, and thus position these islands that much more solidly into the global system of places and peoples. For Vancouver, the territory and the people existed – that was not the problem. What was needed was the proper organization of power, the capacity to recognize an appropriately powerful king who, hopefully, favoured the British crown.

Another explorer in the South Pacific who followed Cook's voyages, both geographically and textually, was Otto von Kotzebue. During his second voyage into the Pacific as a commander, when he lands on Oahu, Kotzebue offers his readers an account of the "rise of the nation,"[50] which is now an "infant state."[51] As in the case of Vancouver, the nation is not what is being created, the nation is rather the subject that is maturing. In the time between Cook and Kotzebue, Tameamea (Kamehameha) "became the supreme governor of the whole Archipelago."[52] Kotzebue describes Tameamea as follows: "Himself endowed with uncommon powers of mind, he entrusted the important offices of state only to such as were capable of discharging them efficiently. He made a very fortunate choice in Karemaku, who, while quite a young man, entered into all the enlightened and comprehensive views of his master, forwarded them with ability and energy, and continued his faithful servant till the death of Tameamea. The English called him the Pitt of the Sandwich Islands."[53]

Tameamea is praised not only because he is a good king, by certain European standards, but also because he was quickly changing the islands in ways that conformed to certain European political ideals. The Sandwich Islanders, as a nation, were thus acquiring a full-fledged state, and were perhaps becoming the pre-eminent nation-state of the Pacific. Cook's narrative of sovereignty thus draws a specific connection between rationality and sovereignty, in which the existence of monarchical sovereign power is one of the primary signs of a developed, civilized, and rational nation.

While the islands of the South Pacific needed states, the organization of Europe needed nations, or at least needed nations and states that were better defined. Of course, the idea that nations had places was not new. What changed in the nineteenth century, however, was the clarity with which those borders had to be articulated. It is significant that it was not until the nineteenth century that the borders of the European nation-states were reworked and clarified by cartographers, surveyors, and politicians, and their ideal was the ideal of the island: sharp divisions, preferably natural, that created distance and separation, if only through markers and the map.[54] Hence Cook's voyages, as the epitome of the scientific exploration narrative, are organized by a conceptual frame that becomes pervasive in the idealizations of politics in European thought.

By imagining the world in terms of territorial nation-states, Cook's voyages echoed the rise of nineteenth-century nationalism. The concept of the modern nation-state depends on a strict and intimate correspondence between the nation and the state, where the nation is a spatially coherent group of people who share language, beliefs, customs, and most importantly, territory. These shared characteristics can exist, however, without "nationalism." Missing in Europe and first offered with the French Revolution, according to E.J. Hobsbawm, was an understanding of the nation as self-conscious and political. In *Nationalism*, Elie Kedourie claimed that in the beliefs of nationalists, "humanity is naturally divided into nations, that nations are known by certain characteristics which can be ascertained, and that the only legitimate type of government is national government."[55] It is not enough that France and Germany exist as linguistic and cultural entities; they must recognize that existence and use it as the basis for the political order for a modern sense of the nation to exist.

While the nation became an important, if not the central, category for articulating the creation and legitimation of the political order, much more intellectual activity was going on at the end of the eighteenth century than the glorification of Rousseau's work. The territorial nation-state became the primary political goal. National consciousness thus depended on the creation of a vast amount of knowledge about the nation – studies of landscapes, of language, of history, of artifacts, of customs, of literature – that is all connected to an emergent national identity that can then be specified, studied, and known. It is not enough to say that the nation ought to rule; what became necessary was to study what the nation was so that it could both rule and be ruled.

Here, Cook's voyages offer a clear model of how to describe a nation. The nation, surrounded by the clear line on the map, could be described in detail. Of course, the ideal of the nation-state in the voyages arises less from political philosophy than from the clarity of descriptions tied to clear geographical articulations. But this almost-natural entity is not the result of conscious human activity. What Cook's voyages help to provide, therefore, was an epistemological basis, a working example, for nationalism. That the voyages gave accounts of primitive nations and states is no criticism; in fact, it only helps to naturalize the entire system and turn nationalists towards their nation's land as much as to their nation's history.

In opposition to historians of ideas who locate the rise of the nation-state in the turmoil of the French Revolution, Benedict Anderson argues in *Imagined Communities* that important aspects of nationalism arose in the Spanish colonies of South America. The relationship between Cook's voyages and the nation-state adds to the global origins of the ideal by pointing to the connection between the ideals of the nation state and the cartographic descriptions of the islands of the South Pacific. Dominant themes in nineteenth-century political thought, focusing on the nation-state, thus operated within a vision of the world in which nations were naturally occurring entities, tied to geographically distinct places. If this characterization is correct, then Cook's voyages can show how the entire conceptual framework holds together, how nationalism is tied to the social sciences, how specific geographical formations became idealized, and why these formations were constructed where they could not be found. The island was not only the daydream of the nation-state, it was an idea that made the nation-state intelligible.

Some historians of ideas who focus on nineteenth-century European romantics, and specifically on writers such as Johann Gottfried Herder and Johann Gottlieb Fichte, argue that nationalism is a reaction to rationalism, offering a spiritual alternative to mechanistic social theories. But the romantics are not the only thinkers to discuss the nation and nationalism. What happens, rather, is that there are two general themes in nineteenth-century nationalism, the first being the romantic nationalism of thinkers such as Herder, and the second being the rationalist nationalism of thinkers such as Edmund Burke and Walter Bagehot. What Cook's voyages helped to establish, in other words, is not so much a way to decide between radical and conservative political projects. Cook may support king and country, but the articulation of the system of nations, states, and territories in the voyages allows for a wide range of political engagements. The voyages are important for the way they established the connections between nations, states, and territories as the primary terrain on which politics must be articulated. Thus, while the South Pacific islanders were the best examples of pure, natural, and unconscious nations, the people of Europe, and of western Europe in particular, were thought of as the best examples of developed, conscious nations, which could not only look back on their own history, but also compare themselves in a methodical way with the other nations of the world. The connection between place and identity thus became a central political concern, and deepening this connection, drawing more inspiration from an imagined autochthonous identity, became a central political project.

As a way to summarize the general point, the connection in European thought between the state, the nation, and the territory can be organized into four distinct stages. The first stage, before the voyages, is where the nation is a concept that is at best loosely tied to the state. Kings might, from time to time, appeal to the shared identity of the nation, but they were more likely to appeal to the loyalty or obligation of their subjects. The second stage, which is an important part of Cook's voyages, is where the nation becomes a clear and natural entity that can be closely tied to the sovereign order. Nations naturally have states, no matter how uncivilized. The third stage is where the ideals of Cook's voyages, based on geometry and tabulated data, become part of the ideal for European states. The connection between the nation and the state is no longer simply natural, but for that very reason it can become self-conscious and rational as well. The fourth stage is where the ideals, worked through the European enlightenment, are turned back on the island nations of the South Pacific, not to confirm their ideal existence, but to now locate them as

infants who, lacking civilization, require the intervention of more enlightened and self-conscious nation-states. The ideal of the insular territorial
nation-state thus becomes the basis on which nineteenth-century ideas of
empire can be justified.

FIVE

Collections

Various articles at Nootka Sound, from Cook's third voyage.

The discussion of points was organized in terms of coordinates and the coordinate system; shapes were discussed in terms of the detailed and the general maps. The discussion of the nation and the state focused on how discrete human groups were identified and described. Now, in this and the next chapter, we will consider how these island-nation-states are consolidated, here as parts of a global system of descriptions, and in the next chapter as parts of a global empire.

As they move from place to place, Cook's ships locate individual entities in a web of sameness and difference. A catalogue of locations, shapes, and inhabitants emerges from the narrative, where the proper names and pictures tie together discrete nation-places that exist within geographies, climates, and habitats. The collection of places is important because it is through this collection that the points of identity, and specifically the territorial nation-states, are finally fixed and placed in relation to each other. It is through this collection that all the places of the world become clear and distinct and in terms of which other collections – biological, geological, and political – can be organized into a single globalized system of knowledge.

Collecting was not an incidental part of Cook's voyages; it was an important aspect of the knowledge that the voyages were intended to create. Cook and his companions collected views, descriptions, and samples from every place the ships went (with the exception of England). We should recall that John Locke organized his account of European voyages in terms of continents, "lest the distance and variety of places should too much distract the reader, if all lay intermixed."[1] The proper, intelligible way to organize places in Locke's world is to locate all the places along a single line, as part of a single narrative, with a single theme or topic, so that distance and variety do not confuse either the text or the reader. In Cook's world, on the other hand, the proper way to collect places in all of their variety is to intermix them on a single ocean, to collect as much variety as possible, and to allow readers to follow their own paths within that variety. Once again, lines become planes, planes become tables, and the knowledge of the world is expanded.

One of the results of Cook's voyages is a small book produced by Alexander Shaw. *A Catalogue of the Different Specimens of Cloth Collected in the Three Voyages of Captain Cook* is remarkable, if only because it contains over thirty pieces of bark cloth (called *tapa* or *kapa* in Polynesian languages), cut to size and sewn into the binding. The first eight pages of printed text contain excerpts from the journals of Anderson and Forster. The book ends with two pages detailing the pieces of cloth, listing the item number (which refers the reader to the appropriate sample), where the piece was taken from, some of its characteristics, and how it was used. There is no indication of who produced the cloth, or, more precisely, the production of the cloth is tied to nations rather than individuals. This collection of cloth, as with collections of artifacts, engravings, and narratives, follows the practices of identification based on the territorial nation-state that have been discussed in previous chapters.

But collecting is something more than acquiring, identifying, and describing. The narratives of acquisition are important ways of establishing the reliability of the objects that are included in the collection, but the collection also depends on broader structures of intelligibility such as global maps and classification systems, which turn individual objects into parts of a larger system of identities. The reader is able to handle the pieces of cloth, to compare them with each other, and to look up where they were from. Taken together, the collections carried back in Cook's ships offer a general image of the Pacific. A place in the world is also a place in the collection and becomes increasingly meaningful in terms of the collection. As Georg Forster notes near the conclusion of his account of the second voyage, "at other seasons we explored the Pacific Ocean between the tropics and in the temperate zone, and then furnished geographers with new islands, naturalists with plants and birds, and, above all, the friends of mankind with various modifications of human nature."[2]

Taken as a *mise en scène* of the entire globe, the collection is created out of representative or exemplary objects from each of the important places, whether the collection is a king's zoo, a child's book of stamps, a set of spoons placed on a mantelpiece, or a group of botanical samples brought back from an exploration and kept in Solander boxes. A new kind of entity, the global collection of national identities, quickly emerges, and different ways of knowing become possible. People no longer travel to places in order to study the world; they travel within the collection.

THE CABINETS OF CURIOSITIES

The geographical organization of the cloth pieces, which is one example of many in which the fragmented geography of the South Pacific becomes the guiding principle for organizing collections, is contrasted with the rooms full of exotic objects that could be found throughout Europe. As Anthony Shelton notes in his discussion of Renaissance collections, "pre-Columbian items were few, and included chiefly for comparison with classical or Christian religion. The cultural origins of these items seem to have been of less importance than their broad geographical provenances. Frequently, the civilizations of the New World – Aztec, Toltec, Mixtec, Maya – were conflated, and the inhabitants of distinct city states and regions were subsumed under general rubrics."[3]

These collection rooms were not the result of an indifference to artifacts. Far from it. Such artifacts were very expensive, were greatly desired, were located in ornate and expansive rooms, and were often the centrepiece of a palace. The collections were also not indifferent to space. The geographical distinctions between Europe and the exotic were crucial to the collection's character. These are the collections of the seventeenth-century Orientalist, or the eighteenth-century primitivist, in which the exotic was externally distinguished from Europe but was internally indistinct. We can still hear Johnson's dismissal of the details offered in Cook's voyages – "All savages are the same" – but this opinion is now coupled with a desire to collect their artifacts.

Collectors also accumulated artifacts from Cook's voyages without regard to location or nationality. They were interested in primitive artifacts, which meant artifacts that were not from either Europe or the Orient, and Cook's voyages probably made those sorts of artifacts less expensive than they had ever been before. The book of cloth samples could be treated in this way. But a different attitude is also evident in Cook's voyages, as suggested by the list of specimens at the end of the book of samples. The samples are not simply marked as savage or Indian, they are described and collected in detailed and systematic ways. As a result, comparing nation-places – the natives of different places – became possible.

Just as Cook's voyages describe how to locate places and identify nations, they also describe and exemplify how to collect the resulting information together into a single system. The collection is an organization of evidence, of possibilities, of comparisons. There is likewise an ontological shift: the world becomes a large storehouse of fixed spaces that are meaningful primarily in terms of the whole. In other words, the division and collection of places in Cook's voyages affirms that the world should be understood not only through the creation of a collection, but also as being a collection that is simply represented in the material collections brought back to England.

COLLECTING NATIONS

In Cook's voyages, the nation became an object of scientific study, which acquired a wide range of attributes (population, customs, resources, artifacts) that are all tied together as much by the shared space as by the shared nationality. When these different nations are arranged together on a single table, it becomes possible to narrate similarities and differences, and as a result it also becomes possible to ask general questions concerning the nature of the Society Islanders, of the Pacific, of savagery, and of humanity. The introduction to the third voyage reflects on this aspect of Cook's project:

> Let us not forget another very important object of study, for which [the voyages of Captain Cook] have afforded to the speculative philosopher ample materials: I mean the study of human nature in various situations, equally interesting as they are uncommon.
>
> However remote or secluded from frequent intercourse with more polished nations the inhabitants of any parts of the world be, if history or our own observation should make it evident that they have been formerly visited, and that foreign manners and opinions, and languages, have been blended with their own, little use can be made of what is observed amongst such people, toward drawing a real picture of man in his natural uncultivated state.[4]

The detailed articulation of nations and places thus offers a well-organized collection of data with which social scientists and other speculative philosophers can formulate and debate general questions concerning human nature and the nature of human development. The contrast between Europe and its other still exists – marked in this passage with the idea of cultivation as it originated in Europe – but the way that the information is organized has changed. Humanity has become fragmented into the places where it lives, and it is here that the history, specifically the physical origins, of national identities can be found.

Just as the islands in the South Pacific became natural examples of the ideal of a pure people, places such as Batavia and the Cape of Good Hope became a natural, or at least unintended, example of the collection. While in Batavia, Tupia's reactions to the diversity of human identities, as well as Cook's reaction to Tupia, are significant. As Cook says, "one of the first things that Tupia remarked, was the various dresses of the passing multitude, concerning which he made many enquiries; and when he was told that in this place where people of many different nations were assembled, every one wore the habit of his country, he desired that he might conform to the custom, and appear in that of Otaheite."[5] It is not surprising that a navigator so intent on specifying the location and character of nations would understand Tupia's reaction to Batavia as a justification for his image of the world. The world is pieced together with territorial nation-states, and Tupia has enough intelligence and curiosity to take up his place in the living diorama. Cook, his crew, and his fellow travellers also take up their nation's place in the city. As the account of Batavia suggests, a considerable amount of differentiation can exist within a completed classification system, and, as a result, the table can celebrate diversity in its own way.

The desire to collect samples of natives "from every climate" into a single space, such as occurred unscientifically in Batavia, could form the basis of a general study of humanity by allowing people to notice, at one sitting, all the varieties of human existence. For some, the ideal gallery involved the acquisition of live specimens. Consider, for instance, John Rickman's vision in the second voyage of a global science of humanity: "It is now, indeed, too late to lament the non importation of a native from every climate, where Nature had marked a visible distinction in the characters of person and mind. As one in each climate might have been procured without force; when assembled together, they would have formed an academy for the study of the human figure, that would have attracted the notice of artists from every country."[6]

In the late eighteenth century, the presentation of national diversity became an important theme in English culture. Dichotomies were not enough. One example is the production of *Omai, or a Trip round the World*, which was a pantomime first produced in 1785. As Bernard Smith writes, "at the end of the pantomime the procession of the 'nations' included representatives from the Cook, Sandwich, and Society Islands, from Easter

Island, and from Kamchatka, Oonalashka (Unalaska), Nootka, and Prince William's Sound."[7] The play, in other words, makes the diversity of national identities visible to every person in the audience at one sitting. Jöppien's analysis of the "gallery of nation" books likewise suggests how diverse and important the popular articulations of national identities were in the late eighteenth century, whether in plays, books, or museums.[8] These representatives may be savages, but they were still representatives of savage nations that, when brought together, indicated the diversity of human existence.

THE PRACTICES OF THE COLLECTION
There is a logical and geographical structure to Cook's collection. The collection begins with acquisitions, whether of locations, shapes, or nations, which are part of the overall exploration narrative. The ships visit a place, document significant aspects of its inhabitants, collect samples, and label everything accordingly. But these acquisitions do not occur in a vacuum, and even if the narrative is organized primarily in terms of the progress of exploration through space and time, it also always exists in terms of a different kind of space. The places where Cook is looking for information, and the kinds of information he is looking for, are permeated by a sense of an already-existing whole in relation to which his voyages are undertaken. Cook does not discover coordinates, he does not discover mapping. Rather, he already lives in a world organized in terms of coordinates and maps, and his project is to fill these spaces with information, to clarify his maps, and in the most expansive way to complete his collection.

But the voyages do more than provide information on specific places and nations; they also help to clarify, or at least affirm, the structure of the collection itself. For the people connected to Cook's voyages, there are many interconnected collections that guide their activities. As travellers, Cook and his companions operate within the system of coordinates and the conventions for describing the physical world (islands, reefs, currents, weather patterns, and so on). As biologists, Cook and his companions operate largely within the hierarchical Linnaean classification system, in which the primary goal is to collect individual species that have not been collected before and to note the existence of already-collected species in different places. As social scientists, Cook and his companions combine the tasks of the navigators and the biologists: collecting nations and sovereignties through a cartographical and physiological description of the native bodies politic. But what is most important in all of this collecting is that a single collection emerges that combines and correlates different kinds of collections into a single system.

Once the collection exists, it becomes possible, if not unavoidable, for people to compare different travel narratives. Of course, this relationship depends on the printing press, which made it easier to identify inconsistencies between accounts and to direct future experiments to resolve the controversy.[9] In an account of the second voyage attributed to John Marra, for example, some discrepancies are noted:

> Our journalist of the *Resolution* [Marra] remarks, that both men and women wanted one of their little fingers; and Tasman who first discovered that island makes a similar remark. They also agree in their description of the manner of painting their bodies from the waist downwards, but they differ as to their hair, which our journalist says is black and frizzled; Tasman, that some wear it cropt and others long. Our journalists represent the men as bold and resolute, armed with clubs of eight or ten pounds weight, and bows and arrows, and of a fierce and dauntless disposition: Tasman, on the contrary, says, they were wholly without arms, friendly and peaceable.[10]

In Marra's opinion, Tasman's account stands in need of correction, and with the publication of Marra's book, Tasman's account is corrected properly. The information is now correct, and readers can ensure that their books are up to date. One of the most important implications of the printing press is that it became possible to produce newer editions of works that corrected earlier mistakes. As Eisenstein notes, "just as the act of publishing errata sharpened alertness to error within the printer's workshop, so too did the preparation of copy pertaining to architectural motifs, regional boundaries, place names, details of dress and local customs."[11]

One of the most important early examples of this process was Sebastian Munster's *Cosmography,* first published in the middle of the sixteenth century. The book had more than forty editions over the next century. Eisenstein notes, "as each edition became bigger, more crammed with data, and more profusely illustrated, each was also provided with more tables, charts, indexes which made it possible for readers to retrieve the growing body of information that was being stored in the work."[12] With

Munster's creation of the *Cosmography*, the published views of the world existed at the end of a methodological line that began with direct observation, or at least with written accounts sent by reliable observers. While writing allowed these accounts to be transmitted to Munster, the printing press allowed the consolidated results to be reproduced in large quantities and distributed again – to be corrected once again.

The claims of newness, the claims of reliability, and the claims of completeness became ever more pervasive and necessary. And Cook's voyages, far from being a marginal event in a global process, became the epitome of that process. Not only do Cook's voyages create a sense of what can be collected, they also create a sense of how other collections can be incorporated into a single, ever more comprehensive and accurate system. Cook adds places, expands on descriptions, and corrects a large number of mistakes made by previous navigators. In this way, Cook's voyages are part of a much larger intellectual and textual process. The published accounts of the voyages are important in part because they updated or created so much information from so many different places. Which compendiums of information could remain current after Cook's voyages? He collects, he is collected, and the structures of his collection come to dominate the subsequent production of books that, along with their readers, can comprehend the world.

In addition to the ongoing verification of information, Cook's voyages also extend the area contained by the collection. Cook's attempt to complete the map of the world was discussed in the first chapter. According to Andrew Kippis, who offered an early summation of the value of Cook's voyages, "before the voyages of the present reign took place, nearly half the surface of the earth was hidden in obscurity and confusion. From the discoveries of our navigator, geography has assumed a new face, and become, in a great measure, a new science; having attained to such a completion, as to leave only some less important parts of the globe to be explored by future voyagers."[13]

In hindsight, Cook's collection was only an early run through the world. He did not complete either the mapping or the description of all the places in the world, but he did claim to have substantially completed the outline of specific areas. However, beyond these specific places – such as Otaheite, New Zealand, and Nootka Sound – the voyages also displayed a logical structure that anticipated and organized further additions, remarks, confirmations, and challenges. Cook claims in the first voyage that "many islands also must have escaped my pencil,"[14] and throughout all three voyages he carefully notes the areas that he had to leave unexplored, due to such things as weather conditions or time restraints. In other words, Cook affirms the structure of the collection and the manner of exploring within and in terms of that collection even when he is unable to collect. Thus, when George Keate published his *Account of the Pelew Islands* in 1788, he, in Smith's words, "wrote his book, he tells us, to present 'a new people' to the world, a people who were 'an ornament to human nature'; and to contravert the opinion that the inhabitants of the Palau Islands were in-human and savage."[15] Pelew was a gap in the collected and collective knowledge of the South Pacific, and Keate's explorations and writings were both directed to fill it. For the South Pacific, completing the process of horizontal exploration took roughly sixty years. By 1831, William Goetzmann notes, "the British Admiralty concluded that no new discoveries beyond those at the antipodes were left to be achieved."[16] By then, there were no significant gaps in the map left to fill.

In addition to the horizontal extension of the collection, Cook's voyages also participate in the vertical extension of the collection, where every place becomes described in greater and greater detail. Anderson, being quoted in the account of the third voyage, notes that "though a very accurate description of the country, and of the most obvious customs of its inhabitants, has been already given, especially by Captain Cook, that much still remains untouched; that, in some instances, mistakes have been made, which later and repeated observation has been able to rectify; and that, even now, we are strangers to many of the most important institutions that prevail amongst these people."[17]

Future navigators are thus directed by the collection, not only to the blank areas on the map, but also to the blank areas in the description. However, as is the case for the maps, Cook's professions of ignorance are coupled with a clear idea of what is not known. These are not vague senses of wonder or of monsters at the edge of the map, but rather a very clear account of what data are missing and where they should be placed.

The collection of published accounts of explorers thus not only creates a heightened awareness of the gaps in the collection, but also allows later navigators to refer readers to previous accounts, for fear of repeating what has been printed before. The fear of repetition is also closely tied to the printing press. The point is to avoid including information that readers can already find in another book. As a result, any particular element of a place only needs to be described once, assuming that it is described well and that the description is readily available in print.

The creation and influence of Cook's collections depended on a series of institutions and practices that turned direct visibility into a broader system of documentation. The British Museum and a host of other collections not only accumulated artifacts and travel journals; they were also the centres of documentation that brought all the nations of the world into a single view. To know something is to collect it, not as a personal activity, but as part of a collective enterprise that brings together people who are describing a wide diversity of places in a standardized way – using the same instruments and organizing the information in the same forms. These institutions helped to authorize particular people to study the world in particular ways, first by determining what counted as a proper account of the world, and second by organizing subsequent explorations based on what was already known. As a result, the development of the collection during and after Cook's voyages connected the acquisition of data with the social and political production of authority and knowledge.

In a footnote near the beginning of his *Anthropology*, Kant discusses the social requirements of the ideal collection. Living in Königsberg and dreaming of a cosmic world, Kant argues that a city such as Königsberg, which is large, the state centre, seat of government provincial councils, site of a university, and seaport connected to the interior through a network of rivers, and therefore having a "location [that] favors traffic with the rest of the country as well as with neighboring or remote countries having different languages and customs, is a suitable place for broadening one's knowledge of man and of the world. In such a city, this knowledge can be acquired even without traveling."[18]

The image of the stationary, knowledgeable collector of places is not new in the late eighteenth century. Daniel Defoe had offered a similar image in *The Complete English Gentleman*, first published in 1730. Defoe writes that a man may "make a tour of the world in books, he may make himself master of the geography of the universe in maps, atlases and measurements of our mathematicians. He may travel by land with the historians, by sea with the navigators. He may go round the globe with Dampier and Rogers, and kno' a thousand times more doing it than all those illiterate sailors."[19]

For Defoe, the primary source of information was the printed book. What is different in Kant's image is the sense of the archival collection and how the world is put together. The collection does not arise primarily from travel narratives; it arises from artifacts, accounts, and everything else being properly labelled, stored, and related. The development of the collection is both ongoing and totalizing.

The collection became a double of the world; for many practical purposes it becomes the world. One indication of this was the way that other books surrounded, affirmed, and fed off Cook's voyages. Consider, for instance, the 1784 publication of Thomas Martyn's *Figures of Non-Descript Shells, Collected in the Different Voyages to the South Seas since the Year 1764.* The book was primarily based on shells in Joseph Banks's collection (now part of the British Museum), but also included shells that other people had collected. Martyn never went to the South Seas, and would never have had to leave London to produce this book. But he could still produce an extensive and well-illustrated printed collection of the shells of the South Seas that were available in Europe.

Martyn's book was not exceptional. Another relevant example, which also suggests the extent to which the collections of nations dominated the representation of human beings, is Jehoshaphat Aspin's *Cosmorama: A View of the Costumes and Peculiarities of All Nations.* This book, published in 1827, contains pictures of people, one male and one female from each place, dressed in national costumes, that serve as the sole representatives of specific places around the world. There are four pictures on each page, and over forty pages of pictures. The conclusion reads, "Having thus, my young friends, rambled with you pretty well over the whole habitable globe, I shall leave you for a short time, that you may ruminate, without interruption, on the diversities of character which have been brought under your observation."[20]

One result of printing all of these collections was that the world became available in ever finer, ever more complete, and ever more available descriptions. What happens, in other words, is that the collection eventually takes over, and any particular fact, or any specific travel journal, must first come to terms with the already-collected world.

BOREDOM AND THE COLLECTION

The collection that Cook creates from one voyage to another becomes an ever more important part of Cook's narrative, to the point where the already-existing collection overpowers any interest that Cook may have had for new discoveries, including the chain of islands that Cook named the Sandwich Islands. He discovers the islands near the end of the third voyage, as his ships were heading from the South Pacific to the northern

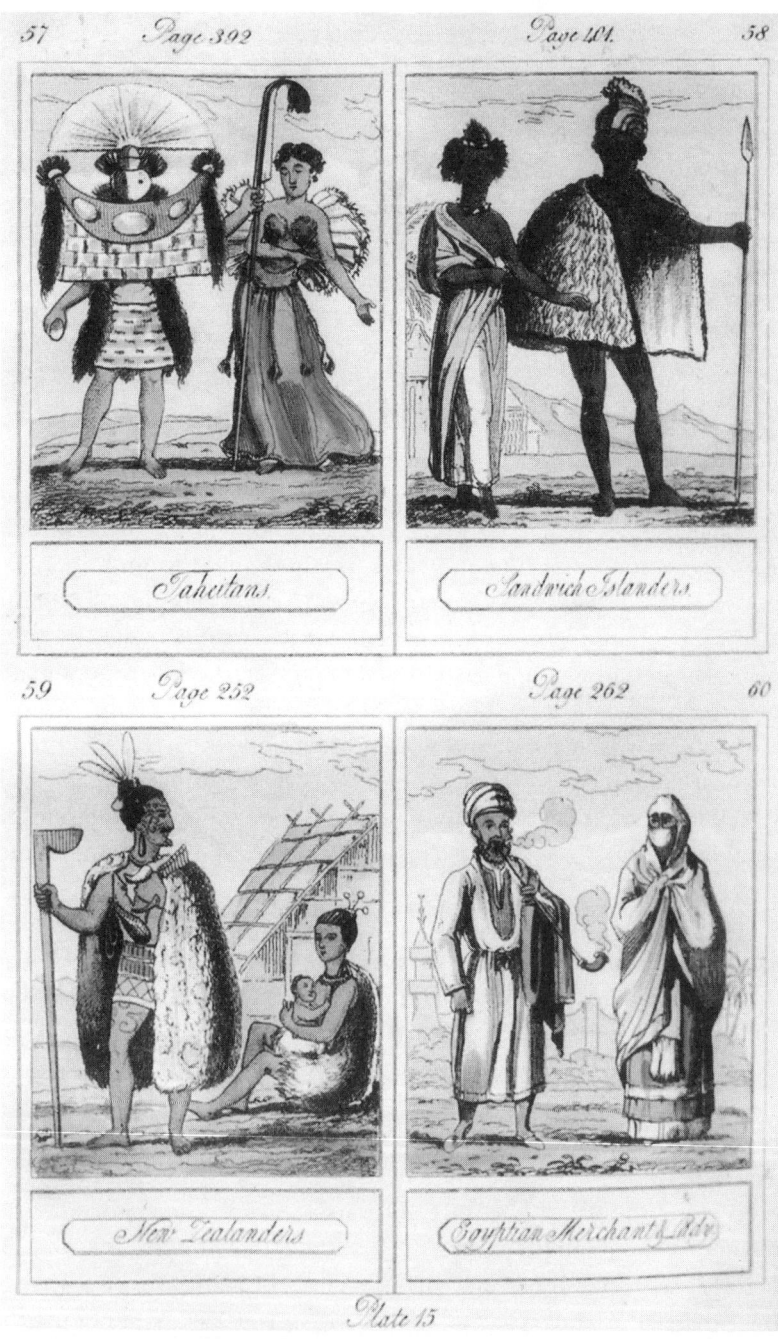

Two pages from Jehoshaphat Aspin's 1827 *Cosmorama: A View of the Costumes and Peculiarities of All Nations*. The picture on the left shows "Taheitans," "Sandwich Islanders," "New Zealanders," and "Egyptian Merchant & Lady." The picture on

the right shows "Danes," "Icelanders," Swedes," and "Finlanders." The book collects together several hundred examples of nations from around the world.

Pacific in search of the Northwest Passage. The table containing the places and peoples of the South Pacific was easily expanded to include the Sandwich Islands and its natives. While some writers, such as Beaglehole, suggest that Cook was physically worn out by the time he set sail on the third voyage,[21] the *scientific* weight of the prior voyages is also noticeable. The discovery of islands and the descriptions of peoples had become routine by that time, and while the mathematical space of the collection urged Cook ever onward to find other places, the collection had become boring. Much like Banks's complaint once specimens of all the species in Botany Bay had been brought on the ship, by the third voyage Cook had no more nation-places to collect. At the very least, the natives of the Sandwich Islands were not different enough from islands in the South Seas to be very interesting.

Consider Cook's initial description of the first of the Sandwich Islands, which occurred as the ships were sailing from the South Pacific (and Otaheite in particular) to the far northern Pacific. In the Admiralty's version of the third voyage, the Sandwich Islands are first mentioned in Chapter 11 of the sixth volume, describing the events of 18 January 1778: "We continued to see birds every day, of the sorts last mentioned; sometimes in greater numbers than others; and between the latitude of 10° and 11°, we saw several turtle. All these are looked upon as signs of the vicinity of land. However, we discovered none till day-break, in the morning of the 18th, when an island made its appearance, bearing north-east by east; and, soon after, we saw more land bearing north, and entirely detached from the former."[22]

The patterns of interaction and the comparisons with the much better-known islands in the South Pacific begin almost immediately. Canoes begin coming from the shore. Cook then says that "we were agreeably surprised to find, that they spoke the language of Otaheite, and of the other islands we had lately visited" and that "one of them offered for sale the piece of stuff that he wore round his waist, after the manner of the other islands."[23] In these first encounters, Cook finds associations between the places that he already knows and the one that he is facing now for the first time. And during all of this time, the people on the English ships are sounding, looking for anchorage, and analyzing the natives, who "seemed very mild" and "though of the common size, were stoutly made." The morais, or religious structures, that were examined and sketched were "like many of those at Otaheite," to which they bear a "great resemblance." The trade between the ship and the island is carried out as it is typically done at other islands. Trifles are exchanged for fruit and pigs, and Cook once again expresses a concern for the spread of venereal disease.

As Cook and his European readers would expect, the natives also steal things, which, according to Cook, "was another circumstance in which they also perfectly resembled those other islanders."[24] And, as both Cook and his readers would expect, Cook responds to the thefts as he generally did, by pursuing the thief, appealing for help from natives who seem to have authority, and recovering the stolen items or at least extracting some form of pain as compensation.

In short, the account of the Sandwich Islands could, with very few exceptions, be exchanged with the account of any one of a number of places throughout the Pacific. Thus, when the voyage tells of how "one of the natives having stolen the butcher's cleaver, leaped overboard, got into his canoe, and hastened to the shore, the boats pursuing him in vain,"[25] the readers are being offered a well-rehearsed story with a familiar narrative and moral content. It is as if the chapter had existed in a skeletal form for many years, and all that Cook had to do was fill in the same blanks that he had filled in a hundred times before. No matter how empty that area of the map, no matter how undescribed the people, these kinds of places had become mundane.

The chapter that follows the first descriptions of the Sandwich Islands also corresponds to the general form of the voyages. Having presented the narrative of the encounter in the first chapter, the second chapter offers an accounting of the place and the people. The chapter heading says it all:

> The Situation of the Islands Now Discovered. – Their Names. – Called the Sandwich Islands. – Atooi Described. – The Soil. – Climate. – Vegetable Productions. – Birds. – Fish. – Domestic Animals. – Persons of the Inhabitants. – Their Disposition. – Dress. – Ornaments. – Habitations. – Food. – Cookery. – Amusements. – Manufactures. – Working-Tools. – Knowledge of Iron Accounted For. – Canoes. – Agriculture. – Account of one of their Chiefs. – Weapons. – Customs Agreeing with those of Tongataboo, and Otaheite. – Their Language the Same. – Extent of this Nation Throughout the Pacific Ocean. – Reflections on the Useful Situation of the Sandwich Islands.[26]

And with that, the islands have been named, located, described, and compared, not only in terms of the islands of the South Pacific but also in terms of European interests and the natural world. The organization of the description does not make the Sandwich Islands an exceptional place.

Like the description of the events, the categories that Cook used to articulate his experiences of the Sandwich Islands are thoroughly unremarkable. Even the chapter headings can be more or less lined up with the headings from other chapters that describe other places. In fact, the headings are designed to be lined up, so that one place could be more easily compared to another, and so the comprehensiveness of the account can be quickly indicated.

Even if the natives of the Sandwich Islands were variations on already-collected themes, they were nonetheless notable for one thing. "In the course of my several voyages," Cook writes, "I never before met with the natives of any place so much astonished, as these people were, upon entering a ship."[27] But this does not make them exceptional. People from many places were astonished by the ship, and if the natives of the Sandwich Islands exist at one end of this extreme, they nonetheless exist on a highly populated continuum. The fact that the discovery of the Sandwich Islands was *not* very significant suggests the extent to which these islands were quickly positioned among already-known places, such as Otaheite and the Marquesas. The Sandwich Islands may have been unexpected, but their discovery was far from surprising or shocking.

The Sandwich Islands were new places in a table that was more or less full, and the newness of the place was, for Cook, primarily geographical and therefore only worth a standard description. The Sandwich Islands, in other words, had been overtaken by the collection almost at the time it was first collected. They bored Cook in the same way that Botany Bay had come to bore Joseph Banks.

Comparisons became more and more important to Cook's voyages, while direct descriptions became more and more mediated by already-existing accounts of other places. Because they arrived so late in Cook's collection of the world, the Sandwich Islands were described primarily in terms of comparisons. Beyond their existence, Cook found nothing that he took to be really new. In the collection, a vast field of information is created, specifying character types, physical builds, cultural practices, material situations, and so on, which turns the presumption of a single human nature into a dispersed articulation of variations or comparisons. More than just organizing data, the collection creates the possibility for a new discourse, not of discovery or identification, but of comparisons, and the scale of these comparisons is global. At one point in the first voyage, for instance, Otaheiteans are placed alongside some inhabitants of South America. One of their garments, for instance, "exactly resembles the garment worn by the inhabitants of Peru and Chili, which the Spaniards call Poncho."[28] The inhabitants of the Sandwich Islands likewise behave in a way that "exempts their national character from the preposterous pride of the more polished Japanese, and of the ruder Greenlander."[29]

Any particular comparison may not be very interesting – most of the comparisons are straightforward and say little that is surprising. But this is the nature of Cook's voyages: the accumulation of banal information transforms the world to the extent that comparisons become more and more possible. These comparisons take various forms: the presence or absence of something, the sameness or difference of something, or the similar functions, looks, practices, customs, and so on. Of course, the most common comparisons are between two groups of natives in the South Pacific. Consider, for instance, a summary offered by Andrew Kippis: "The island of Mangeea is full five leagues in circuit, and of a moderate and pretty equal height. It has upon the whole, a pleasing aspect, and might be made a beautiful spot by cultivation. The inhabitants, who appeared to be both numerous and well fed, seemed to resemble those of Otaheite and the Marquesas in the beauty of their persons; and the resemblance, as far as could be judged in so short a compass of time, takes place with respect to their general disposition and character."[30] Throughout, the island-place is the building block of the comparisons, forming the nation, which is given a "character" or "disposition." The comparisons spread out over the complexity of nations.

On 2 February 1778, Cook's ships left the Sandwich Islands and headed towards the North American coast. The ships returned in November 1778, first sighting land on the 26th. The description continues in the same form. Cook worries about venereal disease spreading to the natives and tries to find a good harbour for his ships. There is a daily accounting of the weather and the provisions that were obtained from the natives. One of the most notable things that happened during his second stay on the island was an eclipse of the moon, which was observed with the requisite instruments and attention. The analysis of the inhabitants of the islands also continued. Cook's final entry in the ship's log, dated 17 January 1779, is also unremarkable: "In the after noon I went a shore to view the place, accompaned by Touahah, Parca, Mr King and others; as soon as we landed Touahah took me by the hand and conducted me to a large Morai, the other gentlemen with Parea and four or five more of the Natives followed."[31] There is a gap of almost a month between this last journal entry and Cook's death on 14 February.[32] If the journal had continued, the next entry would probably have included some mention of the morai, or of the people who had gone with him, or of some noteworthy occurrence that had happened along the way, or of how something that he saw reminded him of something he had seen further south.

Even Cook's death did not significantly set the Sandwich Islands apart from other places around the Pacific. As recounted by others on the voyage, Cook's death occurred while he was trying to recover some stolen article by taking a native chief hostage. He had done this on islands throughout the Pacific, and, as usual, other natives tried to stop him. This time, however, they succeeded. But even in this encounter, the categories through which the places and people were articulated remained intact. Much like his first discovery of these islands, his death may have been unexpected, but it was not exactly shocking.

THE DANGERS OF RELATIVISM

While the values that ground the comparisons in Cook's voyages clearly privilege specific groups, the South Pacific is not always criticized and Europe is not always celebrated. The other becomes the different, which is also sometimes the same or even better. The relative evaluations that become possible with the global table of national identities creates, in turn, the possibility of a profound relativism, where differences can no longer exist alongside a single ideal. Goetzmann notes that "cultural relativism came more naturally as a concept to South Seas adventurers than to any other group long before anthropologists formalized the term."[33] One example from Cook's own life occurs when he eats Forster's dog during the second voyage: "When I began to recover, a favourite dog, belonging to Mr. Forster, fell a sacrifice to my tender stomach. We had no other fresh meat whatever on board; and I could eat of this flesh, as well as broth made of it, when I could taste nothing else. Thus I received nourishment and strength from food which would have made most people in Europe sick; so true it is, that necessity is governed by no law."[34]

The voyages, by combining detailed descriptions of a wide variety of practices with a sense that these practices are connected to a strong and coherent whole (the nation), make it much easier to believe that there are no universal criteria with which to judge different beliefs or practices. Just as every kind of food and action can be desired when it is necessary, every nation exists on its own island and may also exist in its own moral and metaphysical space.

But there are other aspects of Cook's voyages that work against the threats of global relativism, even as the narratives emphasize and extend the descriptions of differences. Cook not only describes nations and locates them in a collection but also evaluates members of that collection in terms of preferences and superlatives. Unlike the absolute exclusion that tends to arise from the division between European and non-European, Cook's articulation of specific variations tends to mix European and non-European peoples in a wide range of categories, a dispersed comparison of many. Just before harshly describing the physical characteristics of the "ape-like" people of Mallicollo, for instance, there is a positive description of their honesty: "As the ship at first had fresh way through the water, several of them dropped astern after they had received our goods, and before they had time to deliver theirs in return. Instead of taking advantage of this, as our friends at the Society Isles would have done, they used their utmost efforts to get up with us, and to deliver what they had already been paid for."[35] Cook argues here that in this aspect of character, the inhabitants of Mallicollo are superior to the natives of the Society Islands.

Some places are better than others for specific things, and some places are the best places of all. When discussing the character of the natives of the island of Amsterdam, for instance, Cook notes in the second voyage that "nothing can be a more demonstrative evidence of their ingenuity than the construction and make of their canoes, which, in point of neatness and workmanship, exceed every thing of this kind we saw in this sea."[36] When characterizing the natives of Ulietea, he notes how "it must be owned, in favour of their cookery, that victuals were never cleaner, nor better dressed."[37] When describing their stay on the island of Middleburgh, Rickman notes, "we also purchased cloth, and many other articles of curious workmanship, the artists of this island, for invention and ingenuity in the execution, exceeding those of all the other islands in the South Seas."[38] On the third voyage, William Ellis notes that "Imaio is, without exception, the most pleasant of all the Society Isles."[39] On the second voyage, at the island of Mallicollo, Cook similarly writes, "had we made a longer stay, we might soon have been upon good terms with this ape-like nation; for, in general, they are the most ugly, ill-proportioned people I ever saw, and in every respect different from any we had met with in this sea. They are a very dark-coloured and rather diminutive race; with long heads, flat faces, and monkey countenances."[40]

The evaluations are frequently moral. In the manuscript of the second voyage, for instance, Cook notes, "I had always looked upon the females of New Zealand to be more chaste than the generality of Indian women."[41] As with other preferences and superlatives, sometimes the Europeans even fare worse. Rickman notes that "the grossest indecencies he ever saw practiced while on the island were by the licentiousness of our own people, who, without regard to character, made no scruple to attempt openly and by force what they were unable to effect with the free voluntary consent of the objects of their desire."[42]

While there is considerable diversity between nations, they are each nonetheless all part of a single system subject to laws of impact and relation.[43] These laws are not only laws of politics, they are also laws of human nature, of cultivation, and of nature. Thus, as nations, states, and territories are all tied together, the laws of the world become one. When Cook notes how "we all agreed, that a South-sea dog was little inferior to an English lamb,"[44] the variations of taste exist within a fixed and universal system of taste, understood as both an aesthetic and a physiological process. What varies are the accidental characteristics of customs, preferences, and local material conditions.

Although there may be variety, there are also ideals – the effective state, the civilized nation – and scientifically grounded ways to move nations towards those ideals. At one point, Cook claims that the New Zealanders are superior to the Spaniards, a nation that Cook has little good to say of in any event: "In this decent article of civil economy they were before-hand with one of the most considerable nations of Europe; for I am credibly informed, that, till the year 1760, there was no such thing as a privy in Madrid, the metropolis of Spain, though it is plentifully supplied with water."[45] Throughout the voyages, the key European groups that are either equivalent or below the natives of the South Pacific are the Spaniards and the lower classes of England. The collection thus moves from descriptions of national difference to descriptions of social rankings, preferences, and superlatives. Not only are places different, but some places are more or less than others. Behind the comparisons, there exists a web of evaluations – sometimes aesthetic, sometimes mathematical, sometimes moral, and sometimes theological – that take up all the differences into a system of rankings.

The dichotomy between England and the Pacific pervades the voyages. When Cook leaves England, his ontological and moral commitments nod at the countryside and promise to make it the ground from which to judge the world. Cook may be from northern England, and he may be from the agricultural working class, but his ideals are the ideals of the Admiralty, the Royal Society, and the landed aristocracy of southern England. But not only are specific ideals and prejudices pervasive in Cook's voyages, they are also tied to the scientific descriptions of nation-places. It is not simply that Cook appeals to stereotypes, but also that these stereotypes infect the basic categories – the variables, the ideal types, the general characters, the goals – through which the functional relationships within and between nations can be described and compared.

At the centre of Cook's comparisons, even if not explicitly present, is an idealized class – civilized, cultivated, rational, lawful, benevolent, and powerful – which is, in the end, also closely tied to the idealized countryside of southeast England. As Eve Darian-Smith has noted, in the eighteenth century, "cultivation became an important ontological frame, and, through its linkage to the English garden landscape, translated into a visual aesthetics of power. The imposing of the English garden across the whole of Britain is a dramatic visual and experiential demonstration of how England was conflated with, and came to represent, the greater British nation."[46] One of the important images that connects Cook's voyages to the English ideal of the countryside of Kent is the garden, and in particular the closely cultivated, geometrically organized garden where a variety of different species of plants were brought together into a single field. Up until the seventeenth century, gardens were almost exclusively for the production of vegetables and herbs for both food and medicine. In the eighteenth century, as Darian-Smith notes, the function of some gardens changed. They became places designed to create an aesthetic experience (whether aromatic or visual) and later for encouraging scientific analyses of plant physiology.[47] Not only was the king's garden at Kew important as a centre of scientific and political activity, it also represented an ideal physical, social, and moral state of being. Thus, when Cook creates a garden for Omai, or when he plants gardens in places around the world, there is more than an immediate practical or scientific goal. He is cultivating the world.

In the voyages Cook understands the issues of human nature with the clarity of a materialist. But in addition to turning the issues of human nature into empirical questions, the voyages also simplify the material world, creating containers that isolate the possible influences and that allow for correlations between geographical, biological, and human systems to be determined.[48] The organization of the world into territorial nation-states forms the basis of a collection that can be used to compare and ultimately explain human diversity. The collected nations of the world may vary, but the laws of their creation and change do not.

The collection also allowed the division of the peoples and places of the world in terms of time. To Georg Forster, for instance, some of the islands of the South Pacific offered a living manifestation of an original, natural state. The people encountered in the South Pacific were living in a different time and could thus be meaningfully compared to a prior period in European history, whether classical Greece, ancient Britain, or the Middle Ages.[49] Time, in other words, had become another way to classify space, where the basic pattern of European history became a classification system for non-European nations. Of course, mapping nations in terms of time does not line up exactly – simple distance, measured from the mature and cultivated places of the Mediterranean or England, was not the only factor. Nonetheless, the temporal order of development (cultivation, civilization, modernization) became a central model for arranging the nations of the world, which in turn reinforced the political and moral status of certain parts of Europe. Every nation becomes part of a single narrative of development, in which western European countries are at the forefront, and the other nations, which exist as living examples of Europe's past, become rightly subjected to Europe through paternalist, if not Darwinist, principles. These temporally backward nations must either be helped or be replaced by temporally superior nations. The savage had returned, but unlike Johnson's dismissiveness, Cook's voyages treat nations that are still living at the beginning of history as important sources of information concerning human nature and the origins of human nations. These natives are examples of humanity in its infancy, as it were, and thus represent a baseline from which to narrate human history.

One set of nations that Cook and his companions were very interested in were those that had never been exposed to European influences. Most of the nations that were encountered in the voyages had already encountered Europeans, often with very unpleasant consequences. The value of the purely non-European nation is evident in Cook's general reflection on the scientific value of all these islands in the third voyage:

> But the islands which our enterprising discoverers visited in the centre of the South Pacific, and are, indeed, the principal scenes of their operations, were untrodden ground. The inhabitants, as far as could be observed, were un-

mixed with any different tribe, by occasional intercourse, subsequent to their original settlement there; left entirely to their own powers for every art of life; and to their own remote traditions for every political or religious custom or institution; uninformed by science; unimproved by education; in short, a fit soil from whence a careful observer could collect facts for forming a judgment, how far unassisted human nature will be apt to degenerate; and in what respects it can ever be able to excel. Who could have thought, that the brutal ferocity of feeding upon human flesh, and the horrid superstition of offering human sacrifices, should be found to exist amongst the natives lately discovered in the Pacific Ocean, who, in other respect appear to be no strangers to the fine feelings of humanity, to have arrived at a certain stage of social life, and to be habituated to subordination and government which tend so naturally to repress the ebullitions of wild passion, and expand the latent powers of the understanding?[50]

Here, Cook collects an image of a human group – an unmixed nation – living in the absolute absence of Europe. But even during Cook's voyages, it was becoming difficult to find such places, and more often than not the primary concern was not to describe the "natural" condition as it was to describe the variations from that condition by considering what impact civilization (Europe) had had.

THE PERSISTENCE OF EXTREME OTHERNESS

Grouping nations by their shared characteristics quickly becomes part of a strategy to reaffirm global dichotomies that echo those appealed to by Johnson and the Orientalists. The increasingly extreme contrast between Europeans and non-Europeans can be noticed, among other places, in the illustrations in later editions of Cook's voyages. In the versions of Cook's voyages edited by John Barrow, for instance, the division between Europeans and non-Europeans is reworked. The interactions are primarily limited to economics and violence, suggestive of the more extreme forms of exploitation that characterized the European and American empires of the nineteenth century. There is very little dialogue, and the non-Europeans are almost irrelevant to the success of the voyages. Tupia, who sailed on the *Endeavour* from Otaheite on Cook's first voyage up to his death in Batavia in 1770, is barely described. This is significant; Tupia played an important role on the *Endeavour,* serving among other things, as a translator throughout the islands of the South Pacific and also as a nautical guide for the ship when it was caught in the Great Barrier Reef.

By excising Tupia from the voyage in this way, Barrow's account sharpens the distinction between Europeans and natives, and ignores the European reliance on the native nations throughout the voyages.

The engravings in later editions of the voyages were also reworked. Not only were the pictures often of a lesser quality and far less numerous, the content of the pictures was changed. One edition of Barrow's account, for instance, includes four colour illustrations, credited to John Williamson. These new illustrations depict two scenes from the first voyage – Cook formally taking possession of New South Wales "in right of his majesty King George III," and the Aborigines setting fire to the grass near the English camp – and two scenes from the second voyage – a native girl dancing at Otaheite, and a violent confrontation at Erromanga (or Erramanga) between the English in the longboat and the natives on shore. There are no coloured illustrations for the third voyage. The coloured illustrations in particular emphasize the sharply defined, often violent encounters between the English and the natives. Warfare is complemented in the first voyage by the extension of English sovereignty and in the second voyage by the European experience of native entertainments. Through these new pictures and the absence of earlier pictures that showed very different interactions, the representation of places and peoples was simplified, and the moral status of England in relation to the rest of the world was emphasized.

The original engraving of the Erromanga encounter can be found in chapter 6 (p. 185). Several differences between the two pictures are noteworthy. The first is that the original engraving provides considerably more detail of the landscape – whereas one can recognize different species of plants in the engraving, the painting provides no details about the place at all. The painting, rather, is an abstract encounter between the English and the savage. Likewise, the character of the confrontation has changed. In the engraving, the English are escaping and, beyond the single musket pointed at the natives on shore, all the other English are either turning back in fright or focusing on escaping and are all but ignoring their attackers. It is only on the second boat, already offshore, that we can see a musket being fired. The main conflict is more of a tug of war. In the painting, on the other hand, three of the four English are in combat with the natives, and while the musket is still present, it is not being used. The focus of the picture, instead, is one of the English sailors punching the most threatening native attacker. The English superiority, then, is not established by firearms or the cannons of the ship, but

Painting from John Barrow's 1925 edition of Cook's voyages depicting Cook's landing at Erromanga during the second voyage. When compared with the original engraving (see p. 185), the function of the picture has evidently changed. The caption here, however, makes no mention of the place and offers no details. Instead, it offers a moralizing account of the relationship between natives and Englishmen.

rather by a physiological superiority. In the engraving, Cook's ship can be seen in the background, almost touching the shore. While the ship's location could make people wonder why the landing was attempted so far away, the ship's function in the picture is more to establish the English presence in the area. The conflict is not just between treacherous savages and strong English individuals, it is between an island with a treacherous king and a system of power and authority that stretches from the shore to the longboat to the English ship and finally to England.

Another relevant work is C.G. Cash's account of Cook's voyages, first published in 1905. *The Life and Voyages of Captain James Cook* was an inexpensive version of the voyages rewritten for younger audiences. There is one black and white picture, at the beginning of the book, which depicts the moment before Cook's death at the Sandwich Islands. In this version

As with the painting from Barrow, the depiction of the death of Captain Cook in C.G. Cash's *The Life and Voyages of Captain James Cook* shows almost no ethnographic, geographic, or moral complexity. The complex divisions into nations and places have given way to the global division between civilization and savagery.

of the voyages, coordinate information is all but gone, as are complaints Cook had of his crew and any hint of the sexual relations between the Europeans and the natives. There are also no maps or tables. The diversity of the collection has again become the sharp contrast between Europeans and savages. The book is written in the first person, but any dialogue that Cook had with other writers or with the people on board is gone. The authorial voice has become clarified, the contrasts have been sharpened, and the description and evaluation of the world has followed suit.

Bernard Smith noted similar transformations in the representations of Cook's death, where Cook becomes more heavenly and the natives of the Sandwich Islands become more stereotypically savage (with a darker skin and a wilder countenance). The result was, in effect, the reaffirmation of the older identity structures that divided the world into civilization and savagery.[51]

THE TRANSCENDENCE OF THE COLLECTOR

There is another kind of otherness created by Cook's voyages, where the primary divisions are not between nations, but between two fundamentally different relationships to the world. The distinction is between the collector and the collected. Cook, of course, is the epitome of the collector. Collecting is also a basic aspect of Cook's account of knowledge: understanding the world properly depends on creating a proper collection. There are in fact two dichotomies here, one between the collector and the collected, and the other between the collector and those who do not collect. These divisions are not the same, although in the end the distinction between them fades as those who do not collect become the collection.

In the late eighteenth century, the collection became part of the public record to which everyone, in principle, had access and was invited to contribute to (as opposed to being an exclusive indicator of social privilege). However, even if the project of scientific collecting was global and ostensibly public, not everyone participated in the same way. Two notable groups in Cook's voyages that are outside of the collective scientific project are the Spanish and the natives. Both of them are criticized for their rejection of the public collection:

> The Spaniards had it more in their power to surmount this bar to instruction; some of them having resided at Otaheite much longer than any other European visitors. As, with their superior advantages, they could not but have had an opportunity of obtaining the fullest information on most subjects

relating to this island, their account of it would, probably, convey more authentic and accurate intelligence than, with our best endeavours, any of us
could possibly obtain. But as I look upon it to be very uncertain, if not very
unlikely, that we shall ever have any communication from that quarter, I
have here put together what additional intelligence about Otaheite and its
neighbouring islands I was able to procure, either from Omai while on board
the ship, or by conversing with the other natives while we remained amongst
them.[52]

The Spaniards, who are recognized as having spent the most time on the
island (and thus as having the best information), are not named or placed
in the collecting narrative. They are, in fact, placed outside of the entire
enlightenment project. Of course, the Spaniards are welcome to share in
the knowledge, and they have the resources to participate as equals if not
superiors, but they have chosen to exclude themselves and to not contribute to the collective European understanding.

The natives of the South Pacific are judged in a similarly negative way.
Cook is concerned to determine whether they have either the skill or the
inclination to collect the world properly. It is simply assumed that these
nations cannot actually create a proper collection because they are not
yet civilized and thus do not yet have the necessary intellectual and social
resources. What is more important for Cook is whether the uncivilized
nations at least *try* to collect. On the third voyage, Cook notes with some
disdain that "their [the natives of Adventure Bay] not expressing that
surprize which one might have expected from their seeing men so much
unlike themselves, and things to which, we were well assured, they had
been hitherto utter strangers, their indifference for our presents, and
their general inattention, were sufficient proofs of their not possessing
any acuteness of understanding."[53] What bothers Cook, for both scientific and moral reasons, is that, while the engaged Europeans are very
concerned to collect information and artifacts from the natives, the natives are uninterested in the Europeans. Along the same lines, Cook is
also interested in testing the ability of the natives to tell Europeans apart.
For instance, in the second voyage Cook writes of how "we told several of
them, that M. de Bougainville came from France, a name they could by
no means pronounce, nor could they pronounce that of Paris much
better." In fact, Cook continues, "they believed that we and Mr.
Bougainville came from the same country; that is, from Pretane, for so
they called our country. They had not the least knowledge of any other

European nation; nor probably will they; unless some of those men should return who had lately gone from the isle."[54] Likewise, Cook remarks in the third voyage that "although we do not think that there is a great similarity between our manners and those of the Spaniards, it is worth observing, that Omai did not think there was much difference."[55] Omai, by not noticing the differences between the English and the Spanish obvious to Cook, demonstrates the superiority of Cook's skills of observation. Omai fails in the most important project of global knowledge because he cannot tell one nation-space from another.

But there are also times when Cook is apparently impressed by the intellectual character of the natives – they are curious or desire European curiosities – and so he tests how much they have advanced in their ideas of collecting. Sometimes the result of these enquiries is disappointing. On the second voyage, for instance, Cook notes how he "took no small pains to know how far their geographical knowledge extended; and did not find that it exceeded the limits of their horizon."[56]

At other times, however, the native world is much more extensive, and Cook attempts to collect the information they have collected. This information is summarized and evaluated, not only in terms of its accuracy, but also its scale. In one passage, for instance, Cook considers the "catalogue" of places of the natives of Wateeoo, with a particular concern for Bougainville's claim that the natives of the South Pacific could navigate over long distances:

> These low isles [near Otaheite] are, doubtless, the farthest navigation, which those of Otaheite and the Society Islands perform at present. It seems to be a groundless supposition, made by Mons. de Bougainville, that they made voyages of the prodigious extent he mentions; for I found, that it is reckoned a sort of prodigy, that a canoe once driven by a storm from Otaheite, should have fallen in with Mopeeha, or Howe's Island, though so near, and directly to leeward. The knowledge they have of other distant islands is no doubt traditional, and has been communicated to them by the natives of those islands, driven accidentally upon their coasts, who besides giving them the names, could easily inform them of the direction in which the places lie from whence they came, and of the number of days they had been upon the sea. In this manner, it may be supposed, that the natives of Wateeoo have increased their catalogue by the addition of Otaheite and its neighbouring isles, from the people we met with there, and also of the other islands these had heard of.[57]

While subsequent research indicates that Cook was wrong, and that long-distance navigation was carried out in the South Pacific, significant here is the way that Cook's judgment connects to how he characterizes collecting, and how collecting becomes one of the key ways to know the world. The greater, more detailed, and more accurate the collection, the more advanced the nation. And in this, of course, Cook and the English become supreme.

The published accounts of Cook's voyages were one of the first, as well as one of the most unequivocal, expressions of the capacity of the English to travel around the world safely. The abstractions of longitude and latitude, the advice concerning the tides, the warnings about the weather, the recommendations of what to eat, and, most importantly, the division and description of the available places in Cook's account of his voyages reads less like an adventure story and more like a travel guide. The most important voyage here is the second, on which improvements in navigational and health techniques were crucial – the chronometer and sauerkraut being two items that have acquired mythical status. As one passage in the second voyage notes, "if I did nothing more, I was at least in hopes of being able to point out to posterity, that these seas may be navigated, and that it is practicable to go on discoveries, even in the very depth of winter."[58] Regardless of what was found, Cook and his crew survived where every European ship before would have suffered extreme hardship if not destruction. But their survival meant that they were able to discover and collect more than anyone else had ever done. The collector, then, becomes the hero, the one who is able to triumph over all the adversities that the world is able to offer.

In Cook's voyages, with his diorama, with his trunks of artifacts, and with his tables of coordinates, the reader is presented with a picture of the world created out of nations and out of all the comparisons that become possible. The collection is not merely an accumulation; it is the basis on which it becomes possible to explore the relative qualities of things – relative, that is, to everything else in the collection. Beyond any particular comparison is the fundamental epistemological claim that nations, existing both in the world and in the collection, can be compared *at all*. And it is this possibility that Cook's voyages prove with neither hesitation nor, apparently, controversy. Likewise, as additional information is published, the form that the information takes remains the same. If anything, the account of places and nations becomes that much more entrenched as more accurate measurements of coordinates and more comprehensive descriptions of places are accumulated. The collection, whether manifested in museums or books, comes to exist beyond any specific account of the world and becomes a primary source of authoritative knowledge about the world. The collection begins to approach the anonymity of a mathematical demonstration.

But with the creation of all these fixed national identities, with the creation of the collection, and with the increased importance of comparisons for the scientific analysis of humanity, Cook remains transcendent. While the world becomes fixed, he remains in motion, and as the world is turned into a collection, he remains forever the collector, forever the one who has explored the world and flattened it between the pages of his book. What remains is for Europe to collect the places of the world again, not as objects in the museum, but as objects in the world. The collections are to become empires.

SIX

Empires

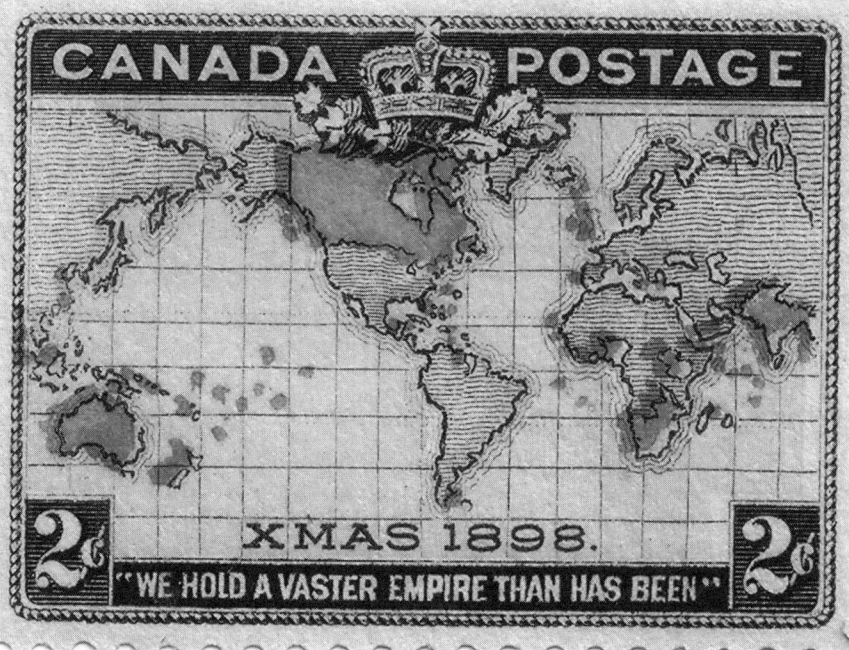

Canadian stamp from 1898 depicting the English empire, with a royal crown over the world and a legend that reads, "We Hold a Vaster Empire Than Has Been." The stamp has the English possessions coloured in red.

The discussion of Cook's world began with coordinates and it will end with empires. The image of a global political system comes last, not only because it is a suitable place to leave Cook's vision of the navigable world, but also because empire exists as the final term in an epistemological system. Like coordinates, nineteenth-century empires are everywhere.

The English acquisition of places around the world is only hinted at in Cook's voyages. There is some talk of sending English colonists to specific places, such as New Zealand. Cook also performs the ceremonies of acquisition at places throughout the world. But in terms of the creation and production of an effective global political system, the voyages are largely silent. However, even if they do not offer an explicit vision of global politics, the voyages are important because they affirm, if not create, the intellectual conditions in which a fragmented global political system could be imagined. The analysis of Cook's voyages offered here has been concerned, in part, with how the official idea of empire became clear in the first place. The image of empire in the nineteenth century was based on a world of naturalized nation-states connected through movement, exchange, and the imperial power of the collector. The empire did not have frontiers, it had collections. It *was* a collection.

In *Culture and Imperialism,* Edward Said points out the obvious but crucial fact that one of the things that the creation and maintenance of an empire depends upon is the idea of *having an empire*.[1] The idea of having an empire can be studied in other fields, such as literature. One example that Said considers is Jane Austen's *Mansfield Park*. First published in 1814, Austen's novel mentions the English plantations in the West Indies, and in the island of Antigua in particular, to which Sir Thomas Bertram must travel at a crucial period in the novel. The references to Antigua are scarce, but for Said, the existence of Antigua in the novel indicates an understanding of how both characters and readers understand their place in the world. Even the most parochial villages in England have some relationship to "the colonies." The novel, in other words, contains a sense of empire, even if the empire is never described in any detail.

In *The Atlas of the European Novel,* Franco Moretti challenges Said's account of the status that the Caribbean colonies had in *Mansfield Park.* Citing economic histories of early-nineteenth-century Britain and internal evidence in the novel that indicates how unimportant the colonies would have been for the fortune of people like Bertram, Moretti argues that the economic (colonial) explanation for Bertram's absence is wrong. Instead, in Moretti's account, Bertram goes to Antigua, "not because he needs the money, but because Austen needs him out of the way. Too strong a figure of authority, he intimidates the rest of the cast, stifling narrative energy, and leaving Austen without a story to tell: for the sake of the plot, he must go."[2] The choice of Antigua, in other words, was purely accidental.

Moretti continues, "the way in which colonial fortunes are introduced – a few hasty commonplaces, period – is itself a good clue to the real state of affairs; and as for the colonies themselves, not one of the thirteen novels [that Moretti is considering at this point] represents them directly; at most, we get a retrospective (and dubious) tale like Rochester's in *Jane Eyre.* This is the mythic geography – *pecunia ex machina* – of a wealth that is not really produced (nothing is ever said of work in the colonies), but magically 'found' overseas whenever a novel needs it."[3] We can grant Moretti's point that the importance of the colony in *Mansfield Park* is not the same as the material or economic importance of colonies in the England of Austen's time. But it is nonetheless significant that a place like Antigua could be included in any form as a "commonplace" in a novel about England. Of course, Bertram's journey to Antigua is crucial for the plot, but the existence of Antigua as a plausible space for an Englishman to travel in the novel indicates that Antigua is a part of the world shared by Austen and her readers. Moretti ignores the way in which Antigua, as a place of plantations, is situated in the textualized world of nineteenth-century England, so that it is plausible (however inaccurately in terms of the historical data) for someone in rural England to be concerned enough to travel there.

As a result, in *Mansfield Park* Austen does not create the idea of having colonies so much as she takes that idea for granted, which encourages her readers to accept colonies as unproblematic aspects of England's relationship to the world. Moretti is correct in claiming that the novel offers almost no information about Antigua. But the passing references, rather than suggesting how unimportant Antigua was, may rather suggest how widespread a basic – that is, a "working" – understanding of the colonies were to the reading public of Austen's time. Bertram's destination could not have been *any* place.

To consider why Austen could include references to Antigua, it is useful to step back from the novel and consider the overall terrain of books and other writings that were available to her readers. For instance, there was a large number of books published throughout the eighteenth century that, like the Abbé Raynal's five-volume *A History of the Settlements and Trade of the Europeans in the East and West Indies* (1774), offered extensive accounts of these places and England's relationship to them. There were also innumerable references to the colonies in the West Indies in newspapers and other periodicals throughout this time. Thus, Antigua could exist as a colony in Austen's novel because it was already located as an English colony in the world of print, a world into which *Mansfield Park* also came to exist.

Focusing on the broader textual world of the eighteenth century leads to more than the accumulation of incidental remarks about colonies. For instance, throughout the eighteenth century one of the most popular genres for printed narratives was the travel journal. From William Dampier's *New Voyage round the World*, first published in 1697, to George Anson's *A Voyage round the World*, first published in 1748, stories of buccaneers, military squadrons, and explorers, whether on the high seas or in distant lands, permeated the textual landscape of the English reading public. But by the late eighteenth century, no travel journal was more pervasive than the voyages of Captain Cook.

For decades after the first publications of the first voyage, in the early 1770s, Cook's voyages were the most popular and best known travel journals in the world. They were quickly reprinted, translated, and reworked, forming an important, almost unavoidable, part of the European world of books. Every member of the European reading public could be expected to know at least something about Cook's voyages. The publication of Cook's voyages thus marked a shift from the localized or Atlantic colonialism of the eighteenth century, where Antigua belonged, to the global order of the nineteenth, offering readers a sense of adventure, of moral purpose, of proper scientific procedures, of the forms that knowledge ought to take, and of the importance and legitimacy of the institutions that would play a central role in nineteenth-century global politics.

When an empire is described in the nineteenth century, the description has two distinct parts: the first concerns which chunks of the world have been collected by the imperial power, and the second concerns the relationship between the collector and the collected. For nineteenth-century writers, the direct possession that can exist in the case of islands has been extended throughout the world, has been tied to nation-places rather than plantations, and has become an object of intense and often public study. These places, understood through the archives of the explorers, have been acquired by European powers through collecting, rather than simply through being "reduced to obedience," as Hobbes would have said. In the nineteenth century, extending political and economic control was not only a matter of extending national territory by planting colonies in other areas, as was generally the case in the seventeenth- and eighteenth-century colonization of the Americas. Rather, or in addition to this, the domination was based on collecting different nations and placing them in a distant but persistent condition of dependence. The native state became a territorial administration, and ultimate sovereignty was brought back to England along with artifacts and government reports. Connecting to the ideals of a global economy based on the division of labour, the global empires of the nineteenth century were thus based on the proliferation of national difference, but difference always contained by the collection.

COOK AND EMPIRE

While Cook's personal responsibility for later political developments varies from one commentator to another, some connection between Cook's voyages and the English empire is widely accepted. Many of those who discuss this connection, however, consider Cook as simply a historical agent who discovered various places that were later incorporated, and who developed or confirmed various technologies that proved useful to people moving around the world. But these writers do not spend any time considering what they mean by empire or how Cook's voyages may have changed the concept itself. Instead, readers are simply offered a history of English activities around the world, and Cook's voyages offer data and techniques, but no ideas.

To equate Cook's voyages so quickly with empire ignores the fact that the concept of empire also has a history. Up until the late eighteenth century, the concept of empire was relatively general, being more or less equivalent to political control or dominion. Derived from the Latin *imperia,* the term "empire" was used to designate any kind of political order, from the union of England, Scotland, and Wales to the "empire of Morroco."[4] Comparing the Latin and English editions of Hobbes's *Leviathan,* for example, one finds that *imperii* is translated as both empire and sovereignty.[5] When Locke uses "empire," it is synonymous with "dominion" or "rule" or "sovereignty," as when he writes of the "fatherly empire" or the "right of empire"[6] that belongs to the ruler. Locke also writes of times when an empire is changed "into a multitude of little governments," which might suggest that empires are larger entities, as they are thought to be now, but then he claims that these new entities are "so many new empires."[7] Finally, Locke refers to the "empire" that individuals give up when they leave the state of nature.[8] "Empire," then, was a general term for power, and did not refer to a specific political system that could be contrasted with other systems, such as a state or a republic.

However, while "empire" was not used to identify a specific political order, some of the basic assumptions that permeated eighteenth-century thought made it difficult to articulate large-scale political systems that were either legitimate or possible. In Hobbes's account, for instance, commonwealths may be large, but the image of the contractual body politic suggests an appropriate size that works against the acquisition of foreign territories and diverse nations. In principle, sovereignty exists wherever there is political power. In practice, however, the organization of sovereignty faces natural limits, which can be seen in the way Hobbes writes about colonies.

In *Leviathan,* colonies are created through procreation:

> The procreation or children of a commonwealth, are those we call plantations, or colonies; which are numbers of men sent out from the commonwealth, under a conductor, or governor, to inhabit a foreign country, either formerly void of inhabitants, or made void then by war. And when a colony is settled, they are either a commonwealth of themselves, discharged of their subjection to their sovereign that sent them ... or else they remain united to their metropolis, as were the colonies of the people of Rome; and then they are no commonwealths themselves, but provinces, and parts of the commonwealth that sent them. So that the right of colonies, saving honour and league with their metropolis, dependeth wholly on their licence or letters, by which their sovereign authorized them to plant.[9]

For Hobbes, a colony is a spatially distinct political entity that has been created in an area that was already empty, or made empty through either expulsion or genocide. Colonists cannot coexist with former inhabitants, and while Hobbes's discussion treats the process as a possibility, logically or practically equal to finding land that is unoccupied, he does not dwell on the brutality of that process. Of course, the belief that there was unoccupied land in the Americas was an important assumption in justifying eighteenth-century colonialism. Hobbes, much less apologetic or deluded than Locke, admits that areas have to be emptied by force. Locke, on the other hand, will assert that the lands are already empty, not of people, granted, but of property owners. The results are more or less the same: European colonists took control of land across the Atlantic, and Europe extended its control over a new continent by sending out colonies.

By articulating colonies as smaller, newer bodies politic, it is difficult to see how Hobbes would articulate the control of the mother country lasting for an extended time. While his image underscores the relationship between the parts (and specifically the powers of government), it suggests that control over colonies will last only as long as the spatially distinct body politic is in its infancy. Colonies may not be automatically independent from their "metropolis," or "mother," but they are at the beginning of a narrative where they will become so. It is simply a matter of maturation.

The other political arrangement that extends dominion in Hobbes's account are provinces, which often include a variety of nations that "remain united to their metropolis." Here, the primary examples are from classical Rome, which created a single administrative system in which their colonies remained connected to the greater body politic: "The Romans who had the sovereignty of many provinces; yet governed them always by presidents, and praetors; and not by assemblies, as they governed the city of Rome, and territories adjacent. In like manner, when there were colonies sent from England, to plant Virginia, and Sommer-islands; though the governments of them here, were committed to assemblies in London, yet did those assemblies never commit the government under them to any assembly there, but did to each plantation send one governor."[10] The idea of the province, however, is dangerous for Hobbes's larger political project, if only because it raises the possibility that the papal power is legitimate – after all, if the Catholic church was built upon the remains of the Roman empire, then why can the Pope not claim to rule the same area through governors that are mistakenly called king? The issue, for

Hobbes, turns on the question of protection. If the province is effectively controlled by the ruling nation or city, then the relationship is legitimate. The extension of control, however, is difficult to imagine when the territories are disconnected, especially when the separated territories can defend themselves. Why should the American colonies remain part of England when they no longer need, or even expect, protection from the English sovereign?

If the commonwealth establishes provinces, the coherence of the entire body politic can be imagined only if the colonies are either contiguous or remain strongly tied in some other way. Otherwise, the contractual and power relations would no longer be in force, and the people would not stand in awe of the centralized sovereign power. As Hobbes writes in an early part of *Leviathan*, "the multitude sufficient to confide in for our security, is not determined by any certain number, but by comparison with the enemy we fear; and is then sufficient, when the odds of the enemy is not of so visible and conspicuous moment, to determine the event of war, as to move him to attempt."[11] Hobbes's political categories are thus awkward as a way to envision a dispersed global empire. Of course, it is possible to *imagine* the creation of such a political arrangement – anyone can submit to anyone else – the problem is in imagining how the dominion could be effective in practice, given that the basis of sovereignty is the protection that arises from a geographically proximate and politically unified system.

Like Hobbes, Locke also talks about the creation of colonies, but these colonies are not described in terms of the military expansion of a pre-existing sovereign power. England is not invading lands in North America. Rather, people from England are moving to an area that no one owns, to begin again a process that has already occurred in Europe. Servants are hired, the land is cleared, families are consolidated, and the creation of responsible government can start. For Locke, there is an inexorable tendency towards political independence; that is, towards the creation of small-scale, territorially limited, representative states. According to Locke's principles, one group of people cannot legitimately invade the territory of another group, provided that the territory has been acquired legitimately. The natives who were living in America were driven off or killed, not because they were the legitimate owners, but because they were hindering the creation of legitimate ownership – that is, ownership based on cleared land, agriculture, and the Christian bourgeois family. For Locke, in other words, the natives were not connected to the land, and they had to be removed in order to allow a proper – that is, propertied – connection to the land to be created.

There are two relevant assumptions shared by Hobbes and Locke that ill-prepared them to conceptualize, let alone justify, the kinds of political structures that would become commonplace in the nineteenth century. The first is their belief that the political community in some way results from conscious individual human activity. They held that the political and social orders are neither natural nor inherently collective. As a result, territory is created, although perhaps never completely settled, by the economic, contractual, and military activities of the commonwealth and its members. The second assumption is that the articulation of political space is built upon the fundamental need for contiguity. Distant colonies are like children in the state of nature – they will rely on the metropolis for some time, but these bonds are eventually broken and the children will wander off on their own.

Another important discussion of empire at the time was Rousseau's. He adopted a position that was more obviously against large-scale political orders. In *On the Social Contract*, Rousseau asks,

> How can a man of a people seize a vast amount of territory and deprive the entire human race of it except by a punishable usurpation, since this seizure deprives all other men of the shelter and sustenance that nature gives them in common? When Nuñez Balboa stood on the shoreline and took possession of the South Sea and all of South America in the name of the crown of Castille, was this enough to dispossess all the inhabitants and to exclude all the princes of the world? On that basis, those ceremonies would be multiplied quite in vain. All the Catholic King had to do was to take possession of the universe all at once from his private room, excepting afterwards from his empire only what already belonged to other princes.[12]

Behind the criticism of the Spanish empire-builders, which parallels criticisms offered by Cook, Rousseau is offering an ideal world composed of naturally occurring territorial nations that are connected to specific areas of the world. By its very nature, an empire cannot exist as a legitimate political order because, at the very least, it disrupts the intimate connection between a nation and a state.

The intellectual problem thus faced by nineteenth-century European imperialists was to imagine a global political system that does not depend on claiming, as an imperial fiat, large areas of the world. But if those claims are not possible, how can an empire be legitimate? What was difficult to imagine was a discontiguous and global empire where the territory is a patchwork of clear and distinct jurisdictions, often intermingled with territories controlled by other powers. Yet it was this image of empire that was so central to nineteenth-century European and eventually American thought. Cook's voyages help solve this problem by considering first the question of acquisition and then the different ways that the parts of the world are related.

EMPIRE AS COLLECTION

By the eighteenth century, it may have become implausible to stand on the coast of a continent and claim the whole thing. But similar claims still occurred. In Cook's voyages, the connection between the claimant and the island is more intimate, though, because claiming depends on some kind of direct knowledge of what is being claimed.

In the first voyage, Cook performs a ritual that he and others performed throughout the Pacific. In Kippis's account of one such event, "the party then fired three volleys of small arms, which were answered by the same number from the ship. When the gentlemen had performed this ceremony upon the island, which they called Possession Island, they reembarked in their boat."[13] The ceremony, which is built on a geographically proximate relationship between the ship and the island, allowed the English sailors, in the name of George III, to claim places in their particularity, even while the Spanish claim the Pacific as their private ocean. Cook does not claim continents or oceans; he claims islands. When those islands are large, the rituals only need to be multiplied. Thus, near the end of the first voyage, Cook narrates his acquisition of the east coast of New Holland (now Australia): "As I was now about to quit the eastern coast of New Holland, which I had coasted from latitude 38° to this place, and which I am confident no European had ever seen before, I once more hoisted English colours, and though I had already taken possession of several particular parts, I now took possession of the whole eastern coast."[14] This is how the empires of the nineteenth century are put together – places are explored, and detailed information is collected. Then the native territorial nation-states can be brought back to the metropolis. Along these lines, Walter Besant, a nineteenth-century biographer and popularizer of Cook's voyages, notes how Cook "had given to his country Australia and New Zealand – nothing less; he had given to Great Britain Greater Britain."[15]

The status of the empire as a gift, as a collection of objects that Cook offered to his nation – even though Cook had actually claimed them for his king as a matter of duty – connects back to the basic account of places (and nations) that has already been considered. Cook does not have to worry about maintaining frontiers. Rather, there are territorial objects that occur naturally in the world, and building an empire is simply a matter of collecting those objects into a single system.

The collection also creates specific relationships between the collector and the collected, which suggests how power relations could be understood and legitimated. Throughout *On Longing*, Susan Stewart has drawn attention to the role the collection plays in creating a sense of control, and the collections connected to Cook's voyages are no exception. The collection offered the information necessary both to justify European domination of non-European places and to plan appropriate economic, social, and theological projects. As Paul Carter wrote, "to debate the ownership of land is to think of the land in question as a region, a geographical object that can be treated in isolation, as a legal or economic unit."[16] We should also recall Said's claims that the goal of the European archives and social sciences is "to deliver the non-European world either for analysis and judgement or for satisfying the exotic tastes of European and North American audiences."[17] There is power in the creation of an imperial archive, not only because the archive depends on power, but also because power is enhanced and organized by the archive.

To extend the relationship between empire and the collection, however, we must notice that the kinds of control that are based on collecting are not necessarily the same as those that are created by traditional forms of conquest. In this new empire, England does not send national colonies to distant lands so much as it brings the nations of distant lands to England. The system of identities and relations, imagined as points, containers, and tables, is infused with power: the power to move, to know, to exchange, and to control. Rather than conquering areas, the understanding of nineteenth-century empires appealed to movements within and around the collection. Thus it is the relationship between the collector and the collected that best distinguishes the empires of the nineteenth century from previous European and global political systems. In Cook's voyages, a scientific and exotic archival text spreads over the world, and imperialism becomes closely tied to ornamentalism, where objects from around the world were put on display as a justification and a microcosm of global power.[18]

All three of Cook's voyages can be read as fables of the contrast between feudal and capitalist forms of exploitation, described in terms of a distinction between Spanish and English colonization. Whereas the Spanish and Portuguese limited travel, suppressed information, and encouraged monopolies, the English published accounts of their explorations and laid the world out for everyone to travel and trade in. Some have described Cook's impact on the world by saying that he "opened" the Pacific. This opening depended on a complicated apparatus of knowledge, growing out of the Admiralty and foreign office (and out of the East India Company), connected to museums, collections, and other institutions of empire. Cook's journals do not simply relate a series of events and places; they help make those places available to any reader capable of travel or study.

The organization of knowledge in Cook's voyages parallels the tracks that he traces in the ocean. A table of places, which creates the primary system for organizing information, presents the world all at once, as in an encyclopedia, where it is possible to move from one place to another at will. This image of global control is evident in a stamp issued by the Dominion of Canada in 1898, where the world is mapped in outline and the British possessions are filled in with red. To print this kind of map on a stamp turns the parts of Britain's empire into something that has been collected. The ideological background of the stamp is fairly straightforward: in an era when "the sun never set on the British Empire," the English crown is set upon a coordinated map with fragments of territory scattered throughout. The collector's greatness arises from the disparate territories it is able to control, but its clarity arises from the sharp shapes it is able to colour confidently.

The table of places became a field of engagement for the conflicts between the European colonial powers. Some of this rivalry had already occurred, such as with the explorers in the late eighteenth century each claiming islands in the name of their respective European monarchs. But in the decades following Cook's death, almost all of the places in the Pacific were acquired by one western power or another. France established protectorates over Otaheite and the Marquesas in 1842 and the main island of New Caledonia in 1853. Britain annexed New Zealand in 1840. By 1860, the scramble for the Pacific was largely over and, beyond the Sandwich Islands, Japan, and parts of the Asian continent, there were very few places that had not officially become parts of one global empire or another. Joining the hunt a little later, the United States acquired control over Guam and the Philippines as a result of the Spanish-American War, and it annexed the Sandwich Islands in 1898. At this time, Samoa was also divided between the United States and Germany. By the late nineteenth century, American writers could publish works such as Charles Morris's *Our Island Empire*, demonstrating that the United States could compete on the same terms as the European powers.

One thing that changed in the South Pacific was the ability to articulate imperialist control that was not monolithic (that is, it did not involve a single power extending over a contiguous area). For the first time, perhaps, it was possible to describe a way for competing empires to mingle in space without having them push up against each other's frontiers.

This scramble for the Pacific hints at a connection between the division of control over Africa, which was organized by European powers in the 1870s, and the formal control over the South Pacific, which was created two or three decades earlier. The division of Africa among European colonial powers followed the pattern that had already occurred in the South Pacific. In the South Pacific, the places already had borders; they could already be imagined as territorial units, and the control over them could thus be determined in a clear and decisive way. For the imperial powers, the question in the Pacific was simply who owned what. As a result, there were no border wars, only colours on a table. When the Europeans divided up Africa, a similar process could be carried out, but only if the territories were treated like islands, with clear cartographic borders and no frontiers. Africa was treated as a waterless ocean and could be divided up accordingly.

EMPIRE AS EXCHANGE

By the time formal possession of specific nation-places was achieved, European influence over the world had already been well established. The relations between Europe and nations in the rest of the world in the nineteenth century were characterized more by movement than by static collection, more by trade than by plantations. To understand how the idea of empire changed in the eighteenth and nineteenth centuries, therefore, it is important to distinguish global economic and political relations from formal sovereign control.

Along with the collection of native identities, Batavia and the Cape of Good Hope are important images of a European-dominated global system of exchange. Consider, for instance, Cook's description when the ships are at the Cape near the end of the second voyage: "We found in the bay, the *Pourvoyeur*, a large French frigate, an American Sloop, and a brig belonging to the place. She had come last from the river Amazon, where she took in a cargo of provisions for the Cape Verde Islands; but, not being able to find them, she steered for this place, where she anchored about half an hour before us."[19]

Each time Cook's ships are returning to England, the third time without Cook, they stop at the Cape. In Batavia during the first voyage, Cook emphasized the costumes of the different nationalities. At the Cape of Good Hope, on the other hand, the account emphasizes the ships of the different European powers. Once Cook had connected to the established trade routes, he had returned to the European world. Emphasizing this connection, Cook notes that during the passage from the Cape of Good Hope to England, Cook's ships were accompanied by ships of the English East India Company, who were following the same well-worn tracks. With the ocean comes travel, and with travel comes exchange.

Once the importance of exchange in Cook's voyages is recognized, the status of the island-nation-place changes. Rather than being the epitome of the autonomous, closed territorial nation-state, the island becomes the epitome of permeability and influence from the outside. What this means is that there is a profound split between places existing as discrete objects of national identity and analysis, and places put into unequal and porous relations with other, typically European, places. The island-nation-state thus exists as both autonomous entity and as an ever more dependent component of a larger structure. The island exists within an ocean that separates the islands, but the ocean is also the plane of European competition.

Cook, looking towards a future where the exchange of commodities would be more developed along the coast of the northern Pacific, writes that trading with the natives of Nootka Sound "would, probably, be much otherwise, were they once habituated to a constant trade with foreigners. This intercourse would increase their wants, by introducing them to an acquaintance with new luxuries; and, in order to be enabled to purchase these, they would be more assiduous in procuring skins, which they would soon discover to be the commodity most sought for; and a plentiful supply of which, I make no doubt, would be had in the country."[20]

Cook's is a tabulated world of relations where people possess a wide variety of things (productions, skills, locations) that can be traded, if only an effective system of exchange can be created. The voyages thus offer an extended picture of the economic conditions of the various places of the

Pacific, including information on what things can be acquired there, what the natives will take in exchange, and how to proceed in establishing suitable trading relations, which over time would include creating a desire for English manufactured goods. Not only will these commodity relations connect distant places to England through economic activities, the people will become better for it.

Creating a market where the ships could trade with the shore was an important part of Cook's interaction with the places of the world. In keeping with the worldview of the voyages, the gift-giving is understood as a relationship between nations as much as between individuals. In the voyages, one of the first steps to creating systems of exchange was to present people, and people of consequence in particular, with gifts. As Cook notes in the second voyage, "three things made them our fast friends. Their own good nature and benevolent disposition; gentle treatment on our part; and the dread of our fire-arm."[21] The goal with these gifts is to create conditions suitable for a market, and specifically one where Cook can exchange trinkets for much-needed supplies. Marcel Mauss has argued in *The Gift* that while gift-giving often appears to be voluntary, in many cases the gift and the reciprocation are obligatory.[22] Cook, however, does not expect a material gift in return; rather, he expects gratitude and, more importantly, the creation of a market where reciprocity will be maintained.

Cook's gift-giving activities typically continued for so long as peaceful relations were maintained, although they tended to occur more at the beginning and the end of any visit, and at key points during important negotiations. Gifts were also used to repair relations, such as when Cook killed a native of Otaheite during the second voyage while the man was rowing to the shore after he had purportedly stolen an iron stanchion from one of the ship's gangways. Cook reports, "I wanted much to have seen him [the man's son], to make him a present, and by other kind treatment to convince him and the others, that it was not from any bad design against the nation, that we had killed his father."[23] After this "unhappy accident," Cook notes how the natives of Otaheite continued to trade with the English "as if nothing had happened." Throughout the three voyages, in fact, Otaheite is one of the most consistent and favourable markets that the English encounter, and it provides Cook with an example of what can be done to improve relations between Europeans and natives of the South Pacific.

While Otaheite is one of Cook's key successes, however, every place in the world is narrated with the same concerns for exchange. The voyages relate what the natives – or, more accurately, what the islands in general – have to offer, what they are willing to take in exchange, and what they value the most. For example, during the stay at Queen Charlotte's Sound during the first voyage, Cook says that "neither did they set much value upon the cloth of Otaheite; but English broad cloth and red kersey were in high estimation; which showed that they had sense enough to appreciate the commodities which we offered by their use, which is more than could be said of some of their neighbours, who made a much better appearance."[24] Cook is representing a specific image of economic exchange, which is based on some notion of reciprocity, fairness, and safety. Cook also relies on the terror of the ship's guns, but he justifies their use in specific, non-military terms. This aspect of Cook's voyages has been discussed in some detail by Bernard Smith, who points out that the engravings from the three voyages indicate a shift in attitude. In the second voyage, and more so in the third, the representations of the interactions between Cook and the natives of the Pacific stressed peaceful themes. As Smith writes, "everywhere Cook goes in the Pacific his arrival is celebrated by Webber in scenes of joyful reception, in dancing, boxing entertainments, gifting, trading. Nothing must disturb this sense of peacefulness. Even Cook's own death, the great trauma of the voyage, is not drawn, nor will it be included in the official publication."[25]

In Cook's voyages, peace is a conditional situation, which depends primarily on the behaviour of the natives and Cook's control of his own crew. If the people who are encountered do not behave appropriately, Cook can become violent. And violence is always threatened: "As I intended to continue in this place five or six days, in order to make an observation of the transit of Mercury, it was absolutely necessary, in order to prevent future mischief, to show these people that we were not to be treated ill with impunity."[26] The peaceful relations depend on military threats as much as on hospitality and fairness. Only then can the market exist. But this is not the violence of either sovereignty or war. Cook never becomes the ruler of the island, and he never describes his violent reactions in terms of warfare. Rather, he is an agent of order and justice, part of a global policing force.

Violence is evident throughout Cook's voyages, not only as an immediate practical requirement but also as an important tool to encourage people to internalize specific legal and moral ideals. The firearms are not always used to drive natives away or to exact revenge, although they are also used for both of these purposes. Firearms are also used to intimidate people, and to ensure that they relate to Cook's crew in particular ways.

Two engravings from the second voyage showing Cook and his crew landing on islands. The peaceful landing is at Tanna and the violent landing is at Erromanga, both islands in the New Hebrides. The landings suggest how complex relationships can be between the English and the nations of the Pacific.

Consider, for instance, Cook's response when Charles Clerke's gun was "snatched from him":

> I sent all the boats off but one, with which I stayed, having a good many of the natives about me, who behaved with their usual courtesy. I made them so sensible of my intention, that long before the marines came, Mr. Clerke's musquet was brought, but they used many excuses to divert me from insisting on the other. At length Mr. Edgecumbe arriving with the marines, this alarmed them so much, that some of them fled. The first step I took was to seize on two large double-sailing canoes, which were in the cove. One fellow making resistance, I fired some small shot at him, and sent him limping off. The natives being now convinced that I was in earnest, all fled; but on my calling to them, many returned; and, presently after, the other musquet was brought, and laid at my feet. That moment I ordered the canoes to be restored, to show them on what account they were detained.[27]

The goal is not simply to get the gun back, but rather to form in the mind of the natives a sense of justice, which involves shooting anyone who resists. On reading accounts of these events, one is reminded of a passage in Friedrich Nietzsche's *On the Genealogy of Morals* in which he is discussing how people internalize a sense of law: "It was in this sphere then, the sphere of legal obligations, that the moral conceptual world of 'guilt,' 'conscience,' 'duty,' 'sacredness of duty' had its origin: its beginnings were, like the beginnings of everything great on earth, soaked in blood thoroughly and for a long time. And might one not add that, fundamentally, this world has never since lost a certain odor of blood and torture?"[28] With Cook the reader is also a target of these moralizing stories.

The creation of an internal moral sentiment is not the only field where violence has its uses. Blood can promote fairness. Blood can encourage a sense of time and place that are appropriate to a global political and economic system. Blood can help outsiders collect nations, and blood can be used to drain those nations away, whether they really existed or not, into the oceanic flows of empire. Blood can paint the ground where direct conquests are carried out. And throughout, the account of place in Cook's voyages helps make the blood look necessary, if not desirable. But this blood is rarely extracted in the name of the English king; it is extracted in the name of civilization, and so even where formal sovereign control is not mentioned, the empire is still there.

Whether the interaction is peaceful or violent, the exchanges are always designed to create and maintain Cook's authority. For instance, there is a significant change in the wording from the manuscript to the print edition. In the Admiralty edition of the first voyage, one encounter is related as follows: "I invited some of them on board; and as they knew they had nothing to fear from us, while they behaved honestly and peaceably, they immediately complied: I made each of them some presents, and dismissed them much gratified."[29] The manuscript version of the same encounter reads, "soon after we had got under sail three large canoes came off to the Ship and several of the People came on board upon the very first invitation; this was owing to their having heard of our being upon the Coast and the manner we had treated the Natives. I made each of those that came on board a small present and after about an hours stay they went away well satisfied."[30] Whereas the manuscript describes Cook's relationship with the natives as if they were equals, and relies instead on Cook's reputation, the Admiralty's reworking describes a legal and authoritarian relation where Cook is the focus of the exchange. While the peaceful relations involved gifts in both accounts, the Admiralty's account also includes threats if the natives behaved improperly, which is apparently how Hawkesworth understood the rather vague phrase "the manner we had treated the Natives." Likewise, whereas the natives "went away" in the manuscript version, they were "dismissed" when the episode was transferred to print.

By setting up interactions and punishments in terms of a shared legal code, Cook creates the possibility that he and his crew will also transgress. One such episode took place in the first voyage, while along the coast of New Zealand:

> In the mean time some of our people, who, when the Indians were to be punished for a fraud, assumed the inexorable justice of a Lycurgus, thought fit to break into one of their plantations, and dig up some potatoes: for this offence I ordered each of them to be punished with twelve lashes, after which two of them were discharged; but the third, insisting that it was no crime in an Englishman to plunder an Indian plantation, though it was a crime in an Indian to defraud an Englishman of a nail, I ordered him back into his confinement, from which I would not release him till he had received six lashes more.[31]

The classical allusion is Hawkesworth's reworking of Cook's words, but the relationship between law and sovereignty permeates all three of the voyages. The voyages not only represent the kind of government that is connected to the nation-state, but also characterize a global ethos that ought to constrain the actions of even the most powerful sovereigns. As a result, during the second voyage, Cook reflected on his relationship to law, not as a subject of George III, but as a representative of a global law whose character he never challenges and whose origin he never accounts for. He tells his reader, "it was ever a maxim with me to punish the least crimes any of my people committed against these uncivilized nations. Their robbing us with impunity, is by no means a sufficient reason why we should treat them in the same manner, a conduct we see they themselves cannot justify. They found themselves injured, and sought for redress in a legal way."[32] If it is hypocritical for a sailor to assume "the inexorable justice of a Lycurgus," it is only because they are being hypocritical, not because the position of Lycurgus is unavailable. Often, it is precisely this kind of position that Cook adopts as he passes judgement on both sailors and natives alike. Rickman reflects on this during the third voyage:

> There are those who have blamed Capt. Cook for his severity to the Indians; but it was not to the Indians alone that he was severe in his discipline. He never suffered any fault in his own people, tho' ever so trivial, to escape unpunished: If they were charged with insulting an Indian, or injuring him in his property, if the fact was proved, the offender was surely punished in sight of the Indians. By this impartial distribution of equal justice, the Indians themselves conceived so high an idea of his wisdom, and his power too, that they paid him the honours as they did their Et-hu-a, or good spirit.[33]

Cook may have often been severe, but he was also generally consistent. As no other European navigator had done, Cook came to represent the voice of an enlightened, global system of justice, which allowed him and those who followed to justify a wide array of acts of force throughout the world. So long as the law was consistent, it could be as harsh as necessary.

The events associated with the *Bounty* indicate some of the issues that arise when the appeal to empire is the dominant political category by which the global relationships that followed in Cook's wake are understood. Consider, for instance, a passage from George Mortimer's account of his voyage into the Pacific in the late 1780s. In the introduction, Mortimer lists the parts of his voyage that will be entertaining to his readers: "lastly, though not of the least importance, was our visit to OTAHEITE; whereby I have been enabled to communicate such intelligence to the Admiralty respecting the probable destination of the mutineers on board his Majesty's ship *Bounty*, as, it is hoped, will enable Captain EDWARDS of the PANDORA frigate, sent out expressly for the purpose of searching for these daring offenders, to bring them to that condign punishment they so justly merit."[34] During this period, the English possessed very few islands in the Pacific, but their ships and their justice were everywhere.[35] Captain William Bligh never left the protection of his sovereign, and the mutineers never left the possibility of punishment.

While justice and economics were universalized, it was still the English who created the larger-scale relations. They traded between islands, they collected and analyzed the data, and they understood the world. The national voyages, books, and archives were signs of the nation's ability to incorporate the outside, to classify it, and to put it up for display as an-thropology or history. The voyages and the collections thus created, to use Cynthia Enloe's phrase, "a sense of world influence," which helped to further justify a global economic and military presence.[36]

The voyages are organized as a triumphal procession of enlightened power. The few exceptions, where Cook made mistakes, are typically ex-pressed in print as confessionals that enhance the credibility of every-thing else Cook does. In terms of the geopolitical struggles between European nations, the immediate impact of Cook's shows of force were minimal. However, the capacity of the English to move freely around the world and to force their will upon natives confers status on a specific kind of European. The collector has both the capacity and the obligation to impose order on the collected.

EMPIRE AS CULTIVATION

Along with the collection of national identities and the set of universal moral and economic rules, Cook's voyages also focus attention on the value of cultivation, understood in terms of both agriculture and nation-ality. The voyages not only identify and collect but also offer images of a better world, a world more like England, or at least a world more like the idealized England that follows Cook through his voyages. Part of Cook's task, as if he had become responsible for his collection, was to encourage specific improvements in the places he collects. As far as Cook's voyages are concerned, history, at least in the South Pacific, begins with the first European contact. The places that are fixed on the table begin to move through time. There are examples throughout the three voyages. On the second voyage, for instance, Cook noted that "we found at these two places, built and building a great number of large canoes, and houses of every kind; people living in spacious habitations, who had not a place to shelter themselves in eight months before; several large hogs about every house; and every other sign of a rising state."[37] We can hear John Locke whispering in Cook's ear: "God gave the world ... to the use of the industrious and rational."[38] For Locke, this was an important way to ignore, if not justify, the extermination of native Americans, whether immediately by war or gradually by disease, poverty, and social exclusion. For Cook, however, European control is organized and justified in a very different way. Whereas there was no connection between natives and the land in Locke, in Cook the connection is quite close, and the task was to show them how to use the land more effectively. They must be trained and provided, typically through exchange, with resources that will improve their place, and ultimately improve the whole world.

When Cook's ships entered the Pacific, they were carrying seeds and animals that were either brought from England or acquired at the Cape of Good Hope, and were intended to be distributed around the islands of the Pacific. During the third voyage, while the ships were at Tongataboo, Cook imagines the future of the Pacific that his seeds and livestock will contribute to: "While I was surveying this delightful prospect, I could not help flattering myself with the pleasing idea that some future navigator may, from the same station, behold these meadows stocked with cattle, brought to these islands by the ships of England; and that the completion of this single benevolent purpose, independently of all other considerations, would sufficiently mark to posterity that our voyages had not been useless to the general interests of humanity."[39]

As the English started to raise animals throughout the world through their intermediaries, husbandry became globalized. The final goal was thus not only to help native nations, it was also to change the places of the world so that Europeans could feel at home. The world was again something that humanity had a general interest in, but now with the English ensuring that people were cultivating the world properly for everyone to use.

In addition to the cultivation of crops and animals, another significant transformative project was in the patterns of economic exchange, where Cook frequently attempted to create more persistent, market-like relationships between the English and the natives. Rather than maintaining a balance of terror, the discourse of safety in Cook's voyages attempts to create a normalized, rationalized, civilized identity that spans human groups (or, rather, extends a particular ideal in a particular group everywhere). In fact, the problems and goals connected to civilizing the natives were often the same as the problems and goals connected to civilizing degenerate groups in Europe itself. Improving the natives was just like improving the poor, the degenerate, or, in Cook's case, his own regular sailors.

One of the common goals throughout Cook's voyages is to encourage natives to imitate Europeans, often through either encouragement or competition. Thus "native curiosity" becomes a useful tool for changing national characters, especially when that curiosity could be used to demonstrate his own superiority. As Cook notes during the first stay at the Sandwich Islands on the third voyage, "it does their sensibility no little credit, without flattering ourselves, that when they saw the various articles of our European manufacture, they could not help expressing their surprise, by a mixture of joy and concern, that seemed to apply the case, as a lesson of humility, to themselves; and, on all occasions, they appeared deeply impressed with a consciousness of their own inferiority; a behaviour which equally exempts their national character from the preposterous pride of the more polished Japanese, and of the ruder Greenlander."[40] As with the comparisons that were carried on within the collection, Cook's transformative engagement acquires a global perspective. Cook encourages natives to compare themselves to Europeans, encourages their participation in European projects, and ultimately encourages them to become like Europeans (though still living in their original places).

Kant is once again a useful writer to connect to the discussion in Cook's voyages. At the beginning of *What Is Enlightenment?* first published in 1784, Kant provides a now-classical definition of the task: "Enlightenment is man's emergence from his self-incurred immaturity. Immaturity is the inability to use one's own understanding without guidance of another."[41] While guidance will ultimately be overcome, for right now it is both pervasive and necessary when someone does not use their "own understanding," that is to say, when they are not the autonomous rational agents that they can, ought, and eventually will be. In a related passage from *The Metaphysics of Morals,* Kant considers whether it is acceptable to either subjugate or colonize "a people that holds out no prospect of civil union" and "bring these human beings (savages) into a rightful condition (as with the American Indians, the Hottentots, and the inhabitants of New Holland)."[42] His answer is that they should not be, although he recognizes the end as a good one. One thing that is important for Kant is that the nations, even though they exist at the opposite extreme to civilization, are, *as a group,* nonetheless owners of the land, and while they are currently excluded from the "prospects of civil union," they are closely united to their places. For Kant, the world is a single system of national identities, a family of nations, where different nations exist in their own places, but where the more mature nations are obligated to improve not only themselves, but also the infant nations that live in places around the world. The goal, in other words, is not to maintain the table of national identities as it is, as if every national species were an unchanging entity, but rather to transform each of them towards a shared ideal.

Whether in Cook or Kant, therefore, the transformative process combines a global system of knowledge with a specific set of cultural, moral, and economic ideals. The collection becomes an intermediate field of information through which the entire world can be cultivated. The idea that nations, while continuing to be distinct, can also change over time, connects Cook's voyages not only to Kant, but also to more general changes in European metaphysics. In *The Order of Things,* Michel Foucault notes how the fixed Linnaean world of species, which was based on comparative anatomy, gave way to a different sense of life in which species were connected to their often-changing material conditions, and thus to a history.[43] The taxonomic table had been replaced by biology. However, while Foucault marks this change with the works of Georges Cuvier, a French biologist of the late eighteenth and early nineteenth centuries, a similar change can be seen in Cook's voyages. In the voyages, however, the creation of the table and the introduction of time coexist. Before the voyages, humanity was organized by one global binary division or another. With the importance of the material conditions central to the articulation of national distinctions, Cook's voyages introduce a taxonomic table of national species and a causal system of cultivation.

EMPIRE AS PANOPTICON

Rather than a fixed table of national identities, the relationship that is created evokes the arrangement of rooms and information that are imagined by Jeremy Bentham in his essay on the panopticon, first written in 1787. If the fixed world of Linnaeus crumbles with the introduction of life (that is, of environment and physiological change), the panoptic collection becomes a way of tracking human life, and therefore a way of disciplining the world.[44] Foucault suggests that Bentham's idea originated with the menagerie at Versailles, a building divided into seven cages with different species of animals. However, the visual relationship that Cook's voyages establishes between the collector and the collected also shares several key features with the ideal of the panopticon.

One significant parallel between the organization of Cook's world and Bentham's panoptic building is that each object of analysis is clearly distinguished in space. In the world of Cook's voyages, however, the prison cell has become the island, and the prisoner has become the nation. In other words, maps and coordinates help create tight containers that support fixed identities, and these identities can be studied, either independently or alongside those in other containers. The world arising from Cook's voyages thus becomes a system for identifying variables, for tracing connections, and for creating a space in the middle for an archival collector of data.

One important aspect of the panopticon is the need for constant observation. Bentham argued against the decision to ship prisoners to Australia in the 1780s, claiming not only that the panopticon was more economical but also that in the panopticon the prisoners would be sources of useful information, which would be impossible if they were shipped out. On the second point, Bentham was wrong. Shipping prisoners to Australia was probably quite expensive, but they were not sent outside of the panopticon because as a surveillance system it followed them to Australia. Whether they were sent to Australia or not, the information could still be collected and consolidated. The key difference was that information was no longer collected from the prisons of England but from the colonies of Australia and then transmitted to England in the form of updates and reports.

The system of exploration and publication also created an almost absolute split between seeing and being seen. In the panopticon, this split was created through the organization of gazes in the tower and the peripheral cells. In Cook's voyages, the split is created through the organization of the sailing ship, the archive, and the printing press. The people from distant places that are encountered during the voyages have some experience of Cook and his companions, but once the information is collected, once the portraits are drawn, they are taken up into an almost wholly European system of communication and exchange that produces learned discussions of native life, artifacts, and the character of primitive humanity in situations throughout the world. After the voyages come to an end, in other words, the nations could still be seen through the artifacts and images in the collection, and therefore could be analyzed by people who never travelled to the South Pacific, or even left the town in which they were born. They could sit at the centre, and look out to any room that they wanted to.

It is important, however, not to carry the connection between Cook and Bentham too far. There is a generalization of humanity into nations that pervades Cook's voyages and that the individualized observations in Bentham's panopticon resist. What Cook is fixing in the space of the map and table is a collective group (the inhabitants, the natives, the nations) and not individuals. Bentham's panopticon, on the other hand, takes the individuated body of the human being as the ground for the production and organization of information. Cook only locates individuals in the table when they are exemplars of national identities. To express this in a different way, what Cook's voyages provided was the encouragement to organize information about a nation as if it were an individual, thus authorizing at a global scale what could be criticized as a fallacy of composition.

While Bentham focuses on individuals and Cook focuses on nations understood as pseudo-individuals, both writers are appealing to a similar arrangement of space. Bentham creates a closed system of observation that separates the subjects from the outside society as much as from each other. Cook's appeal to national identity, on the other hand, allows for the extension of documentation throughout the world. There is still a division between inside and outside, but the outside is now marked by the time Cook spent in the extreme places of the high southern latitudes. Inside the wall of ice are the nations of the world, and beyond there are only penguins. The world thus becomes a single system, as if it were a single city, a single building, or a single filing cabinet.

Given that the world changes, or is changed, and that some of the information becomes outdated, it is essential to collect the world as a process of ongoing surveillance. Cook's voyages not only create the collection, therefore; they also point to the need to update and maintain the collection through time. Only then can the control over the nation-places be maintained. The existence of these scientific institutions and practices, and the ideal of a complete and singular view of the world, encourages, if not demands, that the collection extend through time. Cook's voyages do not simply offer accounts of places, they offer slices of time that can then be taken up by the central collecting institutions and placed into much more extensive temporal sequences. As Besant notes in 1890, "a hundred years more and Cook's descriptions of the Polynesians and Australians will be invaluable as a record of things long since passed away;

even the people of the islands will have disappeared; there will not be a single survivor of the Friendly Islanders, or of the gentle natives of Tahiti, or of the fierce warriors of New Zealand."[45] Besant, reflecting on the impact of European power on the nineteenth century and projecting that impact into the twentieth, creates a sense of the world, complete in both time and space, in which Europe's control of the world is established and the natives, once collected, fade away into the memory of printed books and museum collections. Cook's voyages then become an account of how the world once was, preserving representations of national identities long after those identities no longer exist, long after they have been destroyed by European civilization.

One example of the role that Cook's voyages play in offering a temporal baseline for further descriptions of nation-places can be noted in the descriptions of the Sandwich Islands that were recorded after Cook's voyages. Vancouver describes the Sandwich Islands in much greater detail than Cook had done. The published version of Cook's journals contains roughly 75 pages of text, much of which is taken up by descriptions of coordinates and weather conditions. In contrast, the description of the Sandwich Islands in Vancouver's printed account runs for over 200 pages and contains extended descriptions and detailed charts of the islands. In addition to offering a fuller account, however, Vancouver also discusses the Sandwich Islands in terms of the information that has already been published. He thus recounts the changes that have occurred in the islands since Cook's visit. The Sandwich Islands, as a fixed series of places that had already been located, had now become a place undergoing change, and later navigators would add to the account.

In fact, other navigators were *expected* to add to the account, however trivial the new information might be. The Sandwich Islands had become a topic for all European voyagers in the area. Thus, as Otto von Kotzebue's ship approaches the Sandwich Islands on his second voyage, in 1826, he begins his account by invoking what was becoming a well-worn trope: "My readers, I think, will take some interest in a short account of this people, whose rapid progress in civilization would perhaps by this time have placed them on a level with Europeans, if unfavourable circumstances had not thrown obstacles in the way of their improvement."[46]

As Kotzebue travels through the native islands and the European collections, he notes how much the islands have been transformed. In the fifty years since Cook's visit, the monarchy was organized in western terms and the missionaries had gained considerable influence over the islands.

Kotzebue, like Cook and Vancouver before him, includes a map of the Sandwich Islands. But the maps have become much more iconic. They are useless to navigators (or, at least, much better ones would be readily available in a different kind of book). The map remains an important trope in navigation writing, however. Kotzebue does not need to present the map as a way to create the native territorial nation-state, but the map still helps authorize and situate the update that he is giving.

Other subsequent publications that would update the collection were later editions of Cook's voyages, in which information on the current situation could be included in the introduction, in the footnotes, or in the appendices. For instance, an edition of Cook's voyages published in the 1820s included an appendix that promised to offer "in detail, as we propose, a brief sketch of the remarkable changes in the condition of the several countries which were either in the first instance discovered by Cook, as the Sandwich Islands – or, respecting which we are chiefly indebted to his researches for our most authentic early information, as New Zealand."[47]

After a "rapid survey of the progress of maritime discovery," the appendix moves from place to place, offering a detailed, structured, and often comparative account of each place. Information is garnered from several sources, including Cook's *Voyages*, William Ellis's *Polynesian Researches*, and Thomas Mitchell's 1839 *Three Expeditions into the Interior of Eastern Australia* (for some of the information on New Holland). The Sandwich Islands are discussed in the last entry. The description begins with the physical character of the islands (the number of islands and their location) and then quickly moves from Cook's discovery to the history of the kings of the Sandwich Islands, from King Tamehama onward.[48] Focusing on the history of kings and warfare helps to establish the maturation of the Sandwich Islands as a member of the community of sovereign nations. The detail of these accounts is much greater than what can be found in Cook's voyages, but these accounts, without exception, refer back to the proper names first established in Cook's account.

By the 1820s, another globalizing force had become very important in the Pacific: the de-territorialized missionary organizations. The appendix thus discusses the population and the number of "church members in good standing." The appendix ends with a table, with columns for place name, number of islands, supposed population, state (that is, "Christian," "Mostly Christian," "Partially Christian," or "Heathen"), and the number of missionaries, with a note on which missionary society they are attached to. In some respects, this simple table is the core of Cook's world. Demarcating one place from another and describing each place in terms of fixed categories, the table creates a field of places, each with their specific location, attributes, and historical data. The appendices update the information and thus, if nothing else, affirm the same world and help globalized projects to change it.

What emerges in Cook's voyages, then, is a sense of global control, based on the collection and the political power that supports it, which parallels the relationship between the nation and the state. Now, however, the nation has become humanity, and the state has become, or will become, the empire. But this empire is not the English or the French or the German empire, but empire as such. Cook, in other words, does not simply give Great Britain Greater Britain; he ties the entire world together into a single system of relations, as comprehensive as the coordinate system, as clear and distinct as the map. The world becomes the human world, mediated but never completely owned by men of consequence in Europe.

The sense of empire that emerges from Cook's voyages is thus most clearly imagined through Cook's own relationship to the world. Not only is he a collector who transcends his collection, he is also a person who transcends his national identity. While English, he is also humanity incarnate. As Kippis notes, Cook's voyages were undertaken from "the enlarged and benevolent design of promoting the happiness of the human species."[49] Thus, rather than being the captain of a nation's (a king's) ship, Cook is the captain of an enlightenment ship, and he can claim honour from the world. The account of place in Cook's voyages, therefore, is tied to Cook's own transcendence, not only over his collection, but also beyond any particular national or political attachment. By being the authority behind the voyages, therefore, Cook becomes a citizen of the world, asserting the claims of all the other world citizens (and institutions) to come.

Conclusions

No one had travelled like Captain Cook, and no one will be able to again. Before his voyages, the world was uncertain and dangerous; after them, it was clear and safe. The voyages took the fragmented and obscure printed texts that contained plausible descriptions and consolidated them into a single textual, tabular vision of the entire world. The places of the world were then understood as both fragmented and clear. It was then possible to seriously travel only in Cook's wake, to be always moving either within, or in reaction to the accounts of the world published under his name.

Whatever may be new in Cook's voyages, the account of the world remains a variation on a Cartesian world, where mathematics and physics are tied together, and where the goal of science is the ever more exact representation of natural entities and processes. Specific events are subsumed under general and often highly complex laws, while the world, the cosmos, is viewed as matter in motion, woven together in causal chains. Cook's voyages do not challenge this worldview, but the voyages also affirm the importance of what does not move, of what forms the basis on which changes in the material and specifically human world can be understood. The world is not simply a Cartesian, perfectly flat plane. What is most important in Cook's voyages, and what becomes the key for making the world and all of its inhabitants intelligible, is cartography. The worldview becomes a view of the world: a picture of space taken from far above, as it were, by a geometrically inclined observer who has transcended particular places and has engaged with the terrain of possible locations precisely because he could fixate on particular places so well.

In Cook's voyages, the articulations of place weave together knowledge and power, not only creating new instances of both, but also changing the way that knowledge and power are organized. The shift from coasts to areas, in combination with the ability to accurately measure longitude, reworked political and economic relations. The ability to accurately trace the outlines of places, and to situate those places on a grid that is first geographical, and then national and political, allows the accumulation of considerable information from around the world. The voyages thus also help create the institutions that manage the accumulation of that data. Lastly, the ability to publish all of the elements of this account in books, organized around a single authoritative voice, allows the world and the different ways of understanding it to be unfolded through the text as a single, coherent narrative.

Cook, as a national and global hero, illustrates a specific manifestation of power and authority. The creation of empire depended at first on regulating the other voices (those of the natives, of the English, of the Europeans, and of Cook himself). The authoritarian voice was held together by various European institutions, both scientific and political, that were animated by desires for knowledge and power. The diversity of texts and authors thus existed alongside a series of institutions that helped create and maintain the unity and importance of the voyages. As a result, domination and power were held together through the logic of the voice and the structures of geopolitical intelligibility.

Cook, as a biographical figure, has become someone whose voyages created real knowledge about the world, who presented that knowledge to anyone willing and able to read it, and who offered a model for those who wanted to fill in the parts of the picture that remained empty. He has become the Copernicus of exploration.

Cook's voyages affirm specific ontological commitments concerning, among other things, the relationship between mathematics and space and between human identity and the physical world. The voyages maintain a close connection between geographical and national identities, where human beings, or at least primitive human beings, are primarily created by their environments. Thus, a space is made for civilization, not only as geographical areas in Europe, but also as a series of interventions in the natural world and its uncivilized, naturalized inhabitants. Cook is animated by an imperative to know the world, but he is also animated by a desire to change it. Economic, social, and theological values are intertwined in the relationships between the ships and the shores, and are thus also intertwined with the frequent, sometimes fatal, and often moralized use of force. Greg Dening's *Islands and Beaches*, Alan Moorehead's *Fatal Impact*, and Paul Carter's *Road to Botany Bay* each discuss the relationships in detail.

The explorations offer an idea of empire, not only by creating a mean-ingful terrain on which empires could be imagined, but also by creating a sense of the relations that can and ought to be created between the en-lightened people of Europe and the primitive or savage people every-where, including in Europe itself. Unenlightened people, no matter what nation they belong to, are everywhere the same.

The logic of Cook's account of the places of the world appears trium-phant – in the introductions and subsequent popularizations, it is typi-cally described and celebrated in glorious terms. Not only does Cook clearly demonstrate the existence or non-existence of places, his voyages also offer reliable, accurate accounts of the natural and human world. The move from places to nations is as deductive, it would seem, as the move from points to lines. But perhaps it is the space in between the articulations that is the most important: the likenesses that Cook's voy-ages establish, without and even in spite of the evidence, between islands, nations, states, collections, and empires.

What is finally created by the authors, the books, and the institutions that all take up the manuscripts, by the artifacts and the proper names of the voyages, is a world picture built on maps and narrated through as-tronomical observations and tables of numbers. It is a worldview that is supported by an arrogance – sometimes based on reason, sometimes on civilization, sometimes on theology, and always on available firearms – in which other images of the world, and other ways of life, are under-stood as misguided, superstitious, incomplete, or infantile. The worldview thus not only offers a view of the world, it also creates a position for the viewer: both the collection and the collector are included in the com-plete system.

It is only later that the English acquire their empire, not as a dispersed system of influence, but as a formal collection of places, as if places were stamps. Cook, then, becomes an important point of origin, someone who has articulated the world and given the collected world, as a gift, to his nation. Thus, the two images of empire come to coexist: the one focusing on specific political sovereignty, the other on dispersed moral and economic influence. And it is with these two senses of empire that nineteenth-century Europe organized the world, first in collecting terri-torial units that became formally subject to imperial nations, and then in promoting movements throughout the world that may originate in a sovereign nation, but that travel in the oceanic spaces that connect all the places of the world together.

Notes

INTRODUCTIONS

1 Joseph Conrad, "Geography and Some Explorers," in *Last Essays*, introduction by Richard Curle (New York: Doubleday, 1926), 2.

2 Paul Carter, *The Road to Botany Bay: An Exploration of Landscape and History* (New York: Alfred A. Knopf, 1988), 69.

3 Ibid., 81.

4 Ibid., 12.

5 Ibid., 7.

6 The importance of the printing press for establishing precedence in scientific research is discussed by Elizabeth Eisenstein in *The Printing Press As an Agent of Change: Communications and Cultural Transformations in Early-Modern Europe*, vol. 2 (Cambridge: Cambridge University Press, 1979), passim.

7 Bruce Chatwin, *The Songlines* (London: Penguin Books, 1988), 13.

8 Ibid., 108.

9 Carter, *The Road to Botany Bay*, 7.

10 Marshall Sahlins, *Islands of History* (Chicago: University of Chicago Press, 1985), 109.

11 Paul Kaufmann, *Borrowings from the Bristol Library, 1773-1784* (Charlottesville, VA: Bibliographical Society of the University of Virginia, 1960), 113.

12 See ibid., passim.

13 A detailed historical reconstruction of the impact of the published accounts of Cook's voyages remains to be written. A good example of this sort of book is James Secord's *Victorian Sensation: The Extraordinary Publication, Reception, and Secret Authorship of Vestiges of the Natural History of Creation* (Chicago: University of Chicago Press, 2000), which focuses on the reception of the *Vestiges of the Natural History of Creation*, first published in 1844. A concern for the historical reception of Cook's voyages, however, has been almost completely marginalized by the reception of J.C. Beaglehole's edition of Cook's voyages, which has placed so much emphasis on the manuscripts that it has led people away from a concern for the history of the books, the reprints, the reworkings, and so on.

14 Kaufmann, *Borrowings from the Bristol Library*, 122.

15 The complete title of Sloane's book, which gives a sense of how the places are described, is *A Voyage to the Islands Madiera, Barbados, Nieves, S. Christophers and Jamaica, with the natural history of the herbs and trees, four-footed beasts, fishes, birds, insects, reptiles, &c. &c. of the last of those islands; to which is prefix'd an introduction, wherein is an account of the inhabitants, air, waters, diseases, trade, &c. &c. of that place, with some relations concerning the neighbouring continent, and islands of America.*

16 Susan Stewart, *On Longing: Narratives of the Miniature, the Gigantic, the Souvenir, the Collection* (Baltimore: Johns Hopkins University Press, 1984), 4.
17 Admiralty, *The Voyages of Captain James Cook,* vol. 5 (London: Longman, Hurst, Rees, Orme, and Brown, 1821), 433. References to the *Voyages* are to this edition unless otherwise stipulated.
18 Rickman, *Journal of Captain Cook's Last Voyage to the Pacific Ocean on* Discovery; *Performed in the Years 1776, 1777, 1778, 1779* (1781; facsimile reprint, New York: Da Capo, 1967), 78.
19 Conrad, "Geography and Some Explorers," 19.

CHAPTER 1: POINTS
 1 *Philosophical Transactions,* 8 January 1665-6, in John Locke, *The Whole History of Navigation,* in *The Works of John Locke,* vol. 10 (London: Thomas Tegg, 1823), 508. The attribution of this work to Locke has been challenged by E.S. DeBeer.
 2 Locke, *The Whole History of Navigation,* vol. 10, 405.
 3 Ibid., 372.
 4 Ibid., 401.
 5 Ibid., 391.
 6 Ibid., 427.
 7 Ibid., 431. Paria was along the northern coast of South America, just south of Trinidad.
 8 Glyndwr Williams, *The Great South Sea: English Voyages and Encounters 1570-1750* (New Haven, CT: Yale University Press, 1997), 3.
 9 Ibid., 47.
10 Locke, *The Whole History of Navigation,* vol. 10, 483.
11 Ibid., 484. At the end of the summary of islands associated with America, Locke notes that "the only great island on this side [of] America is California," which is also located in terms of the nearby continent (p. 484).
12 Admiralty, *The Voyages of Captain James Cook,* vol. 1 (London: Longman, Hurst, Rees, Orme, and Brown, 1821), 479.
13 J.C. Beaglehole, *The Life of Captain James Cook* (Stanford, CA: Stanford University Press, 1974), 133. The quote is from a copy of Wallis's manuscript journal, 20 August 1766.
14 Paul Carter, *The Road to Botany Bay: An Exploration of Landscape and History* (New York: Alfred A. Knopf, 1988), 18.
15 Ibid., 14.
16 Ibid., 15.
17 Ibid., 31. Carter overstates the contrast between the natural and cultural orders. There are also natural names throughout Cook's voyages, describing the geographical or biological character of the places, such as Turtle Island and the Isle of Pines.
18 Ibid., 71.
19 See Beulah Tannenbaum and Myra Stillman, *Understanding Maps: Charting the Land, Sea, and Sky* (New York: McGraw-Hill, 1969), ch. 5.
20 Quoted in Glyndwr Williams, *The Great South Sea: English Voyages and Encounters 1570-1750* (New Haven: Yale University Press, 1997), 117.
21 This incident is discussed by Dava Sobel in *Longitude* (New York: Walker Publishing, 1995), 17-20. See also Derek Howse, *Greenwich Time and the Discovery of the Longitude* (Oxford: Oxford University Press, 1980) for a general discussion of the issue.
22 The two techniques were also competing. With the establishment of the Board of Longitude in 1714, Parliament also provided "a Reward, or Sum of Ten Thousand

Pounds, if it Determines the said Longitude to One Degree of a great Circle, or Sixty Geographical Miles; to Fifteen Thousand Pounds, if it Determines the same to Two Thirds of that Distance." Howse, *Greenwich Time and the Discovery of the Longitude*, 51.

23 See J.C. Beaglehole, *The Journals of Captain Cook*, vol. 1 (London: Hakluyt Society, 1968), 119.

24 Admiralty, *Voyages*, vol. 4, 245.

25 Ibid., 40.

26 Quoted in Neil Rennie, *Far-Fetched Facts: The Literature of Travel and the Idea of the South Seas* (Oxford: Clarendon Press, 1995), 30.

27 Ibid., 30.

28 Admiralty, *Voyages*, vol. 3, 316.

29 Ibid., vol. 2, 66.

30 See the discussion of Vancouver's survey of the west coast of North America in Alun Davies, "Testing a New Technology: Captain George Vancouver's Survey and Navigation in Alaskan Waters, 1794," in *Enlightenment and Exploration in the North Pacific*, ed. Stephen Haycox, James Barnett, and Caedmon Liburd (Anchorage, AK: Cook Inlet Historical Society), 103-15.

31 See Otto von Kotzebue, *A Voyage of Discovery into the South Sea and Bering's Straits, for the Purpose of Exploring a North-East Passage, Undertaken in the Years 1815-1818*, vol. 1 (1821; facsimile reprint, New York: Da Capo, 1967), 16.

32 Michel Foucault, "What Is an Author?," in *The Foucault Reader* (New York: Pantheon Books, 1984), 112.

33 Walter Besant, *Captain Cook* (London: Macmillan and Co., 1925), 146.

34 Admiralty, *Voyages*, vol. 3, 153.

35 Ibid., 305.

36 Ibid., vol. 4, 219.

37 Ibid., vol. 2, 5.

38 Ibid., vol. 3, 275.

39 Ibid., vol. 4, 254.

40 Ibid., vol. 3, 314.

41 Ibid., vol. 4, 148.

42 Andrew Kippis, *A Narrative of the Voyages round the World Performed by Captain James Cook, with an account of his life during the previous and intervening periods* (Philadelphia: Henry Coates, [1900?]), 290.

43 Eisenstein, *The Printing Press as an Agent of Change: Communications and Cultural Transformations in Early-Modern Europe*, vol. 2 (Cambridge: Cambridge University Press, 1979), 582.

44 Parkinson, *A Journal of a Voyage to the South Seas, in His Majesty's Ship, the* Endeavour (1773; facsimile reprint, London: Caliban Books, 1984), 86.

45 Admiralty, *Voyages*, vol. 1, 192.

46 Ibid., vol. 3, 264.

47 Ibid., vol. 2, 63.

48 Kippis, *A Narrative of the Voyages*, 202.

CHAPTER 2: SHAPES

1 Aristotle, *Physics*, 212a18 in *The Complete Works of Aristotle*, rev. Oxford translation, vol. 1 (Princeton: Princeton University Press, 1984), 361.

2 Immanuel Kant, *The Metaphysics of Morals*, ed. Mary Gregor (Cambridge: Cambridge University Press, 1996), 121.

3   Admiralty, *The Voyages of Captain James Cook,* vol. 3 (London: Longman, Hurst, Rees, Orme, and Brown, 1821), 255.

4   Francis Bacon, *New Atlantis,* as quoted in Neil Rennie, *Far-Fetched Facts: The Literature of Travel and the Idea of the South Seas* (Oxford: Clarendon Press, 1995), 44.

5   John Rickman, *Journal of Captain Cook's Last Voyage to the Pacific Ocean on* Discovery; *Performed in the Years 1776, 1777, 1778, 1779* (1781; facsimile reprint, New York: Da Capo, 1967), 100.

6   Admiralty, *Voyages,* vol. 3, 271. The manuscript version is essentially the same.

7   Ibid., 41.

8   Ibid., 46. See Smith's discussion of Coleridge in *Imagining the Pacific in the Wake of the Cook Voyages* (Melbourne: Melbourne University Press, 1992), ch. 6.

9   Admiralty, *Voyages,* vol. 3, 56.

10 Ibid., 260.

11 Ibid., 65. As an aside, in 1830 Edward Bulwer-Lytton (1803-73) published *Paul Clifford,* which began, "It was a dark and stormy night; the rain fell in torrents – except at occasional intervals, when it was checked by a violent gust of wind which swept up the streets." Some work has been done to connect Cook's voyages (and the second one in particular) to poets such as Coleridge. Similar work does not seem to exist yet that connects these voyages to gothic novels. Horace Walpole's *The Castle of Otranto,* published in 1764, and Ann Radcliff's *The Mysteries of Udolpho,* published in 1794, were two early works in the genre.

12 Admiralty, *Voyages,* vol. 3, 44.

13 Ibid., 47.

14 Ibid., 75.

15 John Marra, *Journal of the* Resolution*'s Voyage in 1772, 1773, 1774, and 1775, on Discovery to the Southern Hemisphere* (1775; facsimile reprint, New York: Da Capo, 1967), 6.

16 Ibid., 111.

17 Admiralty, *Voyages,* vol. 3, 270.

18 Ibid., 273.

19 Paul Carter, *The Road to Botany Bay: An Exploration of Landscape and History* (New York: Alfred A. Knopf, 1988), 93.

20 Ibid., 245.

21 Admiralty, *Voyages,* vol. 4, 157.

22 Ibid., 263.

23 Ibid., 242.

24 Cook's second voyage took a little over three years (13 July 1772 to 30 July 1775). Anson's voyage had taken three months longer than Cook's second voyage (18 September 1740 to 15 June 1744), while Carteret's voyage had taken roughly two and a half years (22 August 1766 to 20 March 1769).

25 Admiralty, *Voyages,* vol. 3, 272.

26 Joseph Conrad, "Geography and Some Explorers," in *Last Essays,* introduction by Richard Curle (New York: Doubleday, 1926), 5.

27 Admiralty, *Voyages,* vol. 3, 275.

28 Ibid., 150.

29 J.C. Beaglehole, *The Journals of Captain Cook,* vol. 2 (London: Hakluyt Society, 1968), 189.

30 In the first volume of *Hawaiian National Bibliography,* Forbes notes an interesting variation on this public valuation of the islands in Rickman's account of the third voyage.

The first printing of the book contained a general assessment of the discoveries in the Pacific, which referred to "that unfruitful sea, where nothing is to be expected but a few unprofitable islands thinly scattered, and, now and then, as it were by accident, to be touched upon, to reward the toil and hazard of a tiresome and painful search." In many copies of Rickman's work, the leaf that contained this paragraph was excised, and a new one inserted without this negative assessment of the ocean. See David W. Forbes, *Hawaiian National Bibliography, 1780-1900*, vol. 1 (Hawai'i: University of Hawai'i Press, 1993), 24, entry 33.

31 Admiralty, *Voyages*, vol. 4, 128.
32 Ibid., vol. 1, 398.
33 Ibid., vol. 4, 89.
34 Ibid., 90.
35 Ibid., vol. 2, 18.
36 Ibid., vol. 5, 178.
37 Ibid., vol. 4, 193.
38 Ibid., 95.
39 Ibid., 207.
40 Ibid., 202.
41 Thomas Hobbes, *Leviathan*, in *The English Works of Thomas Hobbes*, ed. William Molesworth, vol. 3 (London: John Bohn, 1839), 677.
42 Immanuel Kant, *The Critique of Pure Reason*, trans. Norman Kemp Smith (New York: St. Martin's Press, 1965), 257.
43 See Bernard Smith, *European Vision and the South Pacific* (New Haven, CT: Yale University Press, 1988), 18.
44 Ibid., 109.
45 Admiralty, *Voyages*, vol. 6, 77, footnote.
46 Mary Louise Pratt, *Imperial Eyes: Travel Writing and Transculturation* (London: Routledge, 1992), 23.
47 Humboldt, *Personal Narrative of a Voyage to the Equinoctial Regions*, vol. 1 (n.p., 1822), vii, as quoted in Pratt, *Imperial Eyes*, 24.
48 Carter, *The Road to Botany Bay*, 91.
49 Ibid., 95, 289.
50 Ibid., 92.
51 Bruce Chatwin, *The Songlines* (London: Penguin Books, 1988), 128.

CHAPTER 3: NATIONS

1 James Boswell, *Life of Johnson*, vol. 8 (London: Henry G. Bohn, 1851), 312. The three volumes referred to are the authorized edition of Cook's third voyage, which was first published in 1784.
2 Ibid., vol. 6, 154.
3 Ibid., 124.
4 J.C. Beaglehole, *The Journals of Captain Cook*, vol. 1 (London: Hakluyt Society, 1968), xciv. See also Gavin Daws, *A Dream of Islands: Voyages of Self-Discovery in the South Seas* (New York: W.W. Norton, 1980), 4.
5 Admiralty, *The Voyages of Captain James Cook*, vol. 3 (London: Longman, Hurst, Rees, Orme, and Brown, 1821), 343.
6 Beaglehole, *The Journals of Captain Cook*, vol. 1, 509, Letter to John Walker. The editorial notations are Beaglehole's.

7   Anders Sparrman, *A Voyage round the World with Captain James Cook in H.M.S.* Resolu-
     tion (London: Golden Cockerel Press, 1944), 187-8, as quoted in Neil Rennie, *Far-
     Fetched Facts: The Literature of Travel and the Idea of the South Seas* (Oxford: Clarendon
     Press, 1995), 125.
8   Admiralty, *Voyages*, vol. 4, 61.
9   Bernard Smith, *European Vision and the South Pacific* (New Haven, CT: Yale University
     Press, 1988), 122.
10 Boswell, *Life of Johnson*, vol. 2, 221.
11 Smith, *European Vision and the South Pacific*, 87.
12 Ibid., 12.
13 Admiralty, *Voyages*, vol. 1, 125.
14 Beaglehole, *The Journals of Captain Cook*, vol. 3, 490.
15 Admiralty, *Voyages*, vol. 6, 502.
16 Paul Carter, *The Road to Botany Bay: An Exploration of Landscape and History* (New York:
     Alfred A. Knopf, 1988), 67. "St. George" in the quote should be "King George" – Wallis
     named the island after George III.
17 Admiralty, *Voyages*, vol. 4, 124.
18 Ibid., 194.
19 Ibid., 5.
20 Ibid., 45.
21 Ibid., vol. 6, 255.
22 Ibid., 309.
23 Ibid., vol. 3, 157 and vol. 1, 100.
24 Walter Besant, *Captain Cook* (London: Macmillan and Co., 1925), 136. See also p. 179.
     George Forster was also closely connected to the late-eighteenth- and nineteenth-
     century anthropology, specifically in Germany.
25 Admiralty, *Voyages*, vol. 3, 25.
26 Ibid., vol. 1, 282.
27 Ibid., 282.
28 Ibid., 282.
29 Bernard Smith, *Imagining the Pacific: In the Wake of the Cook Voyages* (Melbourne: Mel-
     bourne University Press, 1992), 77.
30 Admiralty, *Voyages*, vol. 1, 304.
31 Ibid., vol. 4, 109.
32 William Wales, *Remarks on Mr. Forster's Account of Captain Cook's Last Voyage round the
     World in the Years 1772, 1773, 1774, and 1775* (London: J. Nourse, 1778), 28.
33 George Mortimer, *Observations and Remarks Made during a Voyage to the Islands of Teneriffe,
     Amsterdam, Maria's Islands near Van Diemen's Land; Otaheite, Sandwich Islands; Owhyhee,
     the Fox Islands on the North West Coast of America, Tinian, and from thence to Canton, in the
     Brig* Mercury, *Commanded by John Henry Cox, Esq.* (1791; Facsimile reprint, New York:
     Da Capo, 1975), 60.
34 See William Dampier, *The Voyages of Captain William Dampier,* ed. John Masefield, vol. 1
     (London: E. Grant Richards, 1905), 496.
35 Rennie, *Far-Fetched Facts,* 64.
36 Admiralty, *Voyages*, vol. 3, 179.
37 Immanuel Kant, "Review of Herder's *Ideas on the Philosophy of the History of Mankind*,"
     in *Political Writings*, ed. Hans Reiss (Cambridge: Cambridge University Press, 1991),
     214.

38 Elizabeth Eisenstein, *The Printing Press As an Agent of Change: Communications and Cultural Transformations in Early-Modern Europe*, vol. 2 (Cambridge: Cambridge University Press, 1979), 697.

39 Boswell, *Life of Johnson*, vol. 3, 242.

40 Admiralty, *Voyages*, vol. 2, 224.

41 Ibid., vol. 3, 132.

42 Ibid., vol. 5, 185.

43 Ibid., vol. 1, 188.

44 Ibid., vol. 4, 109.

45 John Rickman, *Journal of Captain Cook's Last Voyage to the Pacific Ocean on Discovery; Performed in the Years 1776, 1777, 1778, 1779* (1781; facsimile reprint, New York: Da Capo, 1967), 332.

46 Admiralty, *Voyages*, vol. 1, 381.

47 Ibid., 379.

48 Ibid., 384.

49 Ibid., vol. 3, 248.

50 James Adair, *The History of the American Indians: Particularly those Nations Adjoining to the Mississippi, East and West Florida, Georgia, South and North Carolina, and Virginia* (London: E. and C. Dilly, 1775), 226.

51 Ibid., 228.

52 Admiralty, *Voyages*, vol. 2, 43.

53 Beaglehole, *The Journals of Captain Cook*, vol. 2, 116.

54 Admiralty, *Voyages*, vol. 3, 90.

55 Ruth Dawson, "Mythologizing Pacific Women: Cook's Second Voyage" (paper presented at Pacific Science Congress, 27 May-2 June 1991, Honolulu), 11.

56 Carter, *The Road to Botany Bay*, 8.

57 Ibid., 18.

58 Ibid., 20. The Banks quote is from Banks's journal.

59 Admiralty, *Voyages*, vol. 4, 172.

60 Smith, *European Vision and the South Pacific*, 4.

61 Admiralty, *Voyages*, vol. 5, 193.

62 Ibid., vol. 6, 227.

63 Ibid., 136.

64 Ibid., vol. 3, 285.

65 Beaglehole, *The Journals of Captain Cook*, vol. 1, xciv.

66 Smith, *European Vision and the South Pacific*, 137.

CHAPTER 4: STATES

1 Thomas Hobbes, *Leviathan*, in *The English Works of Thomas Hobbes*, ed. William Molesworth, vol. 3 (London: John Bohn, 1839), 151.

2 Ibid., 568.

3 Ibid., 188.

4 Ibid., 184.

5 Ibid., 201.

6 Hobbes, *Behemoth*, in *The English Works of Thomas Hobbes*, vol. 6, 374.

7 Ibid., 205.

8 John Locke, *Second Treatise on Government*, in *The Works of John Locke*, vol. 5 (London: Thomas Tegg, 1823), section 25.

9 Ibid., section 27.

10 Ibid., section 28. This image will be echoed by Kant.

11 Ibid., section 32.

12 Ibid.

13 Jean-Jacques Rousseau, *On the Social Contract*, in *The Basic Political Writings*, trans. Peter Gay (Indianapolis: Hackett Publishing Company, 1987), 166.

14 Jean-Jacques Rousseau, *The Government of Poland*, trans. Willmore Kendall (Indianapolis: Bobbs-Merrill, 1972), 80.

15 Rousseau, *On the Social Contract*, 170.

16 Rousseau, *The Government of Poland*, 26.

17 Rousseau, *On the Social Contract*, 205.

18 Adam Ferguson, *An Essay on the History of Civil Society* (1767; Edinburgh: Edinburgh University Press, 1966), 120.

19 Rousseau, *On the Social Contract*, 152.

20 Admiralty, *The Voyages of Captain James Cook*, vol. 3 (London: Longman, Hurst, Rees, Orme, and Brown, 1821), 219.

21 Ibid., 213.

22 Ibid., 228.

23 William Ellis, *An Authentic Narrative of a Voyage Performed by Captain Cook and Captain Clerke, in His Majesty's Ships* Resolution *and* Discovery *during the years 1776, 1777, 1778, 1779 and 1780*, vol. 1 (1782; facsimile reprint, New York: Da Capo, 1969), 73.

24 Admiralty, *Voyages*, vol. 4, 147.

25 See Glyndwr Williams, *The Great South Sea: English Voyages and Encounters 1570-1750* (New Haven, CT: Yale University Press, 1997), xiv, for a description of early-eighteenth-century European ships organized in terms of the political factions of the day.

26 Admiralty, *Voyages*, vol. 4, 223.

27 See, for instance, Walter Besant, *Captain Cook* (London: Macmillan and Co., 1925), 179.

28 John Marra, *Journal of the* Resolution's *Voyage in 1772, 1773, 1774, and 1775, on Discovery to the Southern Hemisphere* (1775; facsimile reprint, New York: Da Capo, 1967), 181.

29 Admiralty, *Voyages*, vol. 6, 306.

30 Immanuel Kant, *Idea for a Universal History with a Cosmopolitan Purpose*, in *Political Writings*, ed. Hans Reiss (Cambridge: Cambridge University Press, 1991), 41.

31 See, for instance, Thomas Strack, "Philosophical Anthropology on the Eve of Biological Determinism: Immanuel Kant and Georg Forster on the Moral Qualities and Biological Characteristics of the Human Race," *Central European History* 29, 3 (1996): 285-308.

32 See Bernard Smith, *European Vision and the South Pacific* (New Haven, CT: Yale University Press, 1988), 203.

33 Immanuel Kant, *Anthropology from a Pragmatic Point of View* (The Hague: Martinus Nijhoff, 1974), ix. The published version of Kant's notes was from his own last version, making it impossible to see any changes through time.

34 Ibid., 178. See Eve Darian-Smith's discussion of the channel in *Bridging Divides: the Channel Tunnel and English Legal Identity in the New Europe* (Berkeley: University of California Press, 1999).

35 Kant, *Anthropology from a Pragmatic Point of View*, 178.

36 Ibid., 181.

37 Kant, *Political Writings*, 219; and his *Critique of Judgment* (Indianapolis, IN: Hackett Publishing, 1987), 247.

38 Immanuel Kant, *The Metaphysics of Morals*, ed. Mary Gregor (Cambridge: Cambridge University Press, 1996), 52.

39 Ibid., 56.

40 Ibid., 52.

41 Ibid., 123.

42 Ibid., 50.

43 Kant, *Perpetual Peace*, in *Political Writings*, 114.

44 Kant, *The Metaphysics of Morals*, 53.

45 Ibid., 119.

46 Ibid., 53.

47 Kant, *Perpetual Peace*, 108.

48 Kant, *Idea for a Universal History with a Cosmopolitan Purpose*, 47.

49 Edward Said, *Culture and Imperialism* (New York: Vintage Books, 1994), 254.

50 Otto von Kotzebue, *A Voyage of Discovery into the South Sea and Bering's Straits, for the Purpose of Exploring a North-East Passage, Undertaken in the Years 1815-1818*, vol. 2 (1821; facsimile reprint, New York: Da Capo, 1967), 189.

51 Ibid., 195.

52 Ibid., 191.

53 Ibid., 189.

54 One example of the clarification of borders in the nineteenth century is described in Peter Sahlins, *Boundaries: The Making of France and Spain in the Pyrenees* (Berkeley: University of California Press, 1989).

55 Kedourie, *Nationalism* (Oxford: Basil Blackwell, 1998), 1.

CHAPTER 5: COLLECTIONS

1 John Locke, *The Whole History of Navigation*, in *The Works of John Locke*, vol. 10 (London: Thomas Tegg, 1823), 378.

2 Georg Forster, *A Voyage round the World in His Britannic Majesty's Sloop*, Resolution, *Commanded by Captain James Cook, during the Years 1772, 3, 4, and 5*, vol. 2 (London: B. White et. al., 1777), 606.

3 Anthony Shelton, "Cabinets of Transgression: Renaissance Collections and the New World," in *The Cultures of Collecting*, ed. John Elsner and Roger Cardinal (Cambridge, MA: Harvard University Press, 1994), 184.

4 Admiralty, *The Voyages of Captain James Cook*, vol. 5 (London: Longman, Hurst, Rees, Orme, and Brown, 1821), 67. According to Greg Dening, the early (1950s) analyses offered by Sahlins "belonged to a period in which there was some excitement in the thought of Polynesia as a sort of laboratory in which the observer had some control over the factors which affected the differing evolution of Polynesian societies in their differing environments." Greg Dening, *Islands and Beaches: Discourse on a Silent Land: Marquesas 1774-1880* (Chicago: Dorsey Press, 1980), 285.

5 Admiralty, *Voyages*, vol. 2, 290. See also Sydney Parkinson, *A Journal of a Voyage to the South Seas, in His Majesty's Ship, the* Endeavour (1773; facsimile reprint, London: Caliban Books, 1984), 175.

6 John Rickman, *Journal of Captain Cook's Last Voyage to the Pacific Ocean on* Discovery; *Performed in the Years 1776, 1777, 1778, 1779* (1781; facsimile reprint, New York: Da Capo, 1967), 186.

7 Bernard Smith, *European Vision and the South Pacific* (New Haven, CT: Yale University Press, 1988), 117.

8   See ibid., 113.

9   Elizabeth Eisenstein, *The Printing Press As an Agent of Change: Communications and Cultural Transformations in Early-Modern Europe,* vol. 2 (Cambridge: Cambridge University Press, 1979), 520.

10   John Marra, *Journal of the* Resolution's *Voyage in 1772, 1773, 1774, and 1775, on Discovery to the Southern Hemisphere* (1775; facsimile reprint, New York: Da Capo, 1967), 58.

11   Eisenstein, *The Printing Press As an Agent of Change,* vol. 1, 85.

12   Ibid., 109.

13   Andrew Kippis, *A Narrative of the Voyages round the World Performed by Captain James Cook, with an account of his life during the previous and intervening periods* (Philadelphia: Henry Coates, [1900?]), 405.

14   Admiralty, *Voyages,* vol. 2, 200.

15   Smith, *European Vision and the South Pacific,* 133.

16   William Goetzmann, *New Lands, New Men: America and the Second Great Age of Discovery* (New York: Viking, 1986), 269.

17   Admiralty, *Voyages,* vol. 6, 131. Anderson is being quoted.

18   Immanuel Kant, *Anthropology from a Pragmatic Point of View* (The Hague: Martinus Nijhoff, 1974), 4.

19   Daniel Defoe, *The Complete English Gentleman* (London: David Nutt, 1890), 225.

20   Jehoshaphat Aspin, *Cosmorama: A View of the Costumes and Peculiarities of All Nations* (London: J. Harris, 1827), 404.

21   J.C. Beaglehole, *Cook the Writer* (Sydney: Sydney University Press, 1970), 21.

22   Admiralty, *Voyages,* vol. 6, 176.

23   Ibid., 176.

24   Ibid., 180.

25   Ibid., 181.

26   Ibid., 204.

27   Ibid., 179.

28   Ibid., vol. 1, 191.

29   Ibid., vol. 6, 212.

30   Kippis, *A Narrative of the Voyages,* 299.

31   J.C. Beaglehole, *The Journals of Captain Cook,* vol. 3 (London: Hakluyt Society, 1968), 491.

32   The gap in the journal has received very little attention the literature on Cook's voyages. Beaglehole mentions it in his introduction. See Beaglehole, *The Journals of Captain Cook,* vol. 3, clxxi.

33   Goetzmann, *New Lands, New Men,* 279.

34   Admiralty, *Voyages,* vol. 3, 276.

35   Ibid., vol. 4, 30.

36   Ibid., vol. 3, 222.

37   Ibid., 184.

38   Rickman, *Journal of Captain Cook's Last Voyage to the Pacific Ocean on* Discovery, 126.

39   William Ellis, *An Authentic Narrative of a Voyage Performed by Captain Cook and Captain Clerke, in His Majesty's Ships* Resolution *and* Discovery *during the years 1776, 1777, 1778, 1779 and 1780,* vol. 1 (1782; facsimile reprint, New York: Da Capo, 1969), 146.

40   Admiralty, *Voyages,* vol. 4, 31.

41   Ibid., vol. 3, 142.

42   Rickman, *Journal of Captain Cook's Last Voyage to the Pacific Ocean on* Discovery, 163.

43   See Smith, *European Vision and the South Pacific,* 7.

44 Admiralty, *Voyages,* vol. 1, 196.

45 Ibid., 306.

46 Darian-Smith, *Bridging Divides: The Channel Tunnel and English Legal Identity in the New Europe* (Berkeley: University of California Press, 1999), 45.

47 Ibid., 55-6.

48 One of the themes that arises within this conceptual system is a concern for where in the world the English could belong. Here, the concern is not so much about the impact of "other climates" on English identity – the English encounters with these other climates is transitory. The key question, which is the question of colonialism, is to determine the climates that are similar enough to England for the English to live there.

49 For an example from a different account of the voyage, see Marra, *Journal of the Resolution's Voyage in 1771-1775,* 226.

50 Admiralty, *Voyages,* vol. 5, 67.

51 Bernard Smith, *Imagining the Pacific: In the Wake of the Cook Voyages* (Melbourne: Melbourne University Press, 1992), 233.

52 Admiralty, *Voyages,* vol. 6, 132.

53 Ibid., vol. 5, 191.

54 Ibid., vol. 3, 163.

55 Ibid., vol. 5, 114.

56 Ibid., vol. 4, 73.

57 Ibid., vol. 6, 165. The text is probably from Anderson's manuscript, now lost.

58 Ibid., vol. 3, 142. See also vol. 4, 267.

CHAPTER 6: EMPIRES

1 Edward Said, *Culture and Imperialism* (New York: Vintage Books, 1994), 11.

2 Franco Moretti, *Atlas of the European Novel: 1800 to 1900* (London: Verso, 1998), 26.

3 Ibid., 27.

4 This is a term used by Thomas Salmon in *A New Geographical and Historical Grammar* (London: William Johnston, 1749).

5 Compare, for instance, the headings to the two versions of chapter 30 in *Leviathan,* where the Latin "De Officio Summi Imperii" is equated with "the Office of the Sovereign Representative," and a passage in chapter 10, where "qui regebant imperii limites" is equated with the "bounds of the empire." For the Latin version, see Hobbes, *The Latin Works of Thomas Hobbes,* ed. William Molesworth, vol. 3 (London: John Bohn, 1839), 76. For the English version, see Hobbes, *The English Works of Thomas Hobbes,* ed. William Molesworth, vol. 3 (London: John Bohn, 1839), 83.

6 Locke, *Two Treatises of Government,* in *The Works of John Locke,* vol. 5 (London: Thomas Tegg, 1823), 274, 275.

7 Ibid., 324, 325.

8 Ibid., 411.

9 Hobbes, *Leviathan,* in *The English Works of Thomas Hobbes,* vol. 3, 240.

10 Ibid., 216.

11 Ibid., 155.

12 Jean-Jacques Rousseau, *On the Social Contract,* in *The Basic Political Writings,* trans. Peter Gay (Indianapolis: Hackett Publishing Company, 1987), 152.

13 Andrew Kippis, *A Narrative of the Voyages round the World Performed by Captain James Cook, with an account of his life during the previous and intervening periods* (Philadelphia: Henry Coates, [1900?]), 131.

14 Admiralty, *The Voyages of Captain James Cook*, vol. 2 (London: Longman, Hurst, Rees, Orme, and Brown, 1821), 196.
15 Walter Besant, *Captain Cook* (London: Macmillan and Co., 1925), 84.
16 Paul Carter, *The Road to Botany Bay: An Exploration of Landscape and History* (New York: Alfred A. Knopf, 1988), 136.
17 Said, *Culture and Imperialism*, xvii.
18 For a discussion of nineteenth-century ornamentalism and its connection to the British, see David Cannadine, *Ornamentalism: How the British Saw Their Empire* (London: Allen Lane, 2001).
19 Admiralty, *Voyages*, vol. 4, 258.
20 Ibid., vol. 6, 369.
21 Ibid., vol. 3, 336.
22 See Marcel Mauss, *The Gift: The Form and Reason for Exchange in Archaic Societies* (New York: W.W. Norton, 1990), 8-9.
23 Admiralty, *Voyages*, vol. 3, 302.
24 Ibid., vol. 1, 394.
25 Bernard Smith, *Imagining the Pacific: In the Wake of the Cook Voyages* (Melbourne: Melbourne University Press, 1992), 205.
26 Admiralty, *Voyages*, vol. 1, 322.
27 Ibid., vol. 4, 12.
28 Friedrich Nietzsche, *On the Genealogy of Morals*, trans. Walter Kaufmann (New York: Vintage, 1967), 65.
29 Admiralty, *Voyages*, vol. 1, 341.
30 J.C. Beaglehole, *The Journals of Captain Cook*, vol. 1 (London: Hakluyt Society, 1968), 206.
31 Admiralty, *Voyages*, vol. 1, 355.
32 Ibid., vol. 3, 247. The resonance with Kant's discussion, which was considered in the previous chapter, should be noted here.
33 John Rickman, *Journal of Captain Cook's Last Voyage to the Pacific Ocean on* Discovery; *Performed in the Years 1776, 1777, 1778, 1779* (1781; facsimile reprint, New York: Da Capo, 1967), 301.
34 George Mortimer, *Observations and Remarks Made during a Voyage to the Islands of Teneriffe, Amsterdam, Maria's Islands near Van Diemen's Land; Otaheite, Sandwich Islands; Owhyhee, the Fox Islands on the North West Coast of America, Tinian, and from thence to Canton, in the Brig* Mercury, *Commanded by John Henry Cox, Esq.* (1791; facsimile reprint, New York: Da Capo, 1975), vii.
35 The account of justice that Cook brings to the South Pacific is not exactly an English sense of the justice, at least insofar as there is no appeal to either common law or the intricacies of the actual laws in England. Rather, Cook is attempting to promote a minimal set of laws, justified in terms of rationalized economic and theological principles.
36 The phrase is from Cynthia Enloe, *Bananas, Beaches and Bases: Making Feminist Sense of International Politics* (Berkeley: University of California Press, 1990), 67. Enloe offers a similar analysis of the global presence of the United States in the late twentieth century.
37 Admiralty, *Voyages*, vol. 3, 318.
38 Locke, *Second Treatise on Government*, in *The Works of John Locke*, vol. 5, 357.
39 Admiralty, *Voyages*, vol. 5, 413.
40 Ibid., vol. 6, 212.

41 Immanuel Kant, "What Is Enlightenment?" in *Political Writings*, ed. Hans Reiss (Cambridge: Cambridge University Press, 1991), 54.

42 Immanuel Kant, *The Metaphysics of Morals*, ed. Mary Gregor (Cambridge: Cambridge University Press, 1996), 122.

43 See Michel Foucault, *The Order of Things: An Archaeology of the Human Sciences* (New York: Vintage Books, 1973), 268.

44 For a description of the panopticon, see Michel Foucault, *Discipline and Punish: The Birth of the Prison*, trans. Alan Sheridan (New York: Vintage Books, 1979), 200.

45 Besant, *Captain Cook*, 120.

46 Otto von Kotzebue, *A New Voyage round the World, in the Years 1823, 24, 25, and 26*, vol. 1 (1830; facsimile reprint, New York: Da Capo, 1967), 162.

47 "Appendix" in Admiralty, *The Voyages of Captain James Cook, Illustrated with Maps and Numerous Engravings on Wood: With an Appendix, Giving an Account of the Present Condition of the South Sea Islands, &c.*, vol. 2 (London: W. Smith, 1842), 557.

48 Ibid., 613.

49 Kippis, *A Narrative of the Voyages*, 18.

Bibliography

Adair, James. *The History of the American Indians: Particularly those Nations Adjoining to the Mississippi, East and West Florida, Georgia, South and North Carolina, and Virginia.* London: E. and C. Dilly, 1775.

Admiralty. *Account of the Voyages Undertaken by the Order of His Present Majesty for Making Discoveries in the Southern Hemisphere, and Successively Performed by Commodore Byron, Captain Wallis, Captain Carteret, and Captain Cook, in the* Dolphin, *the* Swallow, *and the* Endeavour. Edited by John Hawkesworth. 2 vols. London: W. Strahan and T. Cadell, 1773.

–. *A Voyage to the Pacific Ocean. Undertaken, by the Command of His Majesty, for Making Discoveries in the Northern Hemisphere, to Determine the Position and Extent of the West Side of North America; its Distance from Asia; and the Practicability of a Northern Passage to Europe. Performed under the Direction of Captains Cook, Clerke, and Gore, in His Majesty's Ships the* Resolution *and* Discovery, *in the Years 1776, 1777, 1778, 1779, and 1780.* Edited by John Douglas. 3 vols. London: Printed by W. and A. Strahan for G. Nicol and T. Cadell, 1784.

–. *A Voyage towards the South Pole, and round the World: Performed in His Majesty's ships the* Resolution *and* Adventure, *in the Years 1772, 1773, 1774, and 1775.* Edited by John Douglas. 2 vols. London: W. Strahan and T. Cadell, 1777.

–. *The Voyages of Captain James Cook.* 7 vols. London: Longman, Hurst, Rees, Orme, and Brown, 1821.

–. *The Voyages of Captain James Cook, Illustrated with Maps and Numerous Engravings on Wood: With an Appendix, Giving an Account of the Present Condition of the South Sea Islands, &c.* 2 vols. London: W. Smith, 1842.

Anderson, Benedict. *Imagined Communities.* London: Verso, 1991.

Anonymous. *Journal of a Voyage round the World, in His Majesty's Ship* Endeavour, *in the Years 1768, 1769, 1770 and 1771.* 1771. Facsimile reprint, New York: Da Capo, 1967.

Anson, George. *A Voyage round the World.* London: J.M. Dent and Sons, 1911.

Anson, George, and Richard Walter. *A Voyage round the World, in the Years M, DCC, XL, I, II, III, IV, by George Anson, Esq., now Lord Anson, Commander in Chief of a Squadron of His Majesty's Ships, Sent upon an Expedition to the South-Seas, Compiled from his Papers and Materials.* Ayr: Printed by J. Wilson, 1790.

Aristotle. *The Complete Works of Aristotle.* Rev. Oxford translation. 2 vols. Princeton: Princeton University Press, 1984.

Armstrong, John. *Nations before Nationalism.* Chapel Hill: University of North Carolina Press, 1982.

Aspin, Jehoshaphat. *Cosmorama: A View of the Costumes and Peculiarities of All Nations.* London: J. Harris, 1827.

Bachelard, Gaston. *The Poetics of Space.* Boston: Beacon Press, 1969.

–. *Waters and Dreams.* Dallas: Pegasus Foundation, 1983.

Bagehot, Walter. *Physics and Politics.* In *The Works of Bagehot,* vol. 4, 427-592. Hartford: Travelers Insurance Company, 1889.

Barrow, John. *Cook's Voyages of Discovery.* London: J.M. Dent and Sons, 1903.

–. *Cook's Voyages of Discovery.* London: A. & C. Black, 1925.

Barthes, Roland. *Image-Music-Text.* New York: Hill and Wang, 1977.

Beaglehole, J.C. *The Journals of Joseph Banks.* 2 vols. Sydney: Angus and Robertson, 1963.

–. *The Journals of Captain Cook.* 4 vols. London: Hakluyt Society, 1968.

–. *Cook the Writer.* Sydney: Sydney University Press, 1970.

–. *The Life of Captain James Cook.* Stanford, CA: Stanford University Press, 1974.

–. *The Exploration of the Pacific,* 3rd ed. London: Adam and Charles Black, 1975.

Beddie, M.K. *Bibliography of Captain James Cook, R.N., F.R.S., Circumnavigator.* Sydney: Mitchell Library, 1970.

Beer, Gillian. *Darwin's Plots: Evolutionary Narrative in Darwin, George Eliot and Nineteenth-Century Fiction.* Cambridge: Cambridge University Press, 2000.

Berry, Christopher. *Social Theory of the Scottish Enlightenment.* Edinburgh: Edinburgh University Press, 1997.

Besant, Walter. *Captain Cook.* London: Macmillan, 1925.

Bloom, Harold, ed. *Romanticism and Consciousness: Essays in Criticism.* New York: W.W. Norton, 1970.

Boswell, James. *Life of Johnson.* 8 vols. London: Henry G. Bohn, 1851.

Brewer, John. *The Pleasures of the Imagination: English Culture in the Eighteenth Century.* New York: Farrar, Straus and Giroux, 1997.

Brown, Stewart, ed. *William Robertson and the Expansion of Empire.* Cambridge: Cambridge University Press, 1997.

Buchan, James. *Crowded with Genius: The Scottish Enlightenment: Edinburgh's Moment of the Mind.* New York: Harper Collins, 2003.

Buck, Peter (Te Rangi Hiroa). *Explorers of the Pacific: European and American Discoveries of Polynesia.* Honolulu: The Bishop Museum, 1953.

Bulwer-Lytton, Edward. *Lytton's Novels.* 28 vols. London: G. Routledge and Sons, 1840-75.

Cannadine, David. *Ornamentalism: How the British Saw Their Empire.* London: Allen Lane, 2001.

Carter, Harold B. *Sir Joseph Banks, 1743-1820.* London: British Museum (Natural History), 1988.

Carter, Paul. *The Road to Botany Bay: An Exploration of Landscape and History.* New York: Alfred A. Knopf, 1988.

Casey, Edward. *The Fate of Place: A Philosophical History.* Berkeley: University of California Press, 1997.

Cash, C.G. *The Life and Voyages of Captain James Cook.* London: Blackie and Sons, 1905.

Castle, Kathryn. *Britannia's Children: Reading Colonialism through Children's Books and Magazines.* Manchester: Manchester University Press, 1996.

Chartier, Roger. *The Order of Books.* Stanford, CA: Stanford University Press, 1994.

Charvat, William. *Literary Publishing in America 1790-1850.* Amherst, MA: University of Massachusetts Press, 1993.

Chatterjee, Partha. *Nationalist Thought and the Colonial World: A Derivative Discourse.* London: Zed Books, 1986.

Chatwin, Bruce. *The Songlines*. London: Penguin Books, 1988.

Chester, Sir Norman. *The English Administrative System: 1780-1870*. Oxford: Clarendon Press, 1981.

Clayton, Daniel. *Islands of Truth: The Imperial Fashioning of Vancouver Island*. Vancouver: UBC Press, 1999.

Conrad, Joseph. "Geography and Some Explorers." In *Last Essays*. Introduction by Richard Curle. 1-21. New York: Doubleday, 1926.

–. *Heart of Darkness*. Edited by Robert Kimbrough. New York: W.W. Norton, 1971.

Dampier, William. *The Voyages of Captain William Dampier*. 2 vols. Edited by John Masefield. London: E. Grant Richards, 1905.

Darian-Smith, Eve. *Bridging Divides: The Channel Tunnel and English Legal Identity in the New Europe*. Berkeley: University of California Press, 1999.

Daws, Gavin. *A Dream of Islands: Voyages of Self-Discovery in the South Seas*. New York: W.W. Norton, 1980.

Dawson, Ruth. "Collecting with Cook: The Forsters and Their Artifact Sales." *Hawaiian Journal of History* 13 (1979): 5-16.

–. "Mythologizing Pacific Women: Cook's Second Voyage." Paper presented at Pacific Science Congress, 27 May-2 June 1991, Honolulu.

Defoe, Daniel. *The Novels and Miscellaneous Works of Daniel de Foe*. London: Thomas Tegg, 1840.

–. *The Complete English Gentleman*. London: David Nutt, 1890.

Deleuze, Gilles, and Felix Guattari. *What Is Philosophy?* Columbia: Columbia University Press, 1994.

Dening, Greg. *Islands and Beaches: Discourse on a Silent Land: Marquesas 1774-1880*. Chicago: Dorsey Press, 1980.

–. "Review of Books." *William and Mary Quarterly*, 3rd series, 54, 1 (January 1997): 253-9.

Dunn, John. *Western Political Theory in the Face of the Future*. Cambridge: Cambridge University Press, 1993.

Dunning A.J. *Extremes: Reflections on Human Behavior*. Translated by Johan Theron. New York: Harcourt Brace Jovanovich, 1992.

Eiseley, Loren. *Darwin's Century: Evolution and the Men Who Discovered It*. New York: Anchor Books, 1961.

Eisenstein, Elizabeth. *The Printing Press As an Agent of Change: Communications and Cultural Transformations in Early-Modern Europe*. 2 vols. Cambridge: Cambridge University Press, 1979.

Ellingson, Ter. *The Myth of the Noble Savage*. Berkeley: University of California Press, 2001.

Elliot, Jane. "The Choosers or the Dispossessed? Aspects of the Works of Some French Eighteenth Century Pacific Explorers." *Oceania* 67 (1997): 234-56.

Ellis, William. *An Authentic Narrative of a Voyage Performed by Captain Cook and Captain Clerke, in His Majesty's Ships* Resolution *and* Discovery *during the years 1776, 1777, 1778, 1779 and 1780*. 2 vols. 1782. Facsimile reprint, New York: Da Capo, 1969.

Elsner, John, and Roger Cardinal, eds. *The Cultures of Collecting*. Cambridge, MA: Harvard University Press, 1994.

Enloe, Cynthia. *Bananas, Beaches and Bases: Making Feminist Sense of International Politics*. Berkeley: University of California Press, 1990.

Fabian, Johannes. *Time and the Other: How Anthropology Makes Its Object*. New York: Columbia University Press, 1983.

Ferguson, Adam. *An Essay on the History of Civil Society.* 1767. Facsimile edition, Edinburgh: Edinburgh University Press, 1966.

Fisher, Robin, and Hugh Johnston, eds. *Captain James Cook and His Times.* Vancouver: Douglas and McIntyre, 1979.

Forbes, David, *Hawaiian National Bibliography.* Vol. 1, *1780-1830.* Honolulu : University of Hawai'i Press, 1999.

Forster, Georg. *A Voyage round the World in His Britannic Majesty's Sloop,* Resolution, *Commanded by Captain James Cook, during the Years 1772, 3, 4, and 5.* 2 vols. London: B. White et. al., 1777.

–. *A Letter to the Right Honourable the Earl of Sandwich, First Lord Commissioner of the Board of Admiralty, &c.* London: G. Robinson et al., 1778.

–. *Reply to Mr. Wales's Remarks.* London: D. White, 1778.

Forster, Reinhold. *Observations during a Voyage round the World.* London: G. Robinson, 1778.

–. *Observations during a Voyage round the World.* Edited by Nicholas Thomas, Harriet Guest, and Michael Dettelbach. Honolulu: University of Hawai'i Press, 1996.

Foucault, Michel. *The Archaeology of Knowledge and the Discourse on Language.* Translated by A.M. Sheridan Smith. New York: Pantheon Books, 1972.

–. *The Order of Things: An Archaeology of the Human Sciences.* New York: Vintage Books, 1973.

–. *Discipline and Punish: The Birth of the Prison.* Translated by Alan Sheridan. New York: Vintage Books, 1979.

–. "What Is an Author?" In *The Foucault Reader,* 101-20. New York: Pantheon Books, 1984.

–. *The History of Sexuality.* Vol. 1, *An Introduction.* Translated by Robert Hurley. New York: Vintage Books, 1990.

Gellner, Ernest. *Nations and Nationalism.* Ithaca, NY: Cornell University Press, 1983.

Gifford, Don. *The Farther Shore: A Natural History of Perception.* New York: Atlantic Monthly Press, 1990.

Gilbert, Thomas. *Voyage from New South Wales to Canton, in the Year 1788, with Views of the Islands Discovered.* 1789. Facsimile reprint, New York: Da Capo, 1968.

Glissant, Edouard. *Poetics of Relation.* Translated by Betsy Wing. Ann Arbor: University of Michigan Press, 1997.

Goetzmann, William. *New Lands, New Men: America and the Second Great Age of Discovery.* New York: Viking, 1986.

Goldsmith, Rev. J. *The British Empire in 1825,* 15th ed. London: G.B. Whittaker, [1825?].

Gregor, Mary. "Kant's Theory of Property." *Review of Metaphysics* 41 (June 1988): 757-87.

Guthrie, William. *Universal Geography Improved, Being a New System of Modern Geography, or, a Geographical, Historical and Commercial Grammar, and Present State of All the Several Kingdoms of the World.* London, 1795.

Harris, Michael. *History of Libraries in the Western World,* 4th ed. Metuchen, NJ: Scarecrow Press, 1995.

Haycox, Stephen, James Barnett, and Caedmon Liburd, eds. *Enlightenment and Exploration in the North Pacific, 1741-1805.* Anchorage, AK: Cook Inlet Historical Society, 1997.

Headrick, Daniel. *The Tools of Empire: Technology and European Imperialism in the Nineteenth Century.* Oxford: Oxford University Press, 1981.

Heater, Derek. *World Citizenship and Government: Cosmopolitan Ideas in the History of Western Political Thought*. London: Macmillan, 1996.

Heidegger, Martin. "The Age of the World Picture." In *The Question Concerning Technology and Other Essays*. Translated by William Lovitt. 113-54. New York: Garland Publishing, 1977.

Hind, Arthur. *A History of Engraving and Etching from the 15th Century to the Year 1914*. New York: Dover, 1963.

Hobbes, Thomas. *The English Works of Thomas Hobbes*. 11 vols. Edited by William Molesworth. London: John Bohn, 1839.

–. *The Latin Works of Thomas Hobbes*. 11 vols. Edited by William Molesworth. London: John Bohn, 1839.

Hobsbawm, E.J. *Nations and Nationalism since 1780: Programme, Myth, Reality*. Cambridge: Cambridge University Press, 1997.

Howe, K.R. "The Making of Cook's Death." *Journal of Pacific History* 31, 1 (1996): 108-18.

Howse, Derek. *Greenwich Time and the Discovery of the Longitude*. Oxford: Oxford University Press, 1980.

Jones, H.S. *Victorian Political Thought*. London: Macmillan Press, 2000.

Jones, M. *The Story of Captain Cook's Three Voyages round the World*. London: Cassell, Petter, and Galpin, 1870.

Judd, Denis. *Empire: The British Imperial Experience from 1765 to the Present*. New York: Basic Books, 1996.

Kant, Immanuel. *The Critique of Judgment*. Indianapolis, IN: Hackett Publishing, 1987.

–. *The Critique of Pure Reason*. Translated by Norman Kemp Smith. New York: St. Martin's Press, 1965.

–. *Anthropology from a Pragmatic Point of View*. The Hague: Martinus Nijhoff, 1974.

–. *Political Writings*. Edited by Hans Reiss. Cambridge: Cambridge University Press, 1991.

–. *The Metaphysics of Morals*. Edited by Mary Gregor. Cambridge: Cambridge University Press, 1996.

Kaufman, Paul. *Borrowings from the Bristol Library, 1773-1784*. Charlottesville, VA: Bibliographical Society of the University of Virginia, 1960.

Keate, George. *An Account of the Pelew Islands*. London: W. Nicoll, 1788.

Kedourie, Elie. *Nationalism*. Oxford: Basil Blackwell, 1998.

Kippis, Andrew. *A Narrative of the Voyages round the World Performed by Captain James Cook, with an account of his life during the previous and intervening periods*. Philadelphia: Henry Coates, [1900?].

Kitson, Arthur. *The Life of Captain James Cook, the Circumnavigator*. London: John Murray, 1907.

Kotzebue, Otto von. *A New Voyage round the World, in the Years 1823, 24, 25, and 26*. 2 vols. 1830. Facsimile reprint, New York: Da Capo, 1967.

–. *A Voyage of Discovery into the South Sea and Bering's Straits, for the Purpose of Exploring a North-East Passage, Undertaken in the Years 1815-1818*. 3 vols. 1821. Facsimile reprint, New York: Da Capo, 1967.

Kroebner, Richard. *Empire*. Cambridge: Cambridge University Press, 1961.

–. *Imperialism*. Cambridge: Cambridge University Press, 1964.

Kuehls, Thom. *Beyond Sovereign Territory*. Minneapolis: University of Minnesota Press, 1996.

Lawson, Philip. *A Taste for Empire and Glory: Studies in British Overseas Expansion, 1660-1800*. Aldershot, UK: Variorum, 1997.

Lefebvre, Henri. *The Production of Space*. Oxford: Basil Blackwell, 1991.

Lewis, Karen. *The Myth of Continents: A Critique of Metageography*. Berkeley: University of California Press, 1997.

Lincoln, Margarette, ed. *Science and Exploration in the Pacific: European Voyages to the Southern Oceans in the 18th Century*. Suffolk: Boydell Press, 1998.

Lipson, Morris. "On Kant on Space." *Pacific Philosophical Quarterly* 73 (1992): 73-99.

Locke, John. *The Works of John Locke*. 10 vols. London: Thomas Tegg, 1823.

Lopez, Barry. *Arctic Dreams: Imagination and Desire in a Northern Landscape*. New York: Bantam Books, 1996.

Mackay, David. *In the Wake of Cook: Exploration, Science, and Empire, 1780-1801*. Wellington, New Zealand: Victoria University Press, 1985.

MacLaren, I.S. "Exploration/Travel Literature and the Evolution of the Author." *International Journal of Canadian Studies* 5 (Spring 1992): 39-68.

Manley, Seon, and Robert Manley. *Beaches: Their Lives, Legends, and Lore*. Philadelphia: Chilton Book Company, 1968.

Marra, John. *Journal of the* Resolution's *Voyage in 1772, 1773, 1774, and 1775, on Discovery to the Southern Hemisphere*. 1775. Facsimile reprint, New York: Da Capo, 1967.

Martyn, Thomas. *Figures of Non-Descript Shells, Collected in the Different Voyages to the South Seas since the Year 1764*. London: N.p., 1784.

Mauss, Marcel. *The Gift: The Form and Reason for Exchange in Archaic Societies*. New York: W.W. Norton, 1990.

Megaw, J.V.S. *Employ'd as a Discoverer: Papers Presented at the Captain Cook Bi-centenary Symposium*. Sydney: A.H. and A.W. Reed, 1971.

Mignolo, Walter. *The Darker Side of the Renaissance: Literacy, Territoriality, and Colonization*. Ann Arbor: University of Michigan Press, 1995.

Mill, John Stuart. *Considerations on Representative Government*. New York: Liberal Arts Press, 1958.

Millar, George Henry. *A New and Universal System of Geography*. London: Alex Hogg, 1782.

Miller, David, and Peter Reill, eds. *Visions of Empire: Voyages, Botany, and Representations of Nature*. Cambridge: Cambridge University Press, 1996.

Miller, Edward. *That Noble Cabinet: A History of the British Museum*. Athens, OH: Ohio University Press, 1974.

Milton, John. *The Prose Works of John Milton*. 7 vols. London: Bensley, 1806.

Moorehead, Alan. *The Fatal Impact: An Account of the Invasion of the South Pacific*. Harmondsworth: Penguin Books, 1985.

Moretti, Franco. *Atlas of the European Novel: 1800 to 1900*. London: Verso, 1998.

Morris, Charles. *Our Island Empire: A Hand-book of Cuba, Porto Rico, Hawaii, and the Philippine Islands*. Philadelphia: J.B. Lippincott Co., 1899.

Mortimer, George. *Observations and Remarks Made during a Voyage to the Islands of Teneriffe, Amsterdam, Maria's Islands near Van Diemen's Land; Otaheite, Sandwich Islands; Owhyhee, the Fox Islands on the North West Coast of America, Tinian, and from thence to Canton, in the Brig* Mercury, *Commanded by John Henry Cox, Esq.* 1791. Facsimile reprint, New York: Da Capo, 1975.

Muldoon, James. *Empire and Order: The Concept of Empire, 800-1800*. London: Macmillan Press, 1999.

Negri, Antonio, and Michael Hardt. *Empire*. Cambridge, MA: Harvard University Press, 2000.

Nietzsche, Friedrich. *On the Genealogy of Morals*. Translated by Walter Kaufmann. New York: Vintage, 1967.

Obeyesekere, Gananath. *The Apotheosis of Captain Cook: European Mythmaking in the Pacific*. Princeton: Princeton University Press, 1992.

–. "'British Cannibals': Contemplation of an Event in the Death and Resurrection of James Cook, Explorer." *Critical Inquiry* 18 (Summer 1992): 630-54.

O'Brian, Patrick. *Joseph Banks: A Life*. Chicago: University of Chicago Press, 1987.

Ó Tuathail, Gearóid. *Critical Geopolitics: The Politics of Writing Global Space*. Minneapolis: University of Minnesota Press, 1996.

Paluka, Frank. *The Three Voyages of Captain Cook*. Pittsburgh: Beta Phi Mu, 1974.

Parker, John. *Discovery: Developing Views of the Earth from Ancient Times to Captain Cook*. New York: Dorset Press, 1972.

Parkinson, Sydney. *A Journal of a Voyage to the South Seas, in His Majesty's Ship, the* Endeavour. London: Printed for Stanfield Parkinson, 1773.

Parry, J.H. *The Discovery of the Sea: An Illustrated History of the Men, Ships and the Sea in the Fifteenth and Sixteenth Centuries*. New York: The Dial Press, 1974.

Pethick, Derek. *First Approaches to the Northwest Coast*. Vancouver, BC: Douglas and McIntyre, 1976.

Piggot, Stuart. *Ancient Britons and the Antiquarian Imagination*. New York: Thames and Hudson, 1989.

Plato. *Republic*. In *The Dialogues of Plato*. Translated by B. Jowett. New York: Charles Scribner and Company, 1871.

Pratt, Mary Louise. *Imperial Eyes: Travel Writing and Transculturation*. London: Routledge, 1992.

Raymond, Joad, ed. *News, Newspapers, and Society in Early Modern Britain*. London: Frank Cass, 1999.

Rennie, Neil. *Far-Fetched Facts: The Literature of Travel and the Idea of the South Seas*. Oxford: Clarendon Press, 1995.

Richards, Thomas. *Imperial Archive: Knowledge and the Fantasy of Empire*. London: Verso, 1993.

Rickman, John. *Journal of Captain Cook's Last Voyage to the Pacific Ocean on* Discovery; *Performed in the Years 1776, 1777, 1778, 1779*. 1781. Facsimile reprint, New York: Da Capo, 1967.

Riess, Hans Siegbert. *The Political Thought of the German Romantics: 1793-1815*. Oxford: Basil Blackwell, 1955.

Riley, Patrick. *Kant's Political Philosophy*. Totowa, NJ: Rowman and Littlefield Publishers, 1983.

Robertson, Jillian. *The Captain Cook Myth*. Sydney: Angus and Robertson, 1981.

Rousseau, Jean-Jacques. *The Government of Poland*. Translated by Willmore Kendall. Indianapolis: Bobbs-Merrill, 1972.

–. *The Basic Political Writings*. Translated by Peter Gay. Indianapolis: Hackett Publishing Company, 1987.

Rousseau, Jean-Jacques, and Johann Gottfried Herder. *On the Origin of Language*. Chicago: University of Chicago Press, 1966.

Ryan, James. *Picturing Empire: Photography and the Visualization of the British Empire*. Chicago: University of Chicago Press, 1997.

Sahlins, Marshall. *Islands of History*. Chicago: University of Chicago Press, 1985.

–. *How "Natives" Think, about Captain Cook, for Example.* Chicago: University of Chicago Press, 1995.

Sahlins, Peter. *Boundaries: The Making of France and Spain in the Pyrenees.* Berkeley: University of California Press, 1989.

–. "Natural Frontiers Revisited: France's Boundaries since the Seventeenth Century." *American Historical Review* 95, 4 (December 1990): 1423-51.

Said, Edward. *Orientalism.* New York: Vintage, 1979.

–. *Culture and Imperialism.* New York: Vintage Books, 1994.

Salmon, Thomas. *A New Geographical and Historical Grammar.* London: William Johnston, 1749.

Samwell, David. *A Narrative of the Death of Captain James Cook, to which are added some particulars, concerning his life and character, and observations respecting the introduction of the venereal disease into the Sandwich Islands.* 1786. Reprinted, San Francisco: David Magee, 1957.

Schama, Simon. *Landscape and Memory.* New York: Alfred Knopf, 1995.

Schofield, Malcolm. *Stoic Idea of the City.* Cambridge: Cambridge University Press, 1991.

Secord, James. *Victorian Sensation: The Extraordinary Publication, Reception, and Secret Authorship of Vestiges of the Natural History of Creation.* Chicago: University of Chicago Press, 2000.

Seidel, Michael. *Robinson Crusoe: Island Myths and the Novel.* New York: Twayne Publishers, 1991.

Shattock, Joanne. *Politics and Reviewers: The Edinburgh and the Quarterly in the Early Victorian Age.* London: Leicester University Press, 1989.

Shaw, Alexander. *A Catalogue of the Different Specimens of Cloth Collected in the Three Voyages of Captain Cook.* London: Alexander Shaw, 1787.

Skinner, Quentin. *The Foundations of Modern Political Thought.* 2 vols. Cambridge: Cambridge University Press, 1980.

Smellie, K.B. *Great Britain since 1688: A Modern History.* Ann Arbor: University of Michigan Press, 1962.

Smith, Bernard. *European Vision and the South Pacific.* New Haven, CT: Yale University Press, 1988.

–. *Imagining the Pacific: In the Wake of the Cook Voyages.* Melbourne: Melbourne University Press, 1992.

Smith Bernard, and Rudiger Joppien. *The Art of Captain Cook's Voyages.* 4 vols. New Haven, CT: Yale University Press, 1988.

Sobel, Dava. *Longitude.* New York: Walker Publishing, 1995.

Sparrman, Anders. *A Voyage round the World with Captain James Cook in H.M.S. Resolution.* London: Golden Cockerel Press, 1944.

Spurr, David. *The Rhetoric of Empire: Colonial Discourse in Journalism, Travel Writing, and Imperial Administration.* Durham: Duke University Press, 1993.

Stavans, Ilan. *Imagining Columbus: The Literary Voyage.* New York: Twayne Publishers, 1993.

Stewart, Susan. *On Longing: Narratives of the Miniature, the Gigantic, the Souvenir, the Collection.* Baltimore: Johns Hopkins University Press, 1984.

Stoddart, D.R. *On Geography and Its History.* Oxford: Basil Blackwell, 1986.

Strack, Thomas. "Philosophical Anthropology on the Eve of Biological Determinism: Immanuel Kant and Georg Forster on the Moral Qualities and Biological Characteristics of the Human Race." *Central European History* 29, 3 (1996): 285-308.

Tannenbaum, Beulah, and Myra Stillman. *Understanding Maps: Charting the Land, Sea, and Sky.* New York: McGraw-Hill, 1969.

Tennyson, Alfred Lord. *The Poetical Works of Alfred Tennyson.* 10 vols. New York: T.Y. Crowell, 1902.

Thomas, Pascoe. *Journal of a Voyage to the South-Seas.* 1745. Facsimile reprint, New York: Da Capo, 1971.

Thornton, A.P. *Doctrines of Imperialism.* New York: John Wiley and Sons, 1965.

Turner, Frederick. *Beyond Geography: The Western Spirit against the Wilderness.* New York: Viking Press, 1980.

Vaughan, Thomas. *Captain Cook, R.N.: The Resolute Mariner.* Portland, OR: Oregon Historical Society, 1974.

Wales, William. *The Original Astronomical Observations, Made in the Course of a Voyage towards the South Pole, and round the World, in His Majesty's ships the* Resolution *and* Adventure, *in the years MDCCLXXII, MDCCLXXIII, MDCCLXXIV, and MDCCLXXV.* London: W. and A. Strahan, 1777.

–. *Remarks on Mr. Forster's Account of Captain Cook's Last Voyage round the World in the Years 1772, 1773, 1774, and 1775.* London: J. Nourse, 1778.

–. *An Inquiry into the Present State of Population in England and Wales.* London: C. Nourse, 1781.

–. *Astronomical Observations, Made in the Voyages Which Were Undertaken by Order of His Present Majesty, for Making Discoveries in the Southern Hemisphere, and Successively Performed by Commodore Byron, Captain Wallis, Captain Carteret, and Captain Cook, in the* Dolphin, Tamer, Swallow, *and* Endeavour. London: C. Buckton, 1788.

Whittaker, C.R. *Frontiers of the Roman Empire.* Baltimore: Johns Hopkins University Press, 1994.

Williams, Glyndwr. *The Great South Sea: English Voyages and Encounters 1570-1750.* New Haven, CT: Yale University Press, 1997.

Willinsky, John. *Learning to Divide the World: Education at Empire's End.* Minneapolis: University of Minnesota Press, 1998.

Index

Account of Corsica, the Journal of a Tour to That Island, An (Boswell), 15
Adair, James, 100-1
Admiralty (English)
  authority represented by Cook, 18
  books as part of Bristol Library, 15-16
  creating Cook's voyages, 12-13
  declares no new discoveries possible in the Pacific, 145
  edition of Cook's voyages compared to journals, 86-7, 102, 150, 187
  reworking Cook's journals, 187
  as source of ideals for Cook, 157
  See also Cape of Good Hope
Admiralty Bay (New Zealand), 30, 31
  Cook's disdain for natives of, 164
Adventure (ship), 10, 35, 74, 82, 122
Adventure Bay (Tasmania), 164
  list of words from, 97
Africa
  as coastal line, 25-8, 31
  Cook coasting, 35
  jungle of understood as ocean, 75
  scramble for compared with scramble for the Pacific, 180
Amazon River, as part of global system, 181
America
  colonial uprisings in, 5
  Condamine's exploration of, 75
  as focus of eighteenth-century European empires, 172
  mentioned in books in the Bristol Library, 14-15
  natives of as example of noble savagery for Rousseau, 81-2
  natives of mentioned by Kant, 191
  as new coastal line for Locke, 25
  northern Pacific coast of, 153
  problem of naming places in, 88-90
  as region for European colonies, 174
  Rousseau criticizes Spanish control over, 176
  South Americans compared with natives of Otaheite, 152-3
Amsterdam Island, 155
Anamooka (island, part of the Friendly Islands), 49
Anderson, Benedict, 133
Anderson, William, 17, 91
  produces a list of words from Adventure Bay, 97
Anson, George
  circumnavigation of, 29
  reliance on coasts and latitude, 23
  reprint of Spanish table of coordinates, 42-3
  use of common track, 32-3
  writings as background to *Mansfield Park*, 169-71
  writings part of the Bristol Library, 14-15
Antarctic
  Cook's map of, 4, 10
  Cook's turn away from, 54, 58
  as extreme place, 49-50
  as horrific place, 51-2
  rise of scurvy in, 51
  view of, 53
  See also penguin
anthropology
  character of debated by Kant and Georg Forster, 208n31
  Cook's voyages as early example of, 91
  Kant's discussion of, 126-7
  problem of relativism in, 154

as sign of national power, 189
Anthropology from a Pragmatic Point of View
   (Kant), 125-7
Antigua, 169-71
antipodes, Cook at, 48
   as last possible area for exploration,
      145
Arab (nation), 79
   See also Orientalism
Arabian Sea, as open ocean, 26
   See also navigation
archives
   as collection of all nations, 96
   connected to image of empire as col-
      lection, 172, 178
   modelled as the South Pacific, 7-8
   and panopticism, 193
   as sign of national power, 189
aristocracy. *See* gentlemen
Aristotle, on spatial divisions, 48
artifacts, collected from Nootka Sound,
   136
   in cabinets of curiosities, 139-40
   connected to institutions, 146
   connected to nations, 91, 98
   stored in the British Museum, 146-7
Asia, as coastal line, 25-6
   Ferguson's account of, 118
   problem of sovereignty in, 131
Aspin, Jehosophat, 147
Assyria (nation), as ideal for Johnson, 80
Astley, Thomas, writings part of the
   Bristol Library, 15
Athens (city), Hobbes's account of
   political order of, 113
   importance of farmlands for political
      space, 114
Atlas of the European Novel, The (Moretti),
   170-1
Austen, Jane, 169-71
Australia
   added to the British Empire, 177
   Cook sailing along coast of, 30
   Cook taking possession of eastern
      coast of, 177
   described by Mitchell, 196
   discussed by Bentham, 193
   eventual extinction of natives discussed
      by Besant, 194-5

explored by the Dutch, 66
Kant's account of native property rights
   in, 129
named New Holland by Dutch, 63
natives mentioned by Kant, 191
painting of Cook taking possession of
   New South Wales, 160
   See also southern continent
Aztec (nation), 139

Bacon, Francis, v, 49
Bagehot, Walter, as nationalist thinker,
   134
Balboa, Nuñez, 176
   Conrad describes first sight of Pacific
      of, 57
Banks, Joseph, 11, 17
   boredom compared to Cook's, 150-1
   collection activities compared to
      Cook's, 103-4
   and explanations of savagery, 85
   shell collection used by Martyn, 147
   tests for cannibalism, 98-9
barbarians, 79
   See also Orientalism; savagery
Barros, John de, 24
Barrow, John, depiction of natives, 159-60
Batavia, 6, 95
   as centre of global exchange, 180-1
   Cook emphasizes the costumes at, 181
   as the end of exploration in Cook's
      first voyage, 30
   as example of global collection, 141
Bay of Plenty, 30
Beaglehole, J.C., 150
   discussion of Otaheite, 107
   focus on journals obscures the recep-
      tion of the voyages, 201n13
Behemoth (Hobbes), 114
Bengal (region), mentioned in books in
   the Bristol Library, 15
Bentham, Jeremy, ideal of panopticon,
   192-4
Bertram, Thomas (character in *Mansfield
   Park*), 169, 170
Besant, Walter, 39, 91
   considers the extinction of south
      Pacific nations, 194-5
   describes Cook as empire builder, 177

Bird Isle, 88
Bligh, William
    and global reach of English justice, 189
    voyage published by Admiralty, 13
Board of Longitude, 13, 202n22
Bolcheretzkoi (region), landscape of,
    106
Borallo, Christopher, 25
borders
    clarified in Europe after Cook's
        voyages, 132
    connected to private property by
        Locke, 115
    lacking in songlines, 10
    marginal in Adair's account of
        America, 100
    marginal in Hobbes's account of
        sovereignty, 114
    obscured by landscapes, 66
    role of island in naturalizing, 87, 132
boredom
    Banks's and Cook's compared, 150-4
    and the collection, 147-54
*Borrowings from the Bristol Library, 1773-
    1784* (Kaufman), 13
Boswell, James, 80, 84
    writings part of the Bristol Library, 15
Botany Bay, 30
    Banks's boredom with, 152
Bougainville, Louis-Antoine de, 39
    Cook disputes account of concerning
        native long distance navigation, 165
    and explanations of savagery, 85
    natives unable to pronounce name of,
        164
    writings part of the Bristol Library,
        14-15
Bounty (ship), 188
    See also Bligh, William
Bouvet, Jean, 35
Brazil, 7
    calculating its distance from Cape of
        Good Hope, 27
    Cook measures the longitude of the
        coast of, 40
Bristol Library, borrowings from, 13-16
Britain (ancient)
    mentioned in books in the Bristol
        Library, 15

nation as substitute for South Pacific
    nations, 108
nation compared to Pacific nations,
    158
    See also England
British Columbia, 89
    See also Nootka Sound
British Mariner's Guide (Maskelyne), 41
British Museum, as destination of arti-
    facts collected on Cook's voyages,
    146-7
Brydone, Patrick, books borrowed from
    the Bristol Library, 14
Buchan, Alexander, 85
    death at Otaheite, 68
Bulwer-Lytton, Edward, 204n11
Burke, Edmund
    as nationalist thinker, 134
    writings part of the Bristol Library, 15
Byron, John, 29, 40

cabinets of curiosities, 139-40
California, described in Drake's voyage,
    27
Caligula (emperor), 84
Canary Islands, 35
Cannadine, David, 212n18
cannibalism
    Banks and Cook testing for presence
        of in natives, 98-9
    importance of in nineteenth-century
        European debates, 108
    See also savagery
Cape Circumcision, 35
Cape Colnett, 63
Cape Farewell, 63, 87
Cape Horn, 33
Cape of Good Hope, 7, 82
    avoided because Cook's ship and crew
        too healthy, 56
    calculating distance of from Congo
        River and Brazil, 27
    as centre of global system of economic
        exchange, 180-1
    contrasted to the Antarctic, 50
    as example of global collection, 141
    not mapped by Cook, 73
    as point where Cook turns to the
        Antarctic in the second voyage, 35

as source of seeds and animals, 190

Cape Verde Islands, as part of global system, 181

Caribbean
in Austen's *Mansfield Park*, 169-71
as example of noble savagery for Rousseau, 81
mentioned in Locke's narrative, 28

Carter, Paul, 8, 30, 199
compares how Banks and Cook collect and classify, 103-4
on Cook's renaming of Otaheite, 87
and debate over control of land, 178
on relationship between ship and shore, 199
on spatial organization of Australia, 55
on use of oceanic imagery when describing interior of Australia, 76

Carteret, Philip, 29
Cook following his track, 59
produces map and landscapes of Pitcairn Island, 66, 68
quality of maps produced by, 71

cartography. *See* maps

Cash, C.G., 161-3

Castle of Otranto, The (book), 204n11

Cataline (emperor), 84

Catalogue of the Different Specimens of Cloth Collected in the Three Voyages of Captain Cook, A (Shaw), 138

Catholic church, connected by Hobbes to Roman Empire, 174

Cavendish, Thomas, voyage of greater duration than Cook's second voyage, 56

Caxton, William, 12

Charlestown, 100

charts. *See* maps

Chatwin, Bruce, 9-10
discussion of different attitudes towards space, 76

Cheerake (Cherokee, nation), discussed by Adair, 100

Chesterfield, Earl of, books borrowed from the Bristol Library, 14

Chile, 153
in Anson's voyage, 33

China, as end of coastal exploration, 25
as place in Orientalism, 80

Christianity, 79
as measurement of national change, 196-7
See also Orientalism

Christmas Sound, portrait of man in, 90

chronometer
importance of to Cook's mythical status, 166
used to calculate longitude, 7, 34

civilization. *See* cultivation; Orientalism

Churchill, John, 22

Clerke, Charles, 186

climate
as explanation of national character, 104, 106
importance of extreme climate in Cook's voyages, 55
as threat to English travel and colonization, 211n48

cloth
collected by Cook, 98
collected by Rickman, 155
English trade cloth from Otaheite at Queen Charlotte's Sound, 183
tapa collected from voyages published by Shaw, 138

coasting. *See* navigation, coasting

Coleridge, Samuel Taylor, 204n11

Collection of Voyages, A (Churchill), 22

colony
concept of in Hobbes and Locke, 174
contrasted to collection, 178
contrasted to province by Hobbes, 174-5
English and Spanish contrasted, 179

Columbus, Christopher
Cook's status in relationship to, 59
favourably described by Locke, 26
reliance on coasts and latitude, 23
use of Regioniontanus's printed tables, 41

common track. *See* navigation, use of common track

Complete English Gentleman, The (Defoe), 146

Condamine, Charles-Marie de la, exploration of South America, 75

Congo River, calculating its distance from Cape of Good Hope, 27

Conrad, Joseph, 7
on Balboa's vision of the Pacific, 57
continents
contrasted to islands, 59
Cook does not discover, 43-4
as focus of explorations prior to
Cook's, 25-9
See also navigation; southern continent
Cook, John, 26
Cook Islands, natives part of a global
national pantomime, 141
coordinates
connected to printing, 39
as ideal location, 37
measuring latitude, 32
measuring longitude, 34
See also maps; navigation
Corsica (island), as ideal for Rousseau,
116
Cosmography (Munster), 143-4
*Cosmorama: A View of the Costumes and
Peculiarities of All Nations* (Aspin),
147-9
costumes
in Batavia, 181
collected and printed by Aspin, 147-9
crew. *See* sailors
Critique of Pure Reason, The (Kant), 64,
124-5
cross-section. *See* landscapes
Crozet, Julien-Marie, 82
Cuba (island), mentioned in Locke's
narrative, 28
cultivation
connected to rise of Christianity, 196-7
empire understood as, 189-92
in Kant's political thought, 129-30
in Locke's account of property, 127
organized through global system of
exchange, 190
See also gardens
Culture and Imperialism (Said), 169
Cuvier, Georges, 192

Dalrymple, Alexander, writings part of
the Bristol Library, 15
Dampier, William, 11, 95
account of navigation, 33
descriptions lack analysis, 91

map from voyage, 20
mentioned by Defoe, 146
voyage of greater duration than
Cook's second voyage, 56
works as background to *Mansfield Park*,
171
Dance, Nathaniel, 3
Darian-Smith, Eve, 157
Darwinism, organizing European atti-
tudes to the world, 158
Davis's Land, 54
Dawson, Ruth, 102
Decads of India (Barros), 24
Defoe, Daniel, 12
books not heavily borrowed from the
Bristol Library, 14
image of the stationary collector, 146
Dening, Greg, on relationship between
ship and shore, 199
Denmark (nation), costume of native
pictured by Aspin, 149
desert, as ocean, 75-6
Diderot, Denis, 85
Discovery (ship), 10, 17, 35, 69
distance, measured by time or geometry,
48
Djakarta. *See* Batavia
dog
compared to lamb, 156
Cook eats Forster's on second voyage,
154
Dorset (region), mentioned in books in
the Bristol Library, 15
Douglas, John, 13
Drake, Francis, 27
reliance on coasts and latitude, 23
use of common track, 33
Dusky Bay, 102

Eahienomauwe (Te Ika a Maui?). *See*
New Zealand
Eaoowe (Eau, island, part of Friendly
Islands), 119
East India Company (Dutch), 24
East India Company (English), 179
as image of global economic actor, 181
Easter Island, 54
discovered by Roggeveen, 58
engravings of natives, 72

landscape of, 71
location first fixed by Cook, 58
map of, 70
natives part of a global national panto-
    mime, 141-2
Edgecumbe, John, 186
Edinburgh, as strategic city in English
    Civil War, 114
Edwards, Edward (captain), 189
Egypt, 80
    mentioned in books in the Bristol
        Library, 15
    native costume pictured by Aspin, 148
Eisenstein, Elizabeth, 41, 96
    importance of errata, 143
    See also printing
Ellis, William, 120, 196
    discussion of Imaio, 155
Endeavour (ship), 10, 58, 63, 87, 159
England
    colonialism contrasted to Spanish, 179
    connection of parochial villages to
        distant colonies, 170
    contrasted to Pacific, 156-7
    as destination of Cook's collection, 140
    discussed by Hobbes, 114
    as focus of Cook's gaze, 5
    as ideal for other places, 190
    maps redone after Cook's voyages, 74
    mentioned by Kant, 125
    nation of supreme collectors, 166
    nation not collected by Cook, 137
    Rousseau discusses king of, 119
    textual landscape of, 171
English Channel, 124
    importance to Kant, 125
enlightenment. *See* cultivation
Enloe, Cynthia, 189
Erromanga (Erramanga, part of
    Vanuatu)
    Barrow's depiction of, 160
    Cook's landing at, 185
Essay on the History of Civil Society, An
    (Ferguson), 117-18
Europe, 79
    mentioned in books in the Bristol
        Library, 15
    See also Orientalism; *specific countries
    and cities*

exchange
    as basis for studying nations, 92
    connected to cultivation, 190
    contrasted to savagery, 183
    violence used to support, 186
exploration. *See* navigation

Fatal Impact, The (Moorehead), 199
Ferguson, Adam, 117
Fichte, Johann Gottlieb, as nationalist
    thinker, 134
Fielding, Henry, books borrowed from
    the Bristol Library, 14
*Figures of Non-Descript Shells, Collected in
    the Different Voyages to the South Seas
    since the Year 1764* (Martyn), 147
Finland, native costume pictured by
    Aspin, 149
firearms. *See* violence
Flinders, Matthew, 11
Florida (region), 100
Forbes, David, 204n30
Forster, Georg
    belief that South Pacific islands offer
        image of natural state, 158
    books borrowed from the Bristol
        Library, 14
    contemporary of Kant, 125
    Cook eats dog of, 154
    debates with Wales over national char-
        acteristics, 93
    importance of place to, 85
    on value of collection for knowledge,
        138
Forster, John Reinhold
    books borrowed from the Bristol
        Library, 14
    importance of place for, 85
Foucault, Michel
    account of the author, 38
    on change from taxonomy to biology,
        192
France, 119
    nation mentioned by Kant, 125
French Revolution, 133
Friendly Islands (Tonga)
    Anamooka mentioned, 49
    eventual extinction of nation dis-
        cussed by Besant, 195

nation described, 106
Frith (river), 114
Furneaux, Tobias
  brings Omai back to England, 95
  death of his crew, 82
  measurement of longitude corrected
    by Cook, 41

Gama, Vasco de, 25
gardens
  Cook carrying seeds to create, 190
  English as ideal for Cook, 157
Geneva (city), idealized by Rousseau,
  116
Genoa (city)
  mentioned in books in the Bristol
    Library, 15
  navigators from, 24
gentlemen
  as participants in ceremonies of pos-
    session, 177
  as source of national ideal, 157
  as source of reliable knowledge, 17
George III (king)
  as focus of Cook's gaze, 5
  painting of Cook taking position of
    New South Wales in the name of, 160
  as recipient of empire, 177
  as source of law, 188
  violence in the name of, 186
  See also England; sovereignty
George's Islands, longitude confirmed
  by Cook, 40
Georgi, Johann Gottlieb, as part of
  collection of all nations, 96
Germany, acquires part of Samoa, 180
gift
  as image of how Cook relates to nations,
    183
  as source of empire, 178
  as way to establish exchange, 182
Giolo, 95
globe. *See* maps
Goetzmann, William 145
  on dangers of relativism, 154
Goldsmith, Oliver, writings part of the
  Bristol Library, 14-15
Government of Poland, The (Rousseau),
  117

Great Barrier Reef, 159
Great Lakes, mentioned in Adair, 100
Greece, 79, 80
  ancient compared to Pacific nations,
    158
  as ideal for Johnson, 99
  mentioned in books in the Bristol
    Library, 15
  used to imagine Otaheite, 66, 68
Greenland (region)
  nation compared by Cook to natives
    of Sandwich Islands, 153, 191
  nation mentioned by Kant, 126
Greenwich (city)
  Cook's relationship to, 5
  as reference for longitude, 34

Hakluyt, Richard, 24
Harrison, John, develops chronometer,
  34
Hawai'i. *See* Sandwich Islands
Hawkesworth, John, 12, 29
  books borrowed from the Bristol
    Library, 14
  and explanations of savagery, 85
  includes maps and landscapes in
    Admiralty edition of voyages, 66
  reworks political aspects of Cook's
    interactions, 187
  use of classical allusions, 187-8
health
  of Cook's sailors, 55-6
  importance of to Cook's mythical
    status, 166
  See also scurvy
heathens, 79
  See also Christianity; Orientalism
Hebrides (islands), 63
Herder, Johann Gottfried
  contemporary of Kant, 125
  and desire to collect all nations, 96
  as nationalist thinker, 133-4
Hicks, Zachary, as source of place name,
  63
high southern latitudes. *See* Antarctic
Hispaniola (island), mentioned in
  Locke's narrative, 28
History of England, The, (Hume), 14
History of India (Osorius), 24

History of the American Indians, The
(Adair), 100
History of the Earth, and Animated Nature
(Goldsmith), 14-15
History of the Life of Henry the Second, The
(Lyttelton), 14
*History of the Present State and Discoveries
Relating to Vision, Light and Colours*
(Priestley), 69
History of the Reign of Charles V, The
(Robertson), 14
*History of the Settlements and Trade of the
Europeans in the East and West Indies*
(Raynal), 14, 171
Hobbes, Thomas, 64
   account of nation, state, and territory,
      112-14
   compared to Ferguson, 118
   compared to Kant, 126-8
   compared to Locke, 114-15
   concept of colony, 174
   concept of empire in, 173
   contrasts province and colony, 174
   could not imagine nineteenth-century
      empires, 176
   empire and obedience in, 172
   importance of security for political
      legitimacy in, 175
   sovereign is necessary for, 121
Hobsbawm, E.J., discussion of nationalism, 132
Hodges, William (painter), 93-4
   landscapes produced by, 69
horror
   in the Antarctic, 51-2
   becomes a theme in English literature
      after Cook's voyages, 204n11
   and cannibalism, 99
   contrasted to manageable dangers,
      55-7
Höst, Georg Hjersing, as part of collection of all nations, 96
Hottentot (nation), 129
   mentioned by Kant, 191
Howe's Island, 165
Howse, Derek, 203n22
Humboldt, Alexander von, 75
   contemporary of Kant, 125

Hume, David, books borrowed from the
   Bristol Library, 14

Iceland, 63
   mentioned in books in the Bristol
      Library, 15
   national costume pictured by Aspin,
      149
*Ideas on the Philosophy of the History of
Mankind* (Herder), 96, 126
Imagined Communities (Anderson), 133
Imaio (Mo'orea, island), compared to
   other Society Islands by Ellis, 155
Imperial Eyes (Pratt), 75
India, 80, 131
Indian
   contrasted to detailed national
      descriptions, 86-91
   as label for Orientalist collections, 139
   nations in North American described
      by Adair, 100-1
Ireland, maps redone after Cook's
   voyages, 74
islands
   as cells in a panopticon, 193
   Cook's idealization of, 7-8
   equivalent to harbours, 64
   fixity compared to Cook's movements,
      123
   of ice connected to confusion by Kant,
      66
   as ideal geometrical entities, 59
   as image of purity for Rousseau, 116
   imagined as a sugarloaf, 60
   Kant's appeal to as ideal political
      space, 128-9
   Kant's use of to idealize knowledge,
      64
   lacking in Adair's description of North
      America, 100-1
   marginal in narratives before Cook,
      26, 27-8
   as natural ideal for Cook, 118
   personified, 62-3
   reappraisal in Rickman's book,
      204n30
   in relationship to the global economy,
      181

as source of ideal knowledge, 89-90
as unattainable ideal for Rousseau,
    118
Islands and Beaches (Dening), 199
Islands of Direction, 30
Islands of History (Sahlins), 11
Isle of Pines, 60
Israel (nation), connected by Adair to
    tribes in North America, 100
Italy, nation mentioned by Kant, 125
    See also Rome

Jackson, George, source of place name,
    30
Jamaica
    mentioned in books in the Bristol
        Library, 15
    mentioned in Locke's narrative, 27-8
Japan, 80
    mentioned in books in the Bristol
        Library, 15
    nation compared by Cook to natives
        of Sandwich Islands, 153, 191
    not controlled after initial European
        expansion into the Pacific, 179
Johnson, Samuel
    account of savagery compared to
        accounts after Cook, 158
    account of savagery undermined by
        descriptions of national diversity, 99
    claims that pity must be cultivated, 84
    connected to orientalist collecting,
        139
    use of language to trace the origins of
        nations, 96
    on the worthlessness of published
        accounts of Cook's voyages, 80
Joseph Andrews (character in novel), 17
Juan Fernandez (island), 33
    Cook's search for, 40, 58
jungle, as ocean, 75-6

Kamchatka (region), natives part of a
    global national pantomime, 141-2
Kamehameha. *See* Tamehameha
Kant, Immanuel
    account of enlightenment, 191-2
    account of global collection, 146

account of nation, state and territory,
    124-30
account of native property, 129
appeal to island as ideal political space,
    128-9
compared to Rousseau, 125
on spatial divisions, 48
use of exploration and island for ideal
    of knowledge, 64
kapa. *See* cloth
Karemaku (Kalanimoku), compared to
    Pitt, 131
Katahba (Catawba, nation), 100,
    described by Adair
Kaufman, Paul, 13
Keate, George, 145
Kedourie, Elie, discussion of nationalism,
    132
Kendall, Larcum, chronometer used to
    calculate longitude, 35
Kent (region), as ideal place, 157
Kepler, Johannes, use of printed tables,
    41
Kew Gardens, 157
King George III's Island. *See* Otaheite
Kippis, Andrew, 40, 45, 144
    account of Cook taking possession of
        land, 177
    characterizes Cook as promoting the
        happiness of the human species,
        197
    compares different natives, 153
knowledge
    connected to taxonomy, 192
    Cook's voyages providing baseline, 196
    and the danger of relativism, 154-9
    idealized as a global system, 137
    importance of newness, reliability and
        completeness to, 144
    place of natives in the production of,
        163-4
Königsberg, as ideal destination of col-
    lection, 146
Kotzebue, Otto von, 11
    account of the rise of the Sandwich
        Islands as a nation, 131
    obtaining instruments to verify and
        create knowledge, 38

updating previous European descriptions of Sandwich Islands, 195-6

Kruzenstern, Ivan (Krusenstern), 11

lamb, compared to dog, 156
land, divided from ocean, 49
landscapes, 66-71
  classical ideal of in first voyage, 85, 93
  contrasted with maps, 71
  influenced by Priestley, 69
  and nationalism, 133
  typical landscapes, 104, 106
  See also Hodges, William; Webber, John
Lapp (nation), mentioned by Kant, 126
latitude. *See* coordinates
law
  Cook's not English, 212n35
  national contrasted with universal, 188
Leith (city), 114
Letters to His Son (Chesterfield), 14
Leviathan (Hobbes). *See* Hobbes, Thomas
library
  books borrowed from Bristol, 13-16
  as collection of places, 15
  See also archives; printing
Life and Voyages of Captain James Cook, The (Cash), 161-2
Life of Johnson (Boswell). *See* Boswell, James
Linnaeus
  classification system connected to Cook's descriptions, 101, 142
  system contrasted to Cuvier's, 192
Lisbon, as reference for longitude, 34
Locke, John, 22
  account of nation, state, and territory, 114-15
  attitude towards American natives, 190
  attribution of *The Whole History of Navigation* challenged, 202n1
  concept of colony, 174
  concept of empire, 173
  could not imagine nineteenth-century empires, 176
  favourable description of Columbus, 26
  importance of agriculture to account of political legitimacy, 175-6
  influence on Cook's account of property, 190
  political thought compared to Kant's, 126-8
  rarely provides longitude, 33
  reliance on coasts and latitude, 24
  simplifies descriptions for practical reasons, 137
London (city)
  as antipode to New Zealand for Cook, 48
  British Museum as destination for Cook's artifacts, 146-7
  collections allow Martyn to produce description of South Seas shells, 147
  as possible focus of Cook's gaze, 5
  as source of accurate scientific instruments, 38
  See also England
longitude. *See* coordinates
Lycurgus, 187-8
Lyttelton, George, books borrowed from the Bristol Library, 14

Macedonia, 119
Madeira (island), mentioned in books in the Bristol Library, 15
Madrid (city), lacking privies, 156
Magellan, Ferdinand de, 26
magnetic needle, 24
Mallicollo (island), 155
  Cook's landing at, 110
Mangeea (Mangaia, island), 153
Mansfield Park (novel), 169-71
maps
  become increasingly iconic, 196
  connected to understanding nations, 198
  constructed of coordinate points, 31
  contrasted with landscapes, 71
  creating a total view of places, 10
  as empty spaces, 43-4
  as field of conflict and control, 197
  filling in the blanks in becomes boring for Cook, 151
  geometrical ideal in Cook's voyages, 71, 73-4
  as image of the collection's structure, 142

Parkinson's use of Cook's map of New Zealand, 43
printed, 3
remapping the world occurred after Cook's voyages, 74
role of in organizing collection of nations and places, 142-3
some places not mapped by Cook, 73
Maria's Island, 41
Marquesas (islands)
  compared to Otaheite, 109
  compared to Sandwich Islands, 152
  France acquires control over, 179
Marra, John, 52, 122
  discussion of Tasman's account of natives, 143
Martyn, Thomas, 147
Maryland (region), 100
Maskelyne, Nevil
  method for calculating longitude, 29, 34
  use of printed tables, 41
Mauss, Marcel, 182
Maya (nation), 139
Meangis Island, 95
Mediterranean (region)
  contrasted to savages and Indians, 86-7
  as ideal for Johnson, 80-1
  as ideal for landscape painters, 68
menagerie, as precursor of panopticon, 192
Mercury, transit of, 183
Metaphysics of Morals, The (Kant), 48, 127-9, 191
Middle Ages, compared to Pacific nations, 158
Middle East, 79
  See also Orientalism
Middleburgh (island), 155
Mitchell, Thomas, 196
Mixtec (nation), 139
Moluccas (islands), mentioned in books in the Bristol Library, 15
Monmouthshire (region), mentioned in books in the Bristol Library, 15
Montaigne, Michel de, connection to Scottish Enlightenment, 117
Montesquieu, Baron de, 85

Moorehead, Alan, on relationship between ship and shore, 199
Moors (nation), mentioned by Kant, 125
Mopeeha (island, Howe's Island), 165
More, Thomas, 12
Moretti, Franco, 170-1
Morris, Charles, 180
Morroco, described as empire, 173
Mortimer, George, 94-5
  description of search for *Bounty* mutineers, 188
Mulgrave, Lord, compared to Omai by Johnson, 81
Munster, Sebastian, *Cosmography* an early example of print's corrective power, 143
Muskohge (nation), described by Adair, 100
Mysteries of Udolpho, The (novel), 204n11

names, 9
  Cook's naming practices along coasts, 31
  Cook's use of native names, 87
  Cook's use of names of people from his career, 30
  importance of natural shapes for, 63-4
  problem of adjoining parts, 88
nationalism
  Cook's voyages as precursor for, 132-4
  as political project, 124
Nationalism (Kedourie), 132
natives
  compared to the Spaniards, 163-4
  contrasted to Indians, 86
  Cook recording physical attributes of, 93
  Cook's description focuses on rulers of, 103
  Cook's severity towards, 188
  Cook's support of property rights of, 187
  description of leads to belief in relativism, 154-9
  explained by climate, 104, 106
  judged by their willingness to collect, 164
  Kant's account of property of, 129

list of words of collected by Europeans,
97

not connected to the land by Locke,
175-6

as objects of cultivation, 189-92

as participants in the production of
knowledge, 163-4

relationship to enlightenment
discussed by Kant, 191-2

and rise of detailed descriptions, 91

as sources of knowledge, 17

See also Giolo; Omai; Tupia

navigation

Admiralty declares exploration ended
in the Pacific, 145

after Cook, 144

before Cook, 7, 11

circumnavigation, 29

coasting, 24-9

coasting not central to Cook's voyages,
31

Cook as ideal navigator, 76

Cook's belief that natives could not
navigate over long distances, 165

creating a catalogue of places, 137

displaying the logical structure of
knowledge, 144

durations of different voyages
compared, 204n24

and Kant's idealization of knowledge,
64

organized as a novel, 16-17

Portuguese and Spanish use of wind
patterns, 28

use of common track, 32-3

verifying previous claims, 36-7

as zig-zagging, 28, 35, 58

New Atlantis (Bacon), 49

New Caledonia (island), 97

French acquire control over, 179

landscape of, 105

natives of described, 93

New Guinea (island), mentioned in
books in the Bristol Library, 15

New Hebrides (islands), 63

Cook's landing at, 184, 185

New Holland. *See* Australia

New South Wales. *See* Australia

New Voyage round the World, A (Dampier),
171

New World. *See* America

New Zealand, 10, 29

account of events changed from
manuscript to print, 102

added to British Empire, 177, 179

contrasted to the Antarctic, 50

Cook sailing along coast, 29-30

Cook's demonstrates that it is two
islands, 60

Cook's description of females of, 156

Cook's voyages a baseline description,
196

death of Furneaux's crew, 82

described as antipode to England, 48

eventual extinction of natives discussed
by Besant, 195

map, 43, 65

nation mentioned by Kant, 126

native costume pictured by Aspin, 148

natives in conflict with the English,
187

as part of a larger logical structure,
144

portrait of native, 94

as possible destination of English colonists, 169

Newfoundland, mentioned in Locke's
narrative, 28

Newton, Isaac, 34

Niebuhr, Carsten, as part of collection
of all nations, 96

Nietzsche, Friedrich, 186

Nootka Sound

collection of artifacts from, 136

native word suggested as place name
by Cook, 89

natives part of a global national pantomime, 141-2

as part of a larger logical structure,
144

possible changes as a result of global
economic activity, 181

Norman (nation), as navigators, 24

Northwest Passage, 6

as escape from boredom for Cook,
147, 150

novel, as organization of exploration narrative, 16-17

Oberea (queen), 102
Observations Made during a Voyage round the World (John Reinhold Forster), 14
Observations on the State of the Nation (Burke), 15
ocean
  associated with jungle and desert, 75
  described as wilderness, 49
  divided by coordinates, 44
  divided from land, 49
  as geometrical plane, 57
  limited by ice, 54
Omai (Mai)
  brought back to England by Furneaux, 95
  Johnson's evaluation, 81
  not able to tell the difference between English and Spanish, 165
  provided with a garden, 157
  as source of information, 164
Omai, or a Trip round the World (play), 141
On Longing (Stewart), 16-17, 178
On the Genealogy of Morals (Nietzsche), 186
On the Social Contract (Rousseau), 116-17, 176
Oonalashka (island)
  Mortimer commends Webber's pictures of natives, 95
  natives part of a global national pantomime, 141-2
Order of Things, The (Foucault), 192
Orient, The, 79
Orientalism
  and collecting, 139
  contrasted to concern for national identities, 84-9
  as division of the globe, 79-84
  Johnson and, 80
  and savagery, 81-4
Original Astronomical Observations Made in the Course of a Voyage towards the South Pole, and round the World, The (Wales), 13
Osorius, Hieronymus, 24

Otaheite (Tahiti, island, part of the Society Islands), 29
  Buchan's death, 68
  compared by Cook to Sandwich Islands, 150-1
  connected to Romanticism, 107
  contrasted to the Antarctic, 50
  Cook steers towards while searching for islands, 39
  Cook's map, 61
  eventual extinction of natives discussed by Besant, 195
  example of Cook's ideal of knowledge, 47
  French acquire control over, 179
  known by natives of Wateeoo, 165
  longitude measured by purser of Wallis's ship, 34
  map compared with map of Pitcairn Island, 73
  name changed by Cook from King George III's Island, 87
  nation an example of noble savagery, 81
  nation compared with Greeks, 66
  nation compared with South Americans, 152
  nation continues to trade after English violence, 182
  nation mentioned by Kant, 126
  nation present in the collection at Batavia, 141
  national costume pictured by Aspin, 148
  part of a larger logical structure, 144
  value of Tahitian cloth in Queen Charlotte's Sound, 183
Our Island Empire (Morris), 180
Owhyhee (Hawai'i). *See* Sandwich Islands

Pacific
  as appropriate challenge for Cook's navigation, 58
  as a collection, 138
  contrasted to England, 156-7
  created as coherent space by Cook's voyages, 107

as empty space, 29
as focus of nineteenth-century empires, 172
as ideal system of national identities, 134
offering image of natural state, 158
Sandwich Islands as boring place within, 147-54
scramble for, 180
as Spanish ocean, 177
painting
of Captain Cook by Nathaniel Dance, 3
changed to reflect different versions of savagery, 159-61
superior to words, 52
used to portray national characteristics, 93-5
Palau (island)
described in Drake's Voyage, 27
Keate's account of, 145
Palestine, 80
See also Orientalism
Palliser, Hugh, as source of place name, 63
Pamela (character in novel), 17
Pandora (ship), 189
panopticon, 192-7
Paoom (island), 60
Paria (region), as part of Locke's narrative, 26, 27
Paris (city)
natives of Otaheite unable to pronounce, 164
as reference for longitude, 34
Parkinson, Sydney
book borrowed from the Bristol Library, 14
as part of collection of all nations, 96
portrait of man of New Zealand, 94
production of landscapes, 68
proponent of importance of place, 85-6
and recording native physical attributes, 93
reprint and use of Cook's map of New Zealand, 43
Parry, J.H., 36
Pecheras (nation), 104

Pelew. *See* Palau (island)
penguin
as early example of the importance of place, 85
at the edge of the national collection, 194
Pennant, Thomas, 85
Perpetual Peace (Kant), 128
Persia (nation), 80, 119
Peru (nation), 153
Philosophical Transactions (journal), 85
Pickersgill, Richard, 120
Pinzon, Vincent Yanez, 26
Pitcairn Island, 66
map compared with map of Otaheite, 73
Point Hicks, 63
Point Jackson, 97
Poland, nation mentioned by Kant, 125, 126
Rousseau's discussion of, 117
Polybius, 63
Polynesian Researches (Ellis), 196
Polynesians, eventual extinction discussed by Besant, 194-5
Poncho, compared to dress of Otaheite by Cook, 153
Port Royal Harbour (Otaheite), 29
Portuguese, navigation methods without longitude, 28
Possession Island, 177
Pourvoyeur (ship), 181
Poverty Bay, 30, 92
Pratt, Mary Louise, 75
Priestley, Joseph, influence over landscape painters, 69
primitivism. *See* savagery
Prince Joely (Giolo), 95
Prince William's Sound, natives as part of a global national pantomime, 141-2
printing, 10, 12
account of Cook's voyages edited for, 102
connected to authority, 199
connected to coordinates, 39
distinguished from manuscripts, 8
and fear of repetition, 145

importance of errata for improving knowledge, 143
use of tables in, 41
See also Eisenstein, Elizabeth; library profiles. *See* landscapes
property, Cook's affirmation of native rights to, 187
province, contrasted to colony by Hobbes, 174-5
Puerto Rico, mentioned in Locke's narrative, 28
Purchas, Samuel, 24
Pytheus, 63

Queen Charlotte's Sound, 183

Radcliff, Ann, 204n11
Rapa Nui. *See* Easter Island
Raynal, Abbé (Guillaume Thomas François)
  books borrowed from the Bristol Library, 14
  works as background to *Mansfield Park*, 171
Regioniontanus, use of tables, 41
relativism
  avoided by appeal to laws of human nature, 156
  Cook's solution for, 155
  dangers of, 154-9
Rennie, Neil, 36
  discussion of Giolo, 95
Resolution (ship), 52, 55, 58
  crew attempting to escape from, 82
Rickman, John, 17, 49, 98, 156
  on Cook's treatment of natives, 188
  discussion of superiority of natives of Middleburgh, 155
  reappraisal of islands in book, 204n30
  vision of a science of humanity, 141
Road to Botany Bay, The (Carter). *See* Carter, Paul
Roberts, Henry, 74
Robertson, William, books borrowed from the Bristol Library, 14
Robinson Crusoe (novel)
  and image of isolated identity, 87
  not part of the Bristol Library, 14

Rogers, Woodes, mentioned by Defoe, 146
Roggeveen, Jacob, 58
Romanticism, 82
  importance of Otaheite, 107
Rome, 80, 99
  empire organized as provinces, 174
  as example of empire for Hobbes, 173
  Hobbes's account of political order of, 113
  importance of frontiers for political space, 114
  knowledge of Thule, 63
  mentioned in books in the Bristol Library, 15
  See also Mediterranean
Rooke, Lawrence (Rook), 22, 31
Rousseau, Jean-Jacques, 81
  account of nation, state, and territory, 116-17
  compared to Kant, 125
  connected to Ferguson, 118
  critique of Spanish control of Americas, 176
  idealized native undermined by national diversity, 99
  impact of Cook's voyages on account of savagery, 108
  response to news of the death of Furneaux's crew, 82
Royal Geographical Society, 37
Royal Navy, 16
  as ideal sovereignty for Cook, 122
Royal Society, 8, 31
  directions for exploration, 22
  as possible focus of Cook's gaze, 5
  as source of ideal, 157
Russia
  attitude to space contrasted with English, 76
  mentioned by Kant, 126
  mentioned in books in the Bristol Library, 15
  See also Kotzebue, Otto von

Sahlins, Marshall, 11
Sahlins, Peter, 209n54
Said, Edward, 79, 131, 178

discussion of empire, 169-70
sailors
  as source of knowledge, 17
  Cook critical of, 191
Salmon, Thomas, 211n4
Samganooda Harbour (on Oonalashka
    island), 64
Samoa (island), control divided between
    Germany and the United States, 180
Samoyed (nation), mentioned by Kant,
    126
Sandwich, Lord, 12
  as source of place name, 63
Sandwich Islands (Hawai'i)
  changes in how Cook's death is pic-
    tured, 161-3
  compared by Cook to Otaheite, 150-1
  Cook's boredom with, 147, 150-4
  Cook's voyages as baseline description
    of, 195
  first mentioned by Cook, 150
  Karemaku compared to Pitt, 131
  nation as part of a global national
    pantomime, 141-2
  native costume pictured by Aspin, 148
  not controlled after initial European
    expansion into the Pacific, 179
  surveyed by Vancouver, 75
  Vancouver's political interventions,
    131
Savage Island, 88
savagery
  as equivalent to Orient, 80
  evaluation of changes over time, 159,
    161
  noble, 107
  not used by Cook as basis for organiz-
    ing the collection, 139
  possible explanations of, 82-5
Scotland
  discussed by Hobbes, 114
  Enlightenment, 117-18
  maps redone after Cook's voyage, 74
  mentioned in books in the Bristol
    Library, 15
scurvy
  affects Cook's crew in the Antarctic, 51
  Anson's crew suffers from, 33

importance of cure to Cook's mythical
    status, 166
Scythia (nation), 119
sea. *See* ocean
Second Treatise on Government (Locke),
    127
Secord, James, 201n13
Seven Years' War, 5
Seward, Anna, 83
Shaw, Alexander, 138
shells, 147
Shelton, Anthony, 139
Sloane, Hans, writings part of the
    Bristol Library, 15
Smith, Adam, 8
Smith, Bernard, 68, 70
  describes global national pantomime,
    141
  on Keate's account of Palau, 145
  on Otaheite and the noble savage, 107
  on primitivism, 84-5
  on the reaffirmation of savagery, 183
  on transformation of how Cook's death
    is pictured, 163
  on typical landscape, 104
Society Islands, 4, 155
  Cook limits their knowledge of the
    Pacific, 165
  mapped by Cook, 73
  natives as part of a global national
    pantomime, 141-2
  pointed to by Cook in Dance's
    portrait, 4
Sommer-islands, 174
Songlines, The (Chatwin), 9-10, 76
South America. *See* America
southern continent, 6
  Cook's proof of the non-existence of,
    44
  See also Australia
southern hemisphere. *See* Antarctic;
    Australia; Pacific
Southern Thule, 63, and Cook's global
    vision
sovereignty
  collecting contrasted to obedience,
    172
  connected to nationalism, 132

Cook's created through exchange, 186
Cook's in relation to his ship and crew, 122
importance for Cook, 102
problem of finding, 120-1
related to nation and territory in Cook's voyages, 123-4
Spain, 119, 153
    challenged by England for control over Pacific, 177
    colonialism contrasted to English, 179
    colonies in South America an early example of nationalist thought, 133
    control of America criticized by Rousseau, 176
    mentioned in Locke's narrative, 28
    people mentioned by Kant, 125
    produced table of coordinates (reprinted by Pascoe Thomas), 43
    use of common track for navigating, 33
    war with the United States, 180
Sparrman, Anders, 206n7
stamp
    collecting as image of global knowledge, 138
    used to picture the nineteenth-century British Empire, 168
Stephens, Philip, source of place name, 30
Sterne, Laurence, books borrowed from the Bristol Library, 14
Stewart, Susan, 16, 178
Strack, Thomas, 208n31
Streights Le Maire, 33, 67
Sturt, Charles, exploration of the interior of Australia, 75
Sumatra (island), mentioned in books in the Bristol Library, 15
Sweden, native costume pictured by Aspin, 149
Swift, Jonathan, 12

Tahiti. *See* Otaheite
Taitbout, M., 85
Tamehameha (Kamehameha, king) described by Kotzebue, 131

discussed in later edition of Cook's voyages, 196
Tanna (island, part of Vanuatu)
    Cook's landing at, 184
    natives of described, 93
    portrait of native from, 78
tapa. *See* cloth
Tasman, Abel, 66
tattoo
    Dampier's description of Giolo's, 95
    heads collected by English, 99
Tayeto (Taiato), death in Batavia before arriving in England, 95
Teneriffe, 7
    not mapped by Cook, 73
Thomas, Pascoe, reprint of Spanish table of coordinates, 43
Three Expeditions into the Interior of Eastern Australia (Mitchell), 196
Thule (island), 63
Todorov, Tzvetan, 16
Toltec (nation), 139
Tom Jones (character in novel), 17
Tongataboo (Tongatapu, island), Cook imagines as cultivated garden, 190
Touahah (native from the Sandwich Islands), 153
Tour through Sicily and Malta, A (Brydone), 14
Traitor's Head, 88
transit of Venus, 6, 29
Tristram Shandy (Sterne)
    borrowed from the Bristol Library, 14
    problem of narrating travel on a plain discussed in, 55
Tupia (Tupaia), 37
    death in Batavia before arriving in England, 95
    importance to first voyage reduced in later versions, 159-60
    relationship to national collection at Batavia, 141
Turkey, mentioned by Kant, 126

Ulietea (Ra'iatea, island), 155
    home of Omai, 95
Unalashka. *See* Oonalashka

United States
  acquires Guam, 179-80
  acquires part of Samoa, 180
  acquires the Philippines, 180
  war with Spain, 180

Van Diemen's Land, 63
Vancouver, George, 11, 131
  surveys the Sandwich Islands, 75
  updates Cook's description of Sandwich Islands, 195
  verifies previous claims, 38
Venice (city), navigators from, 24
Venus. *See* transit of Venus
Versailles (city), 192
Vestiges of the Natural History of Creation (book), 201n13
views. *See* landscapes
violence
  connected to moral sentiment, 186
  Cook reestablishes trade in Otaheite aftermath, 182
  Cook's use for practical goals, 183, 186
  emphasized in later editions of Cook's voyages, 160
  role in establishing political space for Hobbes, 112-14
  role in establishing political space for Kant, 129
  used to create peaceful exchanges between English and natives, 92
Virginia (region), 174
von Kotzebue, Otto. *See* Kotzebue, Otto von
voyage. *See* navigation
Voyage round the World, A (Anson), 14-15, 171
Voyage round the World (Bougainville), 14-15
Voyage to the Islands of Madeira, Barbados ... and Jamaica (Sloane), 15

Wakash, name Cook suggests for the natives of Nootka Sound, 89
Wales (region), mentioned in books in the Bristol Library, 15
Wales, William, 13, 36
  debate with Georg Forster over national characteristics, 93
  measures longitude, 40
Walker, John, 82
Wallis, Samuel, 29
  coastal views, 69
  connected to Romanticism, 107
  Cook's naming practices supersede, 87
  purser's ability to measure longitude, 34
  quality of maps, 71
  use of Otaheite as example of noble savagery, 81
Walpole, Horace, 204n11
watch. *See* chronometer
Wateeoo (Atiu, island, part of the Cook Islands), 165
weapons. *See* violence
Webber, John (painter), 183
  landscapes produced by, 70
  portrait of native of Oonalashka, 95
"What Is Enlightenment?" (Kant), 191-2
Whole History of Navigation, The (Locke), 22-5
wilderness, used to describe ocean, 49
Wilkes, Charles, 75
Williams, Glyndwr, 26
Williamson, John (painter), 160
Works (Fielding), 14
writing, less effective than painting to describe extreme places, 52

Yakut (nation), mentioned by Kant, 126